MUSLIM COSMOPOLITANISM

Southeast Asian Islam in Comparative Perspective

Khairudin Aljunied

EDINBURGH
University Press

Edinburgh University Press is one of the leading university presses in the UK. We publish academic books and journals in our selected subject areas across the humanities and social sciences, combining cutting-edge scholarship with high editorial and production values to produce academic works of lasting importance. For more information visit our website: edinburghuniversitypress.com

First published in hardback 2017

Edinburgh University Press Ltd
The Tun – Holyrood Road
12 (2f) Jackson's Entry
Edinburgh EH8 8PJ

Typeset in 11/15 Adobe Garamond by
Servis Filmsetting Ltd, Stockport, Cheshire,
and printed and bound in Great Britain by
CPI Group (UK) Ltd, Croydon CR0 4YY

A CIP record for this book is available from the British Library

ISBN 978 1 4744 0888 2 (hardback)
ISBN 978 1 4744 2046 4 (paperback)
ISBN 978 1 4744 0889 9 (webready PDF)
ISBN 978 1 4744 0890 5 (epub)

The author and publisher acknowledge a Book Grant from the Faculty of Arts and Social Sciences, National University of Singapore.

CONTENTS

FIGURES

ABBREVIATIONS

ABIM	Angkatan Belia Islam SeMalaysia (Muslim Youth Movement of Malaysia)
ARS	Asatizah Recognition Scheme
CPIRUHAA	Committee for the Promotion of Inter-Religious Understanding and Harmony Among Adherents
DAP	Democratic Action Party
DDII	Dewan Dakwah Islamiyah Indonesia (Islamic Propagation Council)
FMSA	Fellowship of Muslim Students Association of Singapore
FPI	Front Pembela Islam (Muslim Defenders Front)
GDP	gross domestic product
GOLKAR	Partai Golongan Karya (Functional Group Party)
HDB	Housing and Development Board
HMI	Himpunan Mahasiswa Islam (Islamic Students' Association)
IAIN	Institut Agama Islam Negeri (State Institute of Islamic Studies)
ICMI	Ikatan Cendekiawan Muslim se-Indonesia (Indonesian Muslim Intellectuals' Association)
JIL	Jaringan Islam Liberal (Liberal Islam Network)

KISDI	Komite Indonesia untuk Solidaritas Dunia Islam (Committee for the Solidarity of the Muslim World)
MMI	Majelis Mujahidin Indonesia (Indonesian Mujahidin Council)
MUIS	Majlis Ugama Islam Singapura (Islamic Religious Council)
NGO	non-governmental organisation
OWC	Obedient Wives' Club
PAP	People's Action Party
PARPOL ISLAM	Parti Politik Islam (Islamic Political Parties)
PAS	Parti Islam SeMalaysia (Pan-Malaysian Islamic Party)
PERGAS	Persatuan Ulama dan Guru-Guru Agama Islam Singapura (the Singapore Islamic Scholars and Religious Teachers Association)
PITI	Persatuan Islam Tionghoa Indonesia (Organisation of Indonesian Chinese Muslims)
PR	Pakatan Rakyat (People's Alliance)
SIS	Sisters in Islam
UMNO	United Malays National Organisation

ACKNOWLEDGEMENTS

Each page of this book brings with it a whole list of acknowledgements, echoing the contributions of friends, families, colleagues and institutions that have been patient with me for many years. I should begin first with the National University of Singapore for granting me the much-needed time, space and funding for travel to research and write this book till its completion. Joseph Camilleri and Sven Schottmann, both of whom were formerly based at La Trobe University in Melbourne, Australia, invited me to deliver a series of lectures and public talks that shaped my thinking about Muslim cosmopolitanism. The Fulbright Foundation generously supported my stint during fall 2013 at Columbia University, where parts of this book were written. I must thank Karen Barkey and Goh Hwee Lian for making the memorable months there possible.

Whilst in the United States, I benefited from conversations with Talal Asad, Sudipta Kaviraj, Mamadou Diouf and Saskia Schafer. Bruce Lawrence gave much of his precious time reading through my book proposal and questioning my preliminary conceptions of Muslim cosmopolitanism. Ermin Sinanovic invited me to deliver a talk on the main theme of the book at the International Institute of Islamic Thought (IIIT), aside from arranging my use of the institute's extensive Islamic collection.

Participants of lectures and seminars I delivered at the Netherlands Institute of Asian Studies, Prince of Songkla University, State University of Maulana Malik Ibrahim, Naresuan University, the Centre for the Study of Islam and Science (CASIS) at the Universiti Teknologi Malaysia and the University of Brunei asked difficult questions and forced me to rethink my own ideas about Southeast Asian Islam. Beyond universities, a number of local researchers, students and activists such as Shahrudin Ishak, Mohd Raimi, Khairul Anwar, Asri Yusoff, Muhammad Hamzah, Muhammad Zuhal, Mohd Izzuddin and Fadhlina Sidek shared their thoughts and resources that enriched this book in ways I never imagined.

I have benefited much from the intellectual inputs of Maurizio Peleggi, Henk Maier, Timothy Barnard, Bachamiya Hussainmiya and Rommel Curaming. Kamaludeen Nasir read parts of the book and gave his critical comments. Erik Holmberg read the entire book and, as always, turned it into a more polished text. The anonymous reviewers pointed to several useful directions that sharpened my analysis. This book would not have seen the light of day if not for the hard work put in by Nicola Ramsey, Ellie Bush and Rebecca Mackenzie. They are such a joy to work with as part of an excellent production team at Edinburgh University Press.

Above all, I am blessed with a supportive family that stood by me through all the stages of this work. My parents and siblings, my wife Marlina and our six energetic children have yet to come to terms with my writing addiction. This book is for them, as are, God willing, the many more that are to come.

PREFACE:
SEEING LIKE A MUSLIM
COSMOPOLITAN

The school principal refused to yield. For the second time in a month, she called me into her office to unravel an administrative puzzle that had perplexed her. The problem was that my identity card stated my race as 'Malay'. My surname, however, would indicate that I am Arab. The name 'Aljunied' represents a Hadhrami-Arab family in Singapore. What added to the principal's confusion was that the train station adjacent to the school was named Aljunied, in honour of the Arab contribution to the making of modern Singapore. Why, then, wasn't a child of one of Singapore's merchant families paying school fees? Why was I – an Arab by birth – enjoying the same privileges as the Malays, who are acknowledged in the constitution as the indigenous people of Singapore?

I was unsure of how to clarify my fuzzy identity to the principal of the Christian school, where I, a Muslim, was enrolled because my father believed that Muslims could learn a lot from non-Muslims. I vividly remember explaining to the principal that I am Arab through my paternal side and that my mother has Indian ancestry, but that my family brought me up in the Malay culture, that we spoke the Malay language at home and that I was living in a Malay neighbourhood at Jalan Eunos. I was registered as a Malay when I was born, as was my father before me. The matter was left unresolved. The principal, a loyal servant of the state, became even more confused by my explanation but did not get the fees that she wanted. Many years later,

I found out that my responses as a thirteen-year-old teenager were common answers given by localised Arabs when asked about their identities. Like me, they became 'both locals and cosmopolitans' in a region known historically as the 'Malay world'.[1] Like them, I fell in love with the locals and ended up marrying a Malay lady whose mother is half Chinese. My children will have a harder time explaining to school principals what their 'real' identities are, should I choose not to pay their fees.

If I were given another chance to have the same conversation with that principal, my answer might have been different, or perhaps it might have been more nuanced. Beyond the racial categorisations and parochialism of the state and its gatekeepers, my own ambiguous identity and full acceptance into the Malay community reflects an enduring feature of a region that I regard as home: Muslim cosmopolitanism. This book deals with the larger context that shaped my own experiences as a Southeast Asian Muslim whose roots hail from both South Asia and the Middle East, whose feet are firmly planted in the Malay world and whose worldview has been shaped by the visions of cosmopolitans. It is concerned with the historical sociology of Muslim cosmopolitanism in Southeast Asia. It investigates the complex ways by which cosmopolitan ideals have been creatively employed and carefully adapted by Muslim individuals, societies and institutions in Southeast Asia to bring about the necessary contexts for mutual tolerance and shared respect between and within different groups, particularly between religious groups in society.

As a Muslim cosmopolitan myself, whose understanding of Islam has been shaped by the inclusiveness and openness of the people around me, I aim to demonstrate the ways in which the spaces and personalities to which I have been exposed and predisposed throughout my life have laid the conditions for dialogue and shared goals among Muslims and between Muslims and non-Muslims in the region. This book also explores how these relationships have weathered the politics and policies of authoritarian states and the divisive forces that still threaten much of humanity. A work of reflexive and comparative historical sociology rather than narrative history or traditional chronology, this book seeks to interweave the connected Muslim histories of part of the region that has been called 'Muslim Southeast Asia'. I use the term 'Muslim Southeast Asia' to refer to what has also been called the 'Malay world' and is known today as Singapore, Malaysia, Indonesia, Brunei, the Southern Philippines and Southern Thailand.[2]

My angle of vision is centred primarily on Singapore, Malaysia and Indonesia because these countries have been my archive, the primary sites of my historical enquiry and the places that I have been most exposed to throughout my scholarly career. Forming the bulk of Muslim Southeast Asia, the combined population of Singapore, Malaysia and Indonesia is estimated to be close to 280 million. Muslims are a minority in modern-day Singapore (15 per cent of the total population) and are majorities in Malaysia (60 per cent) and Indonesia (close to 90 per cent).[3] Singapore is included in my analysis because it is entirely surrounded by its Muslim-majority neighbouring countries. Moreover, Muslims in Singapore still maintain very close links with their co-religionists in Malaysia and Indonesia to this day.

Despite major differences in terms of demography, land size and the pace of development, these countries share many affinities. The Malays constitute the majority among the Muslims of Muslim Southeast Asia. They are generally Sunni Muslims of the Shafi'ite school of jurisprudence, with the exception of a small minority which subscribes to the Shi'ite faith and its distinctive schools of law. The influence of Sufism is pervasive among Muslims in the region. For many centuries, the Sufis and their *tariqahs* (orders) played creative and vital roles in the Islamisation of the Malay world. Although the influence of this age-old proclivity within Islam is progressively counterbalanced by the spread of Islamic modernism and Salafism, Southeast Asian Sufism is now set on a path of revival as it struggles to sustain its relevance in the twenty-first century.[4]

The Muslim population of Southeast Asia has a youthful profile due to high birth rates and state policies of encouraging marriage. For more than a century, Malay Muslims in Malaysia and Singapore have placed a high premium on having large families, with an average of at least three or more children in each household. The Southeast Asian Muslim youth has been, by and large, globalised in its outlook, plugging into global popular cultures and consumption patterns, and appropriating ideas from Muslim scholars in many parts of the globe to address its own challenges and queries. This 'globalised Muslim youth' manifests an innate tendency in syncretising different influences that emanate from the West, the Middle East and Asia to express unique renderings of Islam that are coloured by local cultures.[5]

The exclusion of Brunei, the Southern Philippines and Southern Thailand from this book does not at all imply that Muslim cosmopolitanism is absent from these countries. Rather, I hope that my findings will encourage future specialists to consider and to bring to light the compelling potential of Muslim cosmopolitanism amidst state enforcement of religious laws in Brunei and the unending separatist violence in the Southern Philippines and Southern Thailand. That being said, I was based at the University of Brunei for a few months as a visiting professor in early 2015 and have conducted fieldwork in the Philippines that culminated in the publication of a number of academic articles on the memories of violence among Muslims.[6] Although I have not stayed for extended periods in Southern Thailand or written anything about it, I have been invited to a number of conferences in Patani and interacted with local researchers. It is clear to me that Muslim cosmopolitanism does exist in these countries. Nevertheless, I have chosen to omit these countries from this study because of my lack of detailed historical and ethnographical knowledge about the Muslim and non-Muslim relations there.

The works of Tariq Ramadan, Manuel Castells and Bruce Lawrence provide the building blocks for the comparative historical methodology used in this study. Tariq advocates the utilisation of the inductive method in the study of cosmopolitanism, particularly in Muslim societies. This can be achieved through critically observing and analysing cosmopolitan practices on the ground 'in order to question, and if necessary challenge, existing philosophical perspectives'.[7] Thus far, writings on cosmopolitanism suffer from the fallacy of indulging in abstract theorising without connecting the concept to 'a set of universal values and principles with local commitments'.[8] Inspired by Tariq's insights, I use edifying vignettes, personal interviews and encounters as well as informative case studies from across Muslim Southeast Asia to provide a panoramic view of Muslim cosmopolitan practices, outlooks and visions in the region. I engage with the prevailing theories of cosmopolitanism, using these postulations as heuristic tools rather than exact depictions of social realities. As such, I hope to interrogate and expand the theoretical discussions surrounding how cosmopolitanism in Asia is lived and thought about. This book grounds Walter Mignolo's concept of 'cosmopolitan localism' within Southeast Asian realities and provides further evidence that there is no need to necessarily take on board Immanuel Kant's ideas as the frame of reference or even the starting point for the study of Muslim cosmopolitanism. Kant, as Mignolo forcefully indicates, 'should be taken as *a local ideal of a cosmopolitan world, the European idea*. Since such imperial cosmopolitanism now is untenable, it is necessary to reduce Kantian legacies to size for there are many other local histories in which cosmopolitan projects emerge'.[9]

As a corollary to this, my critique is directed towards theorists who have attributed the development of religious cosmopolitanism principally to the forces of European globalisation and technological revolutions.[10] In analysing these macro processes, less attention has been given to micro processes, that is, the agency of laypersons who populate markets, mosques and the digital worlds. The masses have played a major role in fostering tolerance, dialogue, pluralism and mutual help among different groups in society, even prior to the coming of globalisation and digital media. This book provides grounded theorisations of religious cosmopolitanism that include both 'elite' and 'subaltern' as well as 'official' and 'vernacular' Muslim cosmopolitanisms within Southeast Asia. I show how variables such as places, personas and politics can contribute to the making and unmaking of various shades of cosmopolitanism in Muslim Southeast Asia, in the present as well as in the distant past. Put differently, Muslim cosmopolitanism can emerge both 'bottom up' and 'top down' from within individuals, communities and activists, just as emerging global factors can aid in the process of sharpening cosmopolitan outlooks in a particular setting. I also foreground the many instances whereby postcolonial states have constricted the evolution of Muslim cosmopolitanism by taming global and local dynamisms to serve their hegemonic ends.

This book brings into sharp relief the history of Muslim cosmopolitanism in Southeast Asia from the 1970s to the early twenty-first century not only because it coincides with my own life story as a Muslim born in the 1970s, but also because it corresponds with what has been described by Manuel Castells as the 'rise of the networked society'. For Castells, the period from the 1970s until the early twentieth century is important methodologically because of the conclusions one can reach about the various structures and processes – both religious and secular – that shaped global societies. Muslim Southeast Asia witnessed the progress and spread of media and informational technology fuelled by the forces of global capitalism during this landmark period. The upshot of this radical disjuncture in human history, according to Castells, was the creation of 'a world of uncontrolled, confusing change' which compels people 'to regroup around primary identities; religious, ethnic, territorial, [and] national'.[11] I will show that, while there is evidence of enclavement, partisanship and provincialism among Muslims in Southeast Asia, cosmopolitan tendencies have persevered and have been augmented by the networked society. In the virtual world, within sites of sociability, through the writings of networked intellectuals and the everyday lives of religious communities in the region, Muslim cosmopolitanism is discussed, disseminated and developed, bringing people closer together.

In showing that Muslim cosmopolitanism in Southeast Asia grew alongside the growth of the networked society, this book positions itself as a counterpoint to the growing perception of Islam and other religions as divisive forces and powerful engines of dissension in society. It contributes to the emerging scholarship that shatters the preponderant thesis that Muslims are prone to violence to achieve what are supposedly their essentially absolutist, divisive and insufficiently rational aims. In this line of reasoning, attempts to reconcile Muslim religious convictions with cosmopolitan ideals are doomed to failure from the very outset. The uncompromising stance that Muslims supposedly assume makes it impossible for any reasonable dialogue to take place. Such presumptions have become entrenched in academia and the media across the globe. These conjectures are mythical, according to William T. Cavanaugh in a provocative book entitled *The Myth of Religious Violence*. The argument that religions such as Islam cause violence or that religion is a source of conflict in society and averse to cosmopolitan tendencies legitimates

> the marginalization of certain types of practices and groups labeled religious, while underwriting the nation-state's monopoly on its citizens' willingness to sacrifice and kill. In foreign policy, the myth of religious violence serves to cast nonsecular social orders, especially Muslim societies, in the role of villain. *They* have not yet learnt to remove the dangerous influence of religion from political life. *Their* violence is therefore irrational and fanatical. *Our* violence, being secular, is rational, peace making, and sometimes regrettably necessary to contain *their* violence. We find ourselves obliged to bomb them into liberal democracy.[12]

On the contrary, this book explains how informed dialogue and engagement in Muslim Southeast Asia has pervaded the work of individuals and collectives wedded to cosmopolitan values. I display a whole variety of groups open to discourses and dialogues to reveal the manner to which Muslims continuously strive to bridge differences between collectives in local societies. Among such groups are Muslim bloggers who have been influential since the last decade, since they function as sources of alternative news and opinions for Southeast Asians.

That Muslim cosmopolitanism in Muslim Southeast Asia could withstand the radical changes that came with the networked society bespeaks of deeper cosmopolitan foundations embedded within local societies. It is here that the writings of Bruce Lawrence are instructive. Drawing upon the ideas of a renowned historian of Islam, Marshall Hodgson, Lawrence calls for an unbiased, global and comparative historical approach to Muslim societies in order to uncover enduring cosmopolitan sensibilities. He urges scholars to move beyond the sensational headlines of the contemporary media about the Islamic threat to look at the passionate interactions between Muslims and non-Muslims in history, especially in cities and urban areas. These connections transcended religious affiliations and were kept alive for a millennium because 'Islam is radically cosmopolitan in its origins'. To Lawrence, 'Muslim cosmopolitanism . . . is nothing less than the urban, trans-cultural arc of an Islam inspired engagement with our common humanity'.[13] *Pace* Lawrence, I trace the roots of Muslim cosmopolitanism in Southeast Asia from the moment when Islam first originated in the region to the near present. By connecting the venture of Southeast Asian Islam with developments in the larger Muslim world, I demonstrate that Muslim cosmopolitanism has remained ensconced in Southeast Asia due in part to the growth of multicultural and pluralised sites such as Singapore, Kuala Lumpur and Jakarta, among many others.

In investigating a topic that has not been given the attention it deserves in the history of religions and forms of religiosity in Southeast Asia, this book pushes the boundaries of the expanding body of literature on the Muslim cosmopolitan outlook and visions to develop a contextualised exposition of the concept that is grounded upon the Southeast Asian experience. Previous studies on Muslim cosmopolitanism have been centred mostly on Europe, the Middle East, Africa, South Asia and East Asia, and are restricted to developments within particular countries such as India, Turkey and Egypt, to name a few. While the term 'Muslim cosmopolitanism' has been put to use by scholars working on these various Muslim regions, no clear definition has been offered. As a concept, Muslim cosmopolitanism thus suffers from being used too loosely and too indiscriminately to describe anything that Muslims say and do which points towards some degree of inclusivity.[14]

Here, I offer a fresh definition of the concept as it has been lived and expressed by Southeast Asian Muslims through an ensemble of ideas, spaces, practices, dispositions, discourses and activities. Muslim cosmopolitanism in Southeast Asia is a style of thought, a habit of seeing the world and a way of living that is rooted in the central tenet of Islam, which is that everyone is part of a common humanity accountable to God and that we are morally responsible towards one another. To embrace Muslim cosmopolitanism is to exhibit a high degree of receptiveness to universal values that are embedded within one's own customs and traditions (*adat*). Internalising Muslim cosmopolitanism enables a person to be at ease with his or her own Islamic and cultural identities, promoting these identities as a means to enrich public understanding about Islam and Muslims while maintaining and embracing a tolerant attitude towards people of other backgrounds. It follows, then, that Muslim cosmopolitans approach varied ways of thinking about Islam and about life in an open-hearted and empowering way in the path to ensure the protection of faith, life, lineage, intellect, property and rights of all groups and individuals in society. As living embodiments of Muslim cosmopolitanism, they are committed to a set of practices and actions that are aimed at enlivening the spirit of compassion (*rahmah*), justice (*adil*) and consensus (*musyawarah*) in order to safeguard public interest (*maslahah*).

Three interlinking issues emerge from such a definition of Muslim cosmopolitanism. First, Muslim cosmopolitanism involves relationships and interactions within the Muslim community, in other words between Muslims of different ideological persuasions and frames of mind. To ensure the vitality of Muslim cosmopolitanism, Muslims in Southeast Asia have attempted, and are unremittingly attempting, to dissolve the bifurcation between traditionalists and modernists and between conservatives and reformists towards assuming a live-and-let-live approach to contentious matters affecting Muslims.

Undeniably, there have been rifts and schisms among Muslims, as seen from my discussion in Chapter 3 on the 'Salafi–Sufi discords' in Malaysia.[15] But such divisions, as this book clarifies, have not undermined the overall cosmopolitan texture of Southeast Asian Islam. It has certainly not led to large-scale sectarian violence.

Second, Muslim cosmopolitanism encompasses ties between Muslims and non-Muslims. As minorities in Malaysia and Indonesia and the majority population in Singapore, non-Muslims have enjoyed mostly harmonious relationships with Muslims across the region. Chapters 1 and 2 on marketplaces and mosques clearly demonstrate this point. In Surabaya, for example, non-Muslims are still visible and are, in fact, dominant in businesses linked to the Muslim consumer market. Muslims and non-Muslims get along extremely well in Sarawak, where Malays are a minority population. They have gone to the extent of sharing sacred spaces to invigorate the spirit of cooperation between the different communities. Muslim cosmopolitanism, from this perspective, is thus not a Muslim-driven enterprise. It can only be made real through the active participation of non-Muslims in the creation of a tolerant society.

Above all, it is obvious that the definition of Muslim cosmopolitanism I offer above draws much from the *maqasid al-shariah* (the goals and purposes of Islamic law).[16] To be sure, much of the thinking and practices of Muslims in Southeast Asia today, and throughout history, is guided by this framework, even though many are often unconscious of it. From the time when Islam first arrived in the region in the eleventh century right up to the present day, prominent Muslim thinkers and preachers have propagated a universalist rather than a communalist conception of Islam. They have espoused the 'maqasidic' maxim that the well-being and public interest of the larger society must be preserved for Muslims to coexist amicably with each other and with other communities. For this and other related reasons, Islamisation in Southeast Asia was described as a 'penetration pacifique'.[17] It was seldom disseminated through the use of force, and predominantly traded through the harmonisation of local customs and beliefs with Islamic teachings. What grew out of this vibrant process, according to Robert Hefner, was the maturing of 'cultural pluralism'.[18] I would go further to suggest that the 'maqasidic' approaches of thinkers and preachers aided in the making of a cosmopolitan Islam. Although the *maqasid al-shariah* were not as intellectu-alised in Southeast Asia as in other parts of the Muslim world until the advent of Islamic reformism in the twentieth century, it was certainly experienced and realised in the everyday lives of the believers.[19] This is clearly seen in the agency of women in Southeast Asia as the torchbearers of cosmopolitan practices. They exhibit a high degree of enthusiasm and commitment in advocating for gender equality, and have also played a big part in nurturing the younger generation's cosmopolitan values through their involvement in advocacy work. One example of such activism by women is the hijab (head-scarf) movement, which is explored at length in Chapter 5 of this book.

Although unique to the Southeast Asian context, many elements of Muslim cosmopolitanism there may well mirror the incarnations of Muslim cosmopolitanism found in other regions, such as along the coasts of the Indian Ocean.[20] I, therefore, depart from Humeira Iqtidar's supposition that 'given the immense variation within the category "Muslim", it is not entirely feasible to conceive of a coherent and stable phenomenon called "Muslim Cosmopolitanism"'.[21] Muslim cosmopolitanism, to my mind, need not be a stable and coherent phenomenon in any given time and space. Much like Islam as a belief system and a cultural reality, different individuals and groups may understand and express cosmopolitanism differently in accordance with the demands of their milieus. They are, however, bounded by the shared conviction that Muslims are accountable to all of humankind and that they learn from each other and from the 'other'. Purveyors of Muslim cosmo-politanism contribute to the making of plural societies, ensuring that peace, harmony and mutual respect are upheld just as they unceasingly oppose the forces of hate and disunity. They all come under the canopy of Muslim cosmopolitanism.

Themes of Muslim Cosmopolitanism

I have structured this book into three thematic parts. Part I explores the processes of cosmopolitanisation across a range of sites and spaces in Muslim Southeast Asia. These chapters highlight the significance of the secular and sacred, virtual and physical places in producing varieties of everyday situated cosmopolitanisms. Such arenas create the conditions for interaction between peoples of varied cultures, origins and ways of life. Chapter 1 looks at spaces where societal actors interact as they buy and sell all sorts of everyday products and services. In the marketplace, where economic activities take place, Muslims and non-Muslims speak, exchange and bargain with one another and thereby sustain peaceful relationships. I look back at history and explore how Southeast Asia developed its reputation of being a region of trading hubs and settlements for diverse communities. Such historical legacies along with the built character of marketplaces in Penang and Kelantan, for example, set the stage for fluid interactions between businessmen, traders and customers, and between Muslims and non-Muslims, each learning the subtleties of their respective cultures while appreciating one another's differences and commonalities alike.

From the marketplace, the book moves on in Chapter 2 to look at sacred spaces. I examine mosques and explain that these institutions are not just devotional places, they are also projections of the cosmopolitan temperaments of Southeast Asian Muslims. This is evidenced in the aesthetics and architecture of the mosques that draw upon so many religious and cultural traditions. Mosques in Muslim Southeast Asia live up to Ulf Hannerz's suggestion that genuine cosmopolitanism entails 'an intellectual and aesthetic openness toward divergent cultural experiences, a search for contrasts rather than uniformity'.[22] The chapter delves into the sharing of sacred space by Muslims and non-Muslims, pointing to the close proximity between mosques and other places of worship. This nearness has encouraged worshippers of different faiths to help one another in a spirit of mutual tolerance and cooperation to ensure the safety and welfare of their respective religious institutions. I also highlight the inclusion of women in the spaces and activities of Southeast Asian mosques, a distinguishing quality that is not so readily found in other parts of the Muslim today.

Chapter 3 of this section scrutinises the virtual world as a space where people coming from different backgrounds gather to share, socialise and partake in discussions about the pertinent issues of their time, thereby attaining clarity about what is at stake for themselves and their societies. The attention here is on Muslim blogs that are aimed at transcending the ideological differences within the Muslim community, the bloggers' strategies in combating Islamophobia and their promotion of ethical conduct online.

Part II of the book highlights the personalities and groups that promote

Muslim cosmopolitanism in Southeast Asia. I explore the manner in which these various groups and individuals exhibit a positive attitude towards differences in society. I underscore their efforts to construct broad allegiances that cut across cultural and social boundaries to address humanitarian problems. In looking at Muslim intellectuals and hijab activists, this part of the book argues that one of the hallmarks of Muslim cosmopolitanism in the region has been the 'obligation to others, obligations that stretch beyond those to whom we are related by ties of kith and kind, or even the more formal ties of citizenship'.[23] Chapter 4 looks at selected Muslim public intellectuals who have actively promoted cosmopolitan attitudes among Muslims in Southeast Asia. These public intellectuals are academics in universities and social commentators who write books and essays calling for cooperation between Muslims and non-Muslims in their countries. They are affiliated to genealogies and networks of intellectuals who inspired them to construct concepts such as 'Qur'anic justice', 'Islam Nusantara' and 'Islamic assertiveness' on the road to thwarting extremism and exclusivism in piety and faith.

The major line of argument pursued in Chapter 5 is that women have contributed extensively to the promotion of gender cosmopolitanism in Southeast Asia. I showcase hijab activists as well as female intellectuals and their interrogation of the excesses of Western feminism. These women have questioned the insularity of a segment of the Southeast Asian community and have courageously campaigned for their inclusion in workplaces that are prejudiced against women who wear headscarves. In campaigning for the hijab and presenting the modesty of Muslim women in innovative ways and styles, these women have revolutionised the concept of modesty in modern societies while reformulating commonplace understandings of gender justice in Muslim Southeast Asia.

Finally, Part III dissects the policies of postcolonial secular states towards Muslim cosmopolitanism across Southeast Asia. I expound on the different tactics that three different states (Indonesia, Malaysia and Singapore) have employed to tame Muslim cosmopolitanism. In so doing, these states have greatly departed from the statecraft of premodern Southeast Asian polities that laid the foundations for the entrenchment of Muslim cosmopolitanism in the region. Despite their varied political trajectories, these states share a common authoritarian objective of constraining and containing the progress of Muslim cosmopolitanism in order to keep it subservient to secular-nationalist projects. Secular states in postcolonial Muslim Southeast Asia, in this analysis, are inhibitors rather than enablers of Muslim cosmopolitanism.

The spectres of secular fundamentalism, nationalist particularism, religious fundamentalism and state intolerance have each challenged Muslim cosmopolitanism in Southeast Asia. Notwithstanding these challenges, Muslim cosmopolitanism has continued to thrive. I invite readers of this book to approach the ensuing pages with new lenses to comprehend what I saw as a teenager and what I continue to see as a scholar living among Muslim cosmopolitans. We must train our eyes to look beyond episodic moments of conflict and dissension. We must begin to see like cosmopolitans and appreciate the practices of the majority, people who have cohabited peacefully for many generations. Indeed, seeing like a cosmopolitan encourages us to pay close attention to those neglected activists and intellectuals who make universal values apparent in their discourses. Seeing like a cosmopolitan enables us to observe carefully the harmonious conversations between strangers in markets and sacred spaces, in the virtual and real worlds, between men and women, and between Muslims and non-Muslims, in whatever costumes they may be wearing, to construct a better world for us all.

Notes

1. Engseng Ho, *The Graves of Tarim: Genealogy and Mobility across the Indian Ocean* (Berkeley: University of California Press, 2006), p. 189. See also Judith Nagata, 'What is Malay? Situational Selection of Ethnic Identity in a Plural Society', *American Ethnologist*, 1, 2 (1974), pp. 331–50.
2. A recent edited volume shares the same conception of Muslim Southeast Asia. See Joseph Camilleri and Sven Schottmann (eds), *Culture, Religion and Conflict in Muslim Southeast Asia: Negotiating Tense Pluralisms* (Abingdon: Routledge, 2012).
3. Max L. Gross, *A Muslim Archipelago: Islam and Politics in Southeast Asia* (Washington, DC: Center for Strategic Intelligence Research, 2007), p. 1.
4. Julia Day Howell and Martin van Bruinessen, 'Sufism and the "Modern" in Islam', in Julia Day Howell and Martin van Bruinessen (eds), *Sufism and the 'Modern' in Islam* (London: I. B. Tauris, 2007), pp. 1–18.
5. Kamaludeen Mohamed Nasir, *Globalized Muslim Youth in the Asia Pacific:*

Popular Culture in Singapore and Sydney (Basingstoke: Palgrave Macmillan, 2016) and Howard Federspiel, *Sultans, Shamans, and Saints: Islam and Muslims in Southeast Asia* (Honolulu: University of Hawai'i Press, 2007), pp. 251–4.

6. Khairudin Aljunied and Rommel Curaming, 'Mediating and Consuming the Memories of Violence in the Philippines', *Critical Asian Studies*, 44, 1 (2012), pp. 227–50; Khairudin Aljunied and Rommel Curaming, 'Social Memory and State-Civil Society Relations in the Philippines: Forgetting and Remembering Jabidah "Massacre"', *Time and Society*, 21, 1 (2012), pp. 89–103; Khairudin Aljunied and Rommel Curaming, 'The Uneven Topography of Personal Memory', in Kah Seng Loh, Stephen Dobbs and Ernest Koh (eds), *Oral History in Southeast Asia: Memories and Fragments* (New York: Palgrave Macmillan, 2013), pp. 83–100.

7. Tariq Ramadan, 'Cosmopolitan Theory and the Dual Pluralism of Life', in Nina Glick Schiller and Andrew Irving (eds), *Whose Cosmopolitanism? Critical Perspectives, Relationalities and Discontents* (Oxford: Berg, 2015), p. 58.

8. Ramadan, 'Cosmopolitan Theory', p. 58.

9. Walter Mignolo, 'Cosmopolitan Localism: A Decolonial Shifting of the Kantian Legacies, *Localities,* 1, (2011), p. 44.

10. Ulrich Beck, *Cosmopolitan Vision* (Cambridge: Polity Press, 2006) and *A God of One's Own: Religion's Capacity for Peace and Potential for Violence* (Cambridge: Polity Press, 2010).

11. Manuel Castells, *The Networked Society*, 2nd edition (Cambridge: Blackwell, 2000), p. 3.

12. William T. Cavanaugh, *The Myth of Religious Violence: Secular Ideology and the Roots of Modern Conflict* (New York: Oxford University Press, 2009), p. 4.

13. Bruce Lawrence, 'Muslim Cosmopolitanism', *Critical Muslim*, 2 (2012), pp. 19–20.

14. Sami Zubaida, 'Cosmopolitanism and the Middle East', in Roel Meijer (ed.), *Cosmopolitanism, Identity, and Authenticity in the Middle East* (Richmond: Curzon Press, 1999), pp. 15–34; Muhammad Qasim Zaman, 'The Scope and Limits of Islamic Cosmopolitanism and the Discursive Language of the Ulama', in Miriam Cooke and Bruce Lawrence (eds), *Muslim Networks from Hajj to Hip Hop* (Chapel Hill: University of North Carolina Press, 2005), pp. 84–104; Karim H. Karim, 'Cosmopolitanism: Ways of Being Muslim', in Amyn B. Sajoo (ed.), *A Companion to Muslim Cultures* (London: I. B. Tauris, 2011), pp. 201–20; Carool Kersten, *Cosmopolitans and Heretics: New Muslim Intellectuals and the Study of Islam* (New York: Columbia University

Press, 2011); Lawrence, 'Muslim Cosmopolitanism'; Mara A. Leichtman and Dorothea Schulz (eds), 'Special Issue on Muslim Cosmopolitanism: Movement, Identity and Contemporary Reconfiguration', *City & Society*, 24, 1 (2012) and Seema Alavi, *Muslim Cosmopolitanism in the Age of Empire* (Cambridge, MA: Harvard University Press, 2015).

15. Dennis Ignatius, 'Wahhabism in Southeast Asia', Asia Sentinel, 27 March 2015, <http://www.asiasentinel.com/society/wahhabism-in-southeast-asia/> (last accessed 1 March 2016).

16. For an excellent summary of the *maqasid al-shariah*, see Jasser Auda, *Maqasid al-Shari'ah: A Beginner's Guide* (London: International Institute of Islamic Thought, 2008).

17. Thomas W. Arnold, *The Preaching of Islam* (Lahore: Ashraf, 1961), p. 363.

18. Robert W. Hefner, *Civil Islam: Muslims and Democratization in Indonesia* (Princeton, NJ: Princeton University Press, 2000), p. 14.

19. My current research, which I hope to publish soon, will elaborate on the development of 'maqasidic' thought among Muslim reformers as exemplified in the works of the famous Indonesian preacher, Haji Abdul Malik bin Abdul Karim Amrullah (Hamka). Hamka, too, discussed the revival of such a line of thinking in many of his historical writings. See Khairudin Aljunied, 'Writing Reformist Histories: A Cleric as an Outsider-History Maker', *The Public Historian*, 37, 3 (2015), pp. 10–28.

20. Kai Kreese and Edward Simpson (eds), *Struggling with History: Islam and Cosmopolitanism in the Western Indian Ocean* (London: Hurst, 2008) and Kai Kreese, 'Interrogating "Cosmopolitanism" in an Indian Ocean Setting: Thinking Through Mombasa on the Swahili Coast', in Derryl N. MacLean and Sikeena Karmali Ahmed (eds), *Cosmopolitanisms in Muslim Contexts: Perspectives from the Past* (Edinburgh: Edinburgh University Press, 2012), pp. 31–50.

21. Humeira Iqtidar, 'Muslim Cosmopolitanism: Contemporary Theory and Social Practice', in Bryan S. Turner, *The Routledge Handbook of Globalization Studies* (London: Routledge, 2010), p. 631.

22. Ulf Hannerz, *Transnational Connections: Culture, People, Places* (London: Routledge, 1996), p. 103.

23. Anthony Appiah, *Cosmopolitanism: Ethics in a World of Strangers* (New York: Norton, 2006), p. xv.

PART I

PLACES

1

EVERYDAY COSMOPOLITANISM IN
THE MARKETPLACE

Visitors to the Tanah Abang area in Jakarta are often amazed by the vast and lavish green building that houses the largest textile market in Southeast Asia. Built in the image of the Islamic monuments of the medieval Arab-Turkish and Persian cities, the Tanah Abang textile mall covers 160,000 square metres, including a mosque within it that can accommodate more than a thousand worshippers. The shops in this iconic mall are sites where bargaining and other commercial exchanges take place daily. Muslim clothing such as long gowns, headscarves, cuffs and tonic tops are sold there, alongside shoes and batik products. What is most amusing about this much talked about mega mall is the pervasive presence of Chinese businessmen and businesswomen. This has not, however, dissuaded the majority Muslims of Southeast Asia from joining the droves of daily shoppers there.[1]

Tanah Abang is not the only modern market (also known as *pasar* in Malay) in Indonesia where such Muslim cosmopolitanism coexists seamlessly with criminals and riff-raff in the Jakarta area.[2] The tenor of affable interreligious and intercommunal exchanges is obvious at Senen, Pasar Baru, Glodok, Mangga Dua, Cempaka Mas and Jatinegara in Indonesia. Elsewhere in Southeast Asia, such a scene is most vividly evident at the Geylang Serai market in the eastern part of Singapore. Known as 'The Malay Emporium of Singapore',[3] a marked presence of diverse communites can be felt at the market. To be sure, Malays in Singapore are fond of buying basic necessities

3

and foodstuffs, clothes and other household products from shops in the area, whether owned by Muslims or non-Muslims. While English is the working language for most Singaporeans today in view of the government's policy of connecting Singapore in a globalising world and of differentiating the country from the rest of Muslim Southeast Asia, where the dominant language is Malay-Indonesian, in Geylang, the more common mode of communication is 'Melayu Pasar' (Market Malay), which is a mixture of Malay and English used by business people and their Muslim patrons to arrive at the best deals for the day. Such linguistic cosmopolitanism is not exclusive to Geylang. It is a common feature among many port cities in the Asia Pacific region, where different cultures encounter one another thus bringing about the creation of creole languages in an interactional setting.[4]

Both the Tanah Abang and Geylang markets, to use the words of a social theorist, are 'cosmopolitan places' where 'new dynamics, interactive moments, and conflicting principles and orientations'[5] between Muslims and non-Muslims are constructed and negotiated. But, this raises a fundamental question: How did these Muslim cosmopolitan spaces emerge and why do their cosmopolitan outlooks endure to this very day? To answer these questions, we need to go as far back as the precolonial and colonial periods. I will then explain the various factors that have ensured the continued vitality of Muslim cosmopolitanism in these spaces. The following pages will explain the role of interactions, the demographic make-up of these markets, and the spatial dynamics that provided the necessary conditions for Muslim cosmopolitanism to flourish. It will become obvious that Muslim cosmopolitanism must, first and foremost, be analysed through the perspective of the marketplace, for these are 'contact zones'[6] where Southeast Asians of all religious faiths and persuasions meet, speak, exchange and fraternise with each other.

The Force of History

We can only fully comprehend the actualisation of these cosmopolitan spaces by looking backwards deep into the precolonial past. Anthony Reid and Leonard Andaya, in their masterly works on early modern Southeast Asia, have painstakingly documented the existence of cosmopolitan port cities where Muslims and non-Muslims congregated to trade, intermarry and persuade one another to accept their respective beliefs, languages and cultures.[7]

This was the 'Age of Commerce' (1400–1650), a watershed period of intense Islamisation of the Malay world, one that witnessed gradual transformations of all aspects of Southeast Asian life. Among such transformations was the creation of hybridised Islamic cultures and cosmopolitan marketplaces across the region. Malacca, Grisek and Makassar, Anthony Reid observes, 'developed from little more than villages to cosmopolitan cities with populations of fifty thousand or more within a century. Aceh, Banten, Patani and Ayudhya also grew to great conurbations'.[8] Meanwhile, the Kingdom of Aceh, according to Leonard Andaya,

> demonstrated its Islamic cosmopolitanism by adhering to the latest religious and secular fashions from the Islamic world. Scholars, traders, and foreign envoys from Muslim lands brought their wares, tracts, and ideas to Aceh. They enticed the ruler and the people to institute changes that would update their society in the image of their illustrious coreligionists in the Ottoman, Safavid, and Mughal Empires. As was characteristic of Southeast Asia, Aceh only selected those aspects that were compatible with the society.[9]

The port city of Malacca was an archetype of this new development. Under the reign of Sri Maharaja Muhammad (1425–45), Malacca developed into a hub of international trade that was facilitated primarily by a Muslim sultanate. The Chinese settled in the city and were allowed to practise their ways of life without fear. In 1436, a scholar who was among the fleet commanded by the legendary Admiral Cheng Ho wrote, 'Pork was eaten by the Chinese who live in Melaka. They lived in a hotel, the chief of which always sends female slaves to serve them and sends their food and drink morning and evening'.[10] Hadhrami Arabs, Chinese, Turks, Malabaris, Bengalis, Javanese, Sumatrans, Armenians, Burmese, Okinawans, Gujaratis and Europeans lived alongside one another in the villages near the river as they engaged in trading activities there. The crowds that thronged the Malaccan streets were said to have used eighty-four languages in their day-to-day conversations, although Melayu (the Malay language) was the lingua franca for trade and diplomacy. Although hyperbolic, this claim 'does convey the idea of the multi-cultural, cosmopolitan atmosphere typical of Southeast Asian towns'.[11] The famed Portuguese traveller, Tomé Pires, noted that women played a significant role in the markets of Malacca and 'sold in every street'.[12] The same hustle and bustle of business among peoples of varied backgrounds could easily be seen in other Muslim marketplaces, such as Pahang, Johor and Brunei. Malacca was the standard for Muslim cosmopolitanism in other parts of Muslim Southeast Asia.

The coming of European colonialism in the sixteenth century changed the general character of these cosmopolitan marketplaces. New regulations were put in place to serve the capitalist and colonising ends of the Portuguese, the Dutch and the Spanish and, later on, the British and the American trading companies. More defined town plans were enacted. Traders from Europe and elsewhere came to visit and settle in Southeast Asian port cities, displacing many local traders with foreign ones. The city of Banten in Indonesia in the seventeenth century, as a case in point, was once a trading hub in Southeast Asia, but became 'a home only for the wretches' under Dutch rule.[13] The dominance of the Arabs in trade across the Southeast Asian region was also broken by the Western powers. Fully integrated into the local community, the Arabs, however, continued to spread Islam across the region through the medium of Sufi orders and by brokering power and favours with local rulers.[14]

European colonialism left other lasting legacies. Another layer of cosmopolitanism was grafted onto the existing ones. Peter van der Veer terms it 'colonial cosmopolitanism', which connotes liberal and evangelical values as well as lifestyles that were disseminated in the colonies and, many a time, imposed upon the local population.[15] This variant of cosmopolitanism refashioned the Muslim cosmopolitanism that was already rooted across Southeast Asia. European-style buildings, churches, missionary societies, schools and other recreational clubs and societies were founded and locals were encouraged to join these institutions and manifest the worldviews, decorums and languages that defined these places. But, that is not all. The colonial powers also opened up new markets that were soon populated, yet again, by Muslim traders and business people, alongside peoples of other backgrounds. These entrepreneurial Muslims, although disliked by the Europeans, were in many instances seen as indispensable for the colonial states to ensure the exuberance of the markets that they had taken over from the local rulers. The famed 'founder' of Singapore, Sir Thomas Stamford Raffles, paradoxically wrote that 'trade would be reduced to less than one-third of even what it is at present, for it is only through the stimulus which they (the Arabs) give to the industry of the country that its resources are to be developed: but let their trade be regulated; and above all, let them not be left in the enjoyment of immunities'.[16] In planning for the development of the municipal area of what would eventually become the prosperous port city of Singapore, Raffles ensured that one of the business districts in Singapore – the Kampung Glam area – was reserved solely for Muslim entrepreneurs and traders.[17] He was acutely cognizant that the rapid growth of the island's economy depended upon the agency of Muslim cosmopolitans.

Two other significant examples pointing to the emergence of a new form of cosmopolitanism built upon encounters with European colonialism are the Tanah Abang Market and the Pasar Kampung Ampel in Surabaya. A Dutchman, Justinus Vinck, established the Tanah Abang Market in 1733. He envisioned it to be the mother of all markets in Java and a conduit for business people from varying backgrounds. To achieve this, Justinus called upon Arab and Chinese traders to settle in the area. Flows of migrants from China, the Arab world and South Asia entered Tanah Abang Market until the early twentieth century. In 1926, the Dutch had to approve the construction of the Masjid Al-Makmur near the market to attract more Muslim traders to frequent the area. Jitneys were introduced to the area in the 1930s, running parallel to the trams, to improve movement from the market to other parts of Jakarta.[18] Three decades after Indonesia's independence in 1949, Tanah Abang had turned into a Muslim economic hub.

The Hadhrami Arabs from Yemen, with assistance from the local population, in turn founded Pasar Kampung Ampel as early as the mid-fifteenth century. These diasporic Arabs came to the area to spread Islam to the local population while engaging in trade. They soon intermarried into the families of the local Javanese aristocracy and contributed to the making of a creole community that was termed *muwallad* by the people of Hadramaut.[19] The *muwallad* developed Pasar Kampung Ampel into a formidable marketplace where products of all sorts, ranging from food and textiles to household items were imported and sold to the locals. By the late nineteenth century, the Dutch anticipated that the market could eventually develop into a conduit where anti-colonial movements would eventually germinate. The Hadhrami

Arabs were, therefore, segregated from the other local, European, Indian and Chinese people who brought into the area.[20] This did not, however, prevent the market from developing into a cosmopolitan site where peoples of different races communicated easily as they engaged in commercial activities. Indeed, so cosmopolitan was Pasar Kampung Ampel during the colonial period and thereafter that it is now recognised as one of the must-go places for anyone who would like to see the cultural diversity of Indonesian life with a slice of Arab-Muslim culture and religiosity.[21]

These broad strokes of history provide evidence that Muslim cosmopolitanism in Southeast Asia has survived the various radical changes in the region. Muslim cosmopolitanism was most palpable in the markets where multicultural and interethnic elements subsisted. The continued survival of Muslim cosmopolitanism, the easy interactions between Muslims of varying backgrounds and between Muslims and non-Muslims were made possible by the tolerance and openness that these diverse communities had for one another. Southeast Asian Muslims, unlike many Muslims in other parts of the Muslim world, are fortunate to have been spared the problem of mass displacement and the exodus of communities from marketplaces. This factor, along with others that are discussed below, has made Muslim cosmopolitanism in Southeast Asia a living reality.

The Power of Fluid Interactions

Fluid interactions or the ability to speak and communicate in an open, calm and warm manner constitute part of everyday Muslim cosmopolitanism in Southeast Asian markets. Indeed, more than any other space, the market is the place where such fluid interactions between diverse groups are carried out, whether spontaneously or more regularly between those who live in close proximity. Ching, Sterling and Denggao, in their study of a Beijing street market, have shown how interactions in the marketplaces generated cosmopolitan tendencies between peoples of differing backgrounds.

> The marketplace is besides its materiality inherently a social place, where different types of interactions take place, not only in the economic realm, but also through the forms of socio-cultural exchange and communication. The vendors in the market consist primarily of internal migrants from other

provinces in China, who, through their immersion in the trade and involvement with a wide range of customers, develop intercultural and linguistic skills and knowledge of consumer trends from a grassroots perspective. An emergent form of everyday cosmopolitanism unfolds in this transformative process.[22]

The same atmosphere is evidenced in the markets that are scattered across Southeast Asia, although the people absorbed in these interactions may not necessarily be conscious that they are producing and reproducing cosmopolitanism in their own environments. This lack of consciousness is not necessarily a bad thing. Rather, the fact that people may take this condition for granted indicates the normalisation and naturalisation of everyday cosmopolitanism that may, in effect, lead to the creation of purposeful networks.[23] Andrew Causey, in an incisive ethnography of Samosir Island in North Sumatra, observes that marketplaces are 'neutral spaces' where both local Batak traders and foreign visitors can communicate in ways that would otherwise be constrained by their own unique cultures, traditions and ways of life.[24] The marketplace is thus an arena where personal biases, cultural barriers, social inhibitions and ideological differences are cast aside, albeit momentarily. When doing business with non-Muslim customers or merchants or with Muslims of contrasting origins, any ordinary Muslim would have to suspend his or her biases or judgements and instead focus on meaningful talk that would lead to a convergence of interests centred upon buying and selling.

There are several types of fluid interaction that transpire in these markets. Taken together, these interactions form the 'social life of the market'.[25] The first and most basic form of interaction involves 'fostering interest'. Potential customers come to various shops of their liking to look at the diverse items that fascinate them. They encounter active sellers who eagerly tell them about their products, from the prices to the products' characteristics, in order to convince the shoppers to buy them. If such explanations are in line with the customers' demands and needs, the second form of interaction comes into being, which is 'sealing the deal'. Sellers and customers come to mutual agreement about which product would satisfy their respective needs and agree upon a price. While most interactions would usually end at this stage, with sellers selling their products and customers paying for the items and then leaving the shop altogether, there are moments where a more sustained interaction takes place. I call this type of interaction 'the production of market acquaintances'. Sellers and customers become close to one another until they have developed long-term ties that may extend beyond buying and selling. They develop a familiarity with one another to such an extent that the customers soon become regular patrons at these markets and the sellers give them discounts and perks to maintain their 'loyalty'. Through this process of interaction, cosmopolitan tendencies are sustained regardless of the backgrounds of the sellers and customers. These interactions also result in a fusion of cultural horizons between shoppers and merchants, in that the cosmopolitan tastes, desires and aspirations of both groups overlap, thus fostering a sustained relationship.

The interactions in these cosmopolitan markets are also made fluid through the activities of women. Linda J. Seligmann notes that women are effective communicators and agents of economic exchange because they are able to 'interweave household economic dynamics with those of a market economy. In particular, women traders in many areas incorporate reciprocity as a primary aspect of their transactions rather than reducing all exchanges to the law of supply and demand'.[26] Put differently, women act as intermediaries in the selling and trading of goods and services just as they are purveyors of the cultures of the societies to which they belong. Other studies have shown that Muslim women in Southeast Asia have superior capabilities in connecting with the people in the marketplaces and beyond while sharing, albeit subtly, the religious beliefs and customs that came with them. They also tap into their own networks and links to generate business within a particular marketplace and ensure that the interactions between sellers and customers, Muslims and non-Muslims are often lively. This is evidenced in the markets of Islamic Ambon and in West Java, where women play major roles as mediators between sellers and customers.[27]

The active participation of women in market economies has been going on since the precolonial period. The British administrator, Raffles, went as far as to stress that, in Java, 'women alone attend the markets and conduct all the business of buying and selling'.[28] This statement corroborates a lengthy historical study done by Barbara Andaya, who showed how Southeast Asian women, both Muslim and non-Muslim, established a reputation of enabling and expanding trade and commerce in the region prior to the coming of the European trading companies. Their participation in the marketplace also occasioned intermarriages between peoples of varying backgrounds and the birth of people of mixed ethnic ancestry.[29]

Markets in Kelantan are excellent illustrations of women's contributions to interactions in markets and the expansion of Muslim cosmopolitanism. Female participation in the markets has been particularly intense for more than a century. Siti Khadijah Market, more specifically, is a place where women have played active roles in selling goods and have also conversed freely with customers of varying ages, genders and cultural backgrounds. Women were most predominant in the selling of 'textiles, clothing, cosmetics, and jewellery, and also in the *songket* and *batik* trade'.[30] A study of the female traders in Kota Bahru in the late 1980s found that, out of a total 200 respondents, 21 per cent could speak languages other than Malay. More than half of that percentage could speak English and some could speak Chinese.[31] My own fieldwork in Kelantan in 2014 would suggest that a majority of the women active in the market can converse in English, albeit at a basic conversational level, just enough to interact if not attract customers to purchase their products. The wide participation of women in the Kelantanese economy is not seen as a source of shame on the part of the local men, nor are the men anxious about the interactions between their wives and strangers in the market. When I asked a local civil servant and researcher, Asri Yussof, why this is the case, he responded in Malay that:

> It has been like that for many generations now. Women in Kelantan are very hardworking and resourceful. They don't depend on men. They do well in business because of the strong connections that they wield among the womenfolk. They learnt the languages of the market to promote their goods. The men support their wives and render help only when they are asked to. Usually, that is not the case because women have for so long been given the freedom to seek their own income for the well-being of their family.[32]

As a matter of fact, the participation of women in the markets is celebrated and encouraged. The ascendancy of women in the markets and their interactive skills have turned Kelantan into a popular tourist destination for Malays in the region, particularly Muslim women in search of high-quality textiles and clothes at reasonable prices.[33]

What is most interesting about Siti Khadijah Market is the presence of non-Muslims who are not only shoppers but also entrepreneurs doing business alongside Muslims. Many scholars have described Kelantan as a state that is conservative and rule-bound (in terms of Islamic law) because of the dominance of Parti Islam SeMalaysia (PAS, the 'Pan-Malaysian Islamic Party') and religious clerics in politics over the last five decades.[34] However, the realities on the ground are somewhat different. At Siti Khadijah Market, Muslim cosmopolitanism flourishes as Muslims and non-Muslims interact easily with one another. A recent study has provided evidence of the existence a substantial number of Chinese and Thai female vendors at the market. They will don the traditional Malay dresses without necessarily wearing the headscarf. Most, if not all, of the non-Muslim businesspersons can converse in Market Malay.[35]

However, there are more absorbing details about Siti Khadijah Market that should be explicated here. Despite the conservatism that has existed in Kelantanese society for many decades, the marketplaces have remained fairly immune to the policies of the Islamic polity. Why is this so? The simple reason has to do with the fact that even the most conservative of governments such as the PAS sees the importance of these markets to the economy of the state. PAS leaders and clerics have also been sensitive to the reality that these sites could function as spaces where the universality of Islam could be exhibited to non-Muslims. Anyone who visits Siti Khadijah Market will notice the stark presence of non-Muslims (usually Chinese), eating with their hands in the Malay style and interacting with Muslims in ways that make them part and parcel of the larger Muslim landscape. Thus, political Islam does not necessarily influence the shape of Muslim cosmopolitanism in the marketplace.

The cosmopolitan interactions visible in the Kelantanese markets have their southern equivalents in the heart of Kuala Lumpur. Ziauddin Sardar, in his insightful study of the city, has observed that Kuala Lumpur is a hub of malls, markets and bazaars, both permanent and transient ones: 'If Petaling Street is the most famous night market, then Bangsar used to be the most famous all-night congress of hawker stalls.'[36] Because the city was the administrative centre of British Malaya, and because it has for many generations been a site of internal and foreign migration, a multicultural, multilingual and multireligious landscape characterises much of Kuala Lumpur today. One particular area that is a hallmark of the city's cosmopolitanism is Jalan Masjid India (Indian Mosque Street). Located at the heart of the city's Indian district, the street is constantly filled with tourists and travellers looking and bargaining for cheap deals. It is reminiscent of the streets of Chennai in India, with Muslims dominating the trade and business and non-Muslims acting as business counterparts earning their daily bread. But there is much more, as Greg Sheridan informs us:

> Now there are many more Malays and plenty of Chinese too, but the area
> retains its Indian flavour, especially through the shops. This is typically KL
> (Kuala Lumpur), shopping areas with particular ethnic associations are not
> enclaves of exclusion but an offering which all Malaysians can enjoy.[37]

Paul Gilroy argues that 'cosmopolitan conviviality' is built upon in part by fluid interactions between different groups in society.[38] Furthering this point, Duruz, Luckman and Bishop conceptualise markets as 'hybrid spaces within postcolonial cities where different ethnic groups come into contact through everyday activity' and where cosmopolitan conviviality is actually lived rather than theorised.[39] These examples of selected markets in Muslim Southeast Asia buttress the observations of Gilroy and his interlocutors. These are places where antagonisms and biases between peoples of differing backgrounds and origins are suspended and sometimes forgotten to give way to forms of talk that can and have brought mutual benefit to both buyers and sellers as well as to locals and strangers. Fluid interactions in markets ensure the well-being of cosmopolitanism: the conversations that take place between peoples in these markets challenge and even subvert the commonly held ways of being 'religious' or, for that matter, of being 'Muslim'. A chauvinistic Muslim may choose to be antisocial and unfriendly towards anyone aside from his co-religionists. But in the markets, where the rules of sociability are seldom congruent with one's religious orientation, compromises and adjustments have to be made for that Muslim to interact with the people around him. Even the most jingoistic Muslim must therefore become a Muslim cosmopolitan, if only temporarily, when engaging in the fluid and profitable interactions of the marketplace.

The Demographic Composition of Markets

Fluid interactions in the markets would not be possible without the existence of polyglot communities within these spaces. The existence of such diversity aided in the making of Muslim cosmopolitanism in Southeast Asia. Still, the fact that Muslims and non-Muslims coexist within specific social spaces need not necessarily imply that they would accept each other's presence or even communicate with each other otherwise. Recall the conflicts between Muslims and Hindus in India, even in cosmopolitan cities such as Gujarat.[40] These communities have lived with each other for many centuries, yet time and again they find themselves in deadly ethnic riots that have led to the loss of hundreds, even thousands, of lives. Granted, Southeast Asian cities such as Jakarta have witnessed violence against the Chinese in the 1990s, but these riots were caused primarily by state failures and economic disparities rather than Muslim or non-Muslim antagonism.[41] What, then, is the difference between the demography of markets in Southeast Asia when compared, for example, with the ones in South Asia?

One essential difference can be traced to the fact that the Muslims who populated these markets in Southeast Asia adhered largely to a syncretic, pluralistic and Sufistic version of Islam. It is a variant of Islam that encourages openness to others, accepting rather than rejecting strangers, welcoming and not excluding them, and being confident and not intimidated by the presence, practices and beliefs of the foreigners who entered Southeast Asia.[42] This inclusivist rather than exclusivist, universalist rather than particularist, understanding of Islam has structured the ways in which Southeast Asians in these marketplaces dealt with non-Muslims and also with Muslims harbouring different religious and ideological persuasions. The legacies of this inclusive version of Islam have developed since the precolonial period and have endured to the present day. A recent survey found that the majority of Indonesian Muslims are open to having non-Muslim neighbours and are willing to interact and trade with them in markets. The study concluded that this has much to do with the texture of Islam in Indonesia that celebrates diversity, peace and respect for people of all faiths and beliefs.[43]

A related demographic factor that is relevant here is the existence of immigrants in Southeast Asian markets. The arrival of the Chinese, Indians and Arabs in large numbers since the thirteenth century into many parts of Muslim Southeast Asia created creole communities in many port cities in the region.[44] Marriages between Arabs, Indians and Malays gave rise to the Arab Peranakan and Jawi Peranakan communities, which were active in business and trading especially in the markets of Singapore, Malacca and Penang. In Penang, the interchanges and intermarriages between Arabs, Indians and Malays also cultivated the birth of mixed languages (*bahasa kacukan*) that are usually used in the markets by persons of mixed blood.[45] The same can still be seen today at the Arab Street area in Singapore. In this street, businesses are run and owned by persons of mixed backgrounds. In many parts of Indonesia and Malaysia, there developed the local Malay-speaking Chinese communities, more commonly known as the 'Baba Chinese Peranakan' communities, which were dynamic in trade and commerce. By virtue of their ability to speak a few languages – Malay, English, Arabic, South Asian and East Asian dialects – and the higher educational status which they yielded, these creole communities served as arbitrators between local business persons and other foreigners who came to Southeast Asia. Indeed, at the present moment in Singapore, the creole Arab and Indian communities are visible in many markets, acting as bridges between migrants from the Middle East and South Asia in dealing with and exchanging goods with the local communities.[46] Creoles, in this sense, are both catalysts and builders of Muslim cosmopolitanism in Southeast Asian marketplaces.

The broadening of the global tourism in the recent decades is closely linked to the functions of creoles in trade. The Singaporean, Malaysian and Indonesian states have invested millions of dollars per year to encourage tourists to visit and boost their countries' gross domestic product (GDP) and to diversify their economies. By virtue of their status as Muslim-majority countries, both Malaysia and Indonesia have gone all out to attract tourists from other Muslim countries, especially those from oil-rich Arab countries, by positioning their countries as a hub for halal and shariah-compliant tourism.[47] Also capitalising on the Muslim tourist market, Singapore has many Muslim amenities and halal restaurants and has upgraded many of its Muslim heritage sites in its successful bid to become 'the most Muslim-friendly destination among non-Muslim countries'.[48] Both Muslim and non-Muslim tourists visit these countries in large numbers every year. From January to March of

2015, Malaysia had 6,482,696 tourist arrivals, Singapore had 3,241,651, while Indonesia attracted 671,211 tourists. The opening up of these countries to as many annual visitors as possible has influenced the changing demography of Southeast Asian markets. In Singapore, Kuala Lumpur and Jakarta, it is common to see European, East Asian and Arab visitors shopping and sightseeing. Joan C. Henderson describes this well:

> The aftermath of the terrorist strikes in the United States in 2001 incited fears of a backlash against Muslims and practical barriers to their travel in the West, redirecting some tourism and prompting a doubling of Malaysia's Arab tourists that year and again in 2002. The capital Kuala Lumpur with its numerous shopping malls attracts eager shoppers; coastal resorts Langkawi and Penang are also popular. Arabs are reported to be lavish spenders (averaging as much as RM10,000 or US$2,800 per person), and stay almost twice as long as other tourists, frequently journeying in large family parties.[49]

The same holds true for other remote parts of Malaysia and Indonesia that have attracted travellers who are absorbed in ecotourism, heritage tourism, cultural tourism and the like. The widespread availability of halal food in Singapore, Malaysia and Indonesia means that these countries are especially friendly to Arab visitors.[50] These tourists are expanding the frontiers of Muslim cosmopolitanism by exposing Muslims in the region to peoples from places they have not visited or encountered before.

Spatial Dynamics of Markets

The spatial dynamics of markets provide another enabling factor for Muslim cosmopolitanism to flourish in Muslim Southeast Asia. Spatial dynamics include a few things. First, these markets are located in and near cities and towns. The network of roads and the other modes of transportation leading to these markets further intensify the encounters between different groups of people. Tanjung Bungah Market in Penang is one such market. Situated close to a bus interchange, a system of small and major roads, hotels, resorts and also residential housing, it is the biggest market in the northern part of Penang Island. Tanjung Bungah is reputed to be a popular destination for many British retirees.[51] Although Muslims are a minority population on the island, they are visible in that market as pedlars, stallholders and shopkeepers, especially on Tuesday nights when the night market is in operation. A famous mosque, Masjid Terapung Tanjung Bungah, is close to the market for Muslim patrons. This area was partly affected by the 2004 Indian Ocean tsunami, but the market soon regained its dynamism. A Penangite, Mohd Izzuddin, described the market in the following manner:

> To me, the Tanjung Bungah market is a microcosm of Penang Island. Visitors come from all cultures and social backgrounds. All necessities and raw produce are sold here to cater to the needs and culinary tastes of all ethnic groups here, Indians, Chinese, Malays and so forth. Why is the market a focal point for interactions between Muslims and non-Muslims, between Malaysians and foreigners? Because it is open for everyone and serves everyone.[52]

The absence of any form of movement restrictions broadens the scope of Muslim cosmopolitanism in these markets. Certainly, one of the prerequisites for cosmopolitanism to thrive in any context is the freedom for people to move and operate within the borders of their own territories and for others from outside to enter and leave without obstruction. A cosmopolitan, as Chris Rumford puts it, 'lives in and across borders'.[53] Non-Muslims can open their shops at any location within most Southeast Asian markets as long as the products they sell do not disturb or disrupt the fundamental sensitivities of the Muslims. There are also no inhibitions shown towards non-Muslims or Muslims of any persuasion roaming around these markets, as long as they do not do or say anything that might cause controversy. The ease of movement within these markets is more apparent during the festive seasons. In the month of Ramadan, for example, bazaars and makeshift shops mushroom in markets across Southeast Asia. Streets are closed to cars and in places such as the Geylang market in Singapore, decorative lights are installed to encourage people from all walks of life to experience the Muslim month.[54]

Above all, Muslim cosmopolitanism has flourished in these markets because the rules governing the use of space are often broken or at least creatively flaunted to make room for more engagement and interaction between different actors. Abdulmaliq Simone, who has crafted a meticulous account of markets in the heart of Jakarta, argues that part of the allure of the market is the way in which the area surrounding the official market facility is so suddenly and completely transformed into a massive trading floor, which has over the years drawn parts of the official facility into an ancillary extension of its operations in a kind of inversion. At the northern periphery of the area, a special market was opened by presidential decree in order to 'join' the proceedings and find a particular niche within it. This conversion of space entails the use of existing infrastructure, such as road dividers, as places of display, the distribution of lights unofficially connected to the grid, the acrobatic movements of carters who quickly parcel out large volumes of products for sale, the near-instantaneous loading and reloading of vehicles, the intricate choreographies of butchering, the make-shift construction of micro fish farms, and the incessant banter of 'market authorities' who collect fees but, more important, take the pulse of the market's mood, coaxing it along, infusing it with revelry at moments of exhaustion. These are just some of the devices acting as lures, lures that effect a sense of intimacy among things, articulate disparate considerations – economic, affective, political, spatial – into a way of acting in concert that is never fully stabilized through the allocation of clear-cut roles or the implementation of unyielding rules.[55]

Such a description could easily be applied to many markets scattered across the Southeast Asia region.

Conclusion

This chapter has explored markets as cosmopolitan places where societal actors from different backgrounds interact as they exchange all sorts of products and services. In the marketplaces, Muslims and non-Muslims speak, trade and bargain with each other, thereby laying the groundwork for peaceful relationships and the trading of cultural practices. We may couch such a phenomenon in the manner of Adam Smith, who designated it as 'commercial cosmopolitanism'. According to Smith, the shared need for things among human beings brings diverse peoples together in given moments and spaces. Politics, ideologies, ethnicities and other differences are pushed aside to give way to goodwill and conversations about who gets what at an agreed price.[56] In other words, commercial cosmopolitanism has transformed markets into contact zones for peoples of many different backgrounds, each of whom has encountered familiar faces and strangers, looking and speaking to them when necessary and learning to accept 'others' as they are.

Markets are, of course, not the only places where Muslim cosmopolitanism is nurtured and sustained throughout Muslim Southeast Asia. Other sites of sociability, such as coffee shops, cafes, cinemas, recreational parks and other hang-outs at the heart of communities in the region perform a similar function. Seen in this light, we need to sensitise ourselves to those neglected areas where the common folk have acted out their cosmopolitan visions and, at the same time, brought to the fore their strategies of adapting to the presence of the strangers in their midst. By focusing our eyes on these neglected sites where Muslim cosmopolitanism has been kept alive, our understanding of the Muslim and non-Muslim relations that have evolved from and within these places can be deepened to enable us to recover the 'small voices of history'.[57]

Notes

1. P. J. Leo, 'Bargains Galore at Tanah Abang', *The Jakarta Post*, 1 June 2011, <http://www.thejakartapost.com/news/2011/06/01/bargains-galore-tanah-abang.html> (last accessed 22 January 2016).
2. Ian Douglas Wilson, *The Politics of Protection Rackets in Post-New Order Indonesia* (London: Routledge, 2012), pp. 67–85.
3. Rahil Ismail, "'Di waktu petang di Geylang Serai'" Geylang Serai: Maintaining Identity in a Globalised World', in Rahil Ismail, Brian J. Shaw and Ooi Giok Ling (eds), *Heritage in a Globalising World: Diverging Identities in a Dynamic Region* (Surrey: Ashgate, 2009), p. 23.
4. Alastair Pennycook and Emi Otsuji, *Metrolingualism: Language in the City* (London: Routledge, 2015), p. 145.
5. Gerard Delanty, *The Cosmopolitan Imagination: The Renewal of Critical Social Theory* (Cambridge: Cambridge University Press, 2009), p. 15.
6. Mary Louise Pratt, *Imperial Eyes: Travel Writing and Transculturation* (London: Routledge, 1992), p. 7.
7. See Anthony Reid, *Southeast Asia in the Age of Commerce*, vol. 1 (New Haven, CT: Yale University Press, 1988).
8. Anthony Reid, *Charting the Shape of Early Modern Southeast Asia* (Chiang Mai, Thailand: Silkworm Books, 1999), p. 23.

9. Leonard Y. Andaya, *Leaves of the Same Tree: Trade and Ethnicity in the Straits of Melaka* (Honolulu: University of Hawai'i Press, 2008), p. 124.
10. Kernial Singh Sandhu, 'Chinese Colonization of Malacca, 1500 to 1957 AD', *Journal of Tropical Geography*, 15 (1961), p. 3.
11. Barbara Watson Andaya and Leonard Y. Andaya, *A History of Early Modern Southeast Asia, 1400–1830* (Cambridge: Cambridge University Press, 2015), p. 87.
12. Tome Pires, *The Suma Oriental of Tome Pires*, translated by Armando Cortesao (London: Hakluyt Society, 1944), p. 274.
13. Quoted in Craig A. Lockard, *Southeast Asia in World History* (Oxford: Oxford University Press, 2009), p. 100.
14. Mohammad Redzuan Othman, 'The Origins and Contributions of Early Arabs in Malaya', in Eric Tagliacozzo (ed.), *Southeast Asia and the Middle East: Islam, Movement and the* Longue Durée (Stanford, CA: Stanford University Press, 2009), p. 86.
15. Peter van der Veer, 'Colonial Cosmopolitanism', in Robin Cohen and Steve Vertovec (eds), *Conceiving Cosmopolitanism* (Oxford: Oxford University Press, 2002), pp. 165–80.
16. Thomas Stamford Raffles, *The History of Java*, vol. 1 (London: John Murray, 1817), p. 228.
17. Ellen C. Cangi, 'Civilizing the People of Southeast Asia: Sir Thomas Stamford Raffles' Town Plan for Singapore: 1819–1832', *Planning Perspectives*, 8, 2 (1993), pp. 166–87, and Hadijah Rahmat, 'Portraits of a Nation: The British legacy for Malay Settlement in Singapore', *Indonesia and the Malay World*, 36, 106 (2008), pp. 359–74.
18. Howard W. Dick, 'Urban Public Transport: Jakarta, Surabaya and Malang', *Bulletin of Indonesian Economic Studies*, 17, 1 (1981), pp. 66–82.
19. Frode F. Jacobsen, *Hadrami Arabs in Present-Day Indonesia* (London: Routledge, 2009), p. 23.
20. Nasution, *Ekonomi Surabaya pada masa colonial, 1830–1930* (Surabaya, Indonesia: Pustaka Intelektual, 2006), p. 19.
21. Soledad and the Sisters Co (SATSCO), 'Pasar Kampung Ampel (2014)' [YouTube video], posted on 20 March 2015, <https://www.youtube.com/watch?v=I9ViAfA-WLw> (last accessed 26 January 2016) and Tri Joko Sri Haryono, 'Integrasi Etnis Arab dengan Jawa dan Madura di Kampung Ampel Surabaya', *Biokultur*, 2, 1 (2013), pp. 13–26.
22. Ching Lin Pang, Sara Sterling and Denggao Long, 'Cosmopolitanism, Mobility

and Transformation: Internal Migrant Women in Beijing's Silk Street Market, *Asian Anthropology*, 13, 2 (2014), p. 125.

23. Jenny Onyx et al., 'Scaling up Connections: Everyday Cosmopolitanism, Complexity Theory and Social Capital', *Cosmopolitan Civil Societies Journal*, 3, 3 (2011), pp. 37–67.

24. Andrew Causey, *Hard Bargaining in Sumatra: Western Travellers and Toba Batak in the Marketplace of Souvenirs* (Honolulu: University of Hawai'i Press, 2003).

25. Rachel E. Black, *Porta Palazzo: The Anthropology of an Italian Market* (Philadelphia: University of Pennsylvania Press, 2002), p. 23.

26. Linda J. Seligmann, 'Introduction: Mediating Identities and Marketing Wares', in Linda J. Seligmann (ed.), *Women Traders in Cross-Cultural Perspective: Mediating Identities, Marketing Wares* (Stanford, CA: Stanford University Press, 2002), p. 6.

27. Keebet von Benda-Beckmann, 'Joint Brockerage of Spouses in Islamic Ambon' and Ines Smyth, 'Indonesian Women as (Economic) Mediators: Some Comments on Concepts', in Sita van Bemelen, Madelon Djajadiningrat-Nieuwenhuis, Elsbeth Locher-Scholten and Elly Touwen-Bouwsma (eds), *Women and Mediation in Indonesia* (Leiden: KITLV Press, 1992), pp. 13–32 and pp. 33–46.

28. Raffles, *History of Java*, p. 353.

29. Barbara Andaya, *The Flaming Womb: Repositioning Women in Early Modern Southeast Asia* (Honolulu: University of Hawai'i Press, 2006), p. 133.

30. Nor Aini Haji Idris and Faridah Shahadan, 'The Role of Muslim Women Traders in Kelantan', in Mohamed Arif (ed.), *The Muslim Private Sector in Southeast Asia* (Singapore: ISEAS, 1991), p. 127.

31. Haji Idris and Shahadan, 'Role of Muslim Women Traders', p. 131.

32. An online interview with Asri Yussof conducted on 20 February 2015.

33. Siti Fatihah Awang, 'Pasar Siti Khadijah berwajah baru', Sinar Online, 22 February 2014, <http://www.sinarharian.com.my/edisi/kelantan/pasar-siti-khadijah-berwajah-baru-1.253370> (last accessed 22 January 2016).

34. Joseph C. Liow, *Piety and Politics: Islamism in Contemporary Malaysia* (New York: Oxford University Press, 2009), pp. 102–5.

35. Muhammad Bin Ahmad et al., 'The Islamic Image of a Marketplace in Malaysia: A Case Study Presentation', *South East Asia Journal of Contemporary Business, Economics and Law*, 2, 1 (2013), pp. 86–8.

36. Ziauddin Sardar, *The Consumption of Kuala Lumpur* (London: Reaktion Books, 2000), p. 94.

37. Greg Sheridan, *Cities of the Hot Zone: A Southeast Asian Adventure* (Sydney: Allen and Unwin, 2003), p. 19.

38. Paul Gilroy, *After Empire: Melancholia or Convivial Culture?* (London: Routledge, 2004), p. xi.

39. Jean Duruz, Susan Luckman and Peter Bishop, 'Bazaar Encounters: Food, Markets, Belonging and Citizenship in a Cosmopolitan City', *Continuum: Journal of Media and Communication Studies*, 25, 5 (2011), p. 601.

40. Ward Berenschot, *Riot Politics: Hindu–Muslim Violence and the Indian State* (New York: Columbia University Press, 2011).

41. Jemma Purdey, *Anti-Chinese Violence in Indonesia, 1996–1999* (Honolulu: University of Hawai'i Press, 2006).

42. On Sufi Islam in Southeast Asia, see Anthony H. Johns, 'Sufism in Southeast Asia: Reflections and Reconsiderations', *Journal of Southeast Asian Studies*, 26, 1 (1995), pp. 169–83.

43. Saiful Mujani, 'Civil Society and Tolerance in Indonesia', in Azra Azyumardi and Wayne Hudson (eds), *Islam Beyond Conflict: Indonesian Islam and Western Political Theory* (Aldershot: Ashgate, 2008), p. 183.

44. Engseng Ho, 'Before Parochialization: Diasporic Arabs Cast in Creole Waters', in Huub de Jonge and Nico Kaptein (eds), *Transcending Borders: Arabs, Politics, Trade and Islam in Southeast Asia* (Leiden: KITLV Press, 2002), pp. 11–35.

45. Noriah Mohamed, 'Malay Language (Bahasa Melayu): Its Early History and Variation in Penang', in Muhammad Haji Salleh (ed.), *Early History of Penang* (Penang, Malaysia: Penerbit USM, 2012), pp. 74–6.

46. Rahil Ismail, 'Ramadan and Bussorah Street: The Spirit of Place', *GeoJournal*, 66, 3 (2006), pp. 243–56.

47. Ibrahim Nafee, 'Malaysia's Halal Tourism Attracts Muslims from All Over the World', *Arab News*, 28 May 2014, <http://www.arabnews.com/news/577851> (last accessed 27 January 2016) and Lily B. Libo-on, 'Indonesia Targets UAE, Middle East as Potential Tourism Markets', *Khaleej Times*, 29 May 2009, <http://www.khaleejtimes.com/article/20090528/ARTICLE/305289919/1002> (last accessed 27 January 2016).

48. Melissa Lin, 'Singapore Named the Most Muslim-friendly Destination among Non-Muslim Countries', *The Straits Times*, 4 March 2015.

49. Joan C. Henderson, 'Islam and Tourism: Brunei, Indonesia, Malaysia and Singapore', in Noel Scott and Jafar Jafari (eds), *Tourism in the Muslim World* (Bingley: Emerald, 2010), p. 82.

50. Johan Fischer, *Islam, Standards, and Technoscience: In Global Halal Zones* (London: Routledge, 2016), p. 33.

51. Paul Green, 'British Later-Life Migrants in Malaysia', in Michael Janoschka and Heiko Haas (eds), *Contested Spatialities, Lifestyle Migration and Residential Tourism* (London: Routledge, 2014), p. 149.

52. An interview conducted on 27 November 2015, Penang Island.

53. Chris Rumford, 'Theorizing Borders', *European Journal of Social Theory*, 9, 2 (2006), p. 163.

54. Editorial, 'Geylang Serai to Turn into a Street of Tradition and Religion for Hari Raya Light Up 2014', *The Straits Times,* 20 June 2014.

55. Abdulmaliq Simone, *Jakarta: Drawing the City Near* (Minneapolis: University of Minnesota Press, 2014), p. 8.

56. Fonna Forman-Barzilai, *Adam Smith and the Circle of Sympathy: Cosmopolitanism and Moral Theory* (Cambridge: Cambridge University Press, 2010), p. 215.

57. Ranajit Guha, 'The Small Voice of History', in Shahid Amin and Dipesh Chakrabarty (eds), *Subaltern Studies: Writings on South Asian History and Society* 9 (Delhi: Oxford University Press, 1996), pp. 1–12.

2

THE COSMOPOLITAN MOSQUE

In the heart of Singapore's bustling Chinatown stands a nearly two-century-old mosque known as Jamae Mosque (Masjid Jamae, also called 'Chulia Mosque'). Painted green throughout, the location and design of the mosque reflects the cosmopolitan nature of the people who built it. It is in the middle of an old Chinese settlement, a place populated by markets, businesses and all things non-Muslim. Standing majestically a few metres from the mosque is the oldest Hindu temple in Singapore, Sri Mariamman Temple, revered by Hindu worshippers in the city-state and from all over the world. The temple shares many legacies with the mosque. It was built in 1827 around the same time when the mosque was established. Since the foundation of these buildings, Hindu and Muslim worshippers have walked along a common path to their respective sanctuaries. The common architectural forms that both buildings share will strike any discerning passer-by. The twin minarets of Jamae Mosque are constructed with Indic forms that are akin to the main facade of Sri Mariamman. Both the mosque and the temple boast large gates that reveal the interiors of these houses of worship to onlookers. Jamae Mosque is an archetype of how Muslim sacred spaces can function as cosmopolitan spaces. Mosques are reflections, expressions, manifestations, representations and symbols of Muslim cosmopolitanism.

This chapter examines mosques in Muslim Southeast Asia as spaces where Muslim cosmopolitanism is showcased, promoted and celebrated. A mosque, as Roemer van Toorn noted in his study of mosques in the European con-text, 'is not *just* a house to honour God, but a place to come together, a col-lective space for the community. In short, a mosque as a space can provide a counterweight to the "public" space of the individualized and consuming human being'.[1] I would extend this illuminating reflection further to argue that mosques in Southeast Asia are also places that enable different faiths, per-suasions, ideologies and temperaments to interact, collaborate and amalgamate to give rise to a dynamic environment. To demonstrate this point, I will first dissect the aesthetics of the mosque. This is followed by an examination of the tolerance and cooperation between the worshippers at these mosques and dev-otees of other faiths at nearby religious sites. I delve into the inclusive nature of mosques, allowing non-Muslims to utilise the space for their own purposes. Finally, I discuss the place of women in Southeast Asian mosques, as well as the ready acceptance by men of women's presence and function in sites that can be seen as exclusively male provinces in other parts of the Muslim world.

The Evolution of Mosques in Muslim Southeast Asia

The successful diffusion and continuous vitality of Islam in Southeast Asia is partly attributed to the rapid expansion of mosques in all corners of the region. The region's oldest surviving mosque, Masjid Agung Demak, was built in the thirteenth century in Central Java, Indonesia. The structure and functions of this mosque became a sort of model that was emulated by other mosque founders and builders in later years. It 'was made up, reproduced, and rearticulated, along with other practices, products, and discourses demar-cated over time in Javanese society'.[2]

The colonial period saw a sustained expansion of mosque-building throughout Southeast Asia. The Dutch and the British, in particular, spon-sored the founding of many mosques as part of their strategy to gain the support of local rulers and Muslim elites. However, they maintained a close surveillance of all mosque activities, committee members and publications to keep track of anticolonial movements that all too often emerged from these religious sites.[3] Together with local Muslim leaders and elites, European architects experimented with new designs, incorporating Turkish, Indian, Persian, Chinese and even European architectural styles to create mosques that soon become national monuments in the postcolonial period.

The British, for example, drew upon the various forms of Hindu, Western and Indian-Islamic architecture that they had experimented with in India and transplanted these styles to the building of new mosques in their Southeast Asian colonies.[4] Onion-shaped domes were introduced and these domes later became an indispensable feature of mosques in Muslim Southeast Asia. Abdul Halim Nasir, a historian of mosques in Muslim Southeast Asia, has highlighted the extent to which domes have become essential to mosques in the region:

> Many people feel that a mosque is not really complete without the onion-shaped dome. This feeling has created restlessness and as a result mosques built during the pre-colonial and colonial period without the onion-shaped domes have had the roofs radically modified so that an onion-shaped dome can be built.[5]

Examples of mosques in Singapore with domes introduced by colonial architects include Abdul Ghafoor Mosque, Alkaff Mosque, Haji Yusoff Mosque, the above-mentioned Jamae Mosque (see Figure 2.1), and the ornamental Hajjah Fatimah Mosque in Beach Road in Singapore that incorporates the architectural forms of diverse religious buildings.

There is a dearth of information about the total number of mosques that currently exist in Muslim Southeast Asia. In the small island-state of Singapore, official records state that there are currently more than sixty mosques, with two more under construction.[6] The number of mosques found in Malaysia and Indonesia would probably be a few hundred times the number in Singapore, given the size of these countries and the number of Muslims populating them. Undoubtedly, mosques in Southeast Asia have become the most visible and the most emblematic of all Muslim religious sites due to state sponsorship of mega-mosque projects.

Under the Sukarno and Suharto regimes from 1949 to the end of the 1990s, there were programmed attempts on the part of the Indonesian presidents to build dozens of grand mosques as a means of bolstering their political legitimacy. Similarly, in Malaysia during the same period, mosques were built at a rate of almost one a year, with each mosque surpassing the one that came before it in terms of its aesthetic beauty as well as its sheer size.[7] Conversely, in Singapore, the number of mosques actually saw a marked decline after

Figure 2.1 Jamae Mosque in Singapore.

independence. Small mosques were demolished to make way for new generation mosques that could accommodate larger numbers of worshippers and to
ensure the state supervision of all mosques in Singapore through the Majlis
Ugama Islam Singapura (MUIS, the 'Islamic Religious Council').[8] As in the
case of mosque-building in the Arab world,[9] Iran and Turkey during this era,
the majority of these mosques were 'state mosques as well as ambassadorial
gifts, monumentalizing the political ambitions of their patrons. Their audience is the local user as well as the international community, for whom they
represent a particular vision of global Islam'.[10]

Architectural historians have divided the development of mosques in
Southeast Asia into three overlapping phases:

- phase 1: the building of vernacular mosques with styles that display strong
  local Malay and Indic influences (thirteenth century to the present);
- phase 2: the introduction of colonial-sponsored mosques that blend
  classical and Moorish styles (early nineteenth century to the 1950s);
- phase 3: the establishment of modern mosques which encompass the styles
  drawn from the Arab world, Turkey, and Iran (1950s to the present).[11]

The mosques that are currently standing in different parts of Muslim Southeast Asia comprise community-funded mosques, mosques supported by generous endowments as well as state-sponsored mosques. While Singaporean and Malaysian mosques are highly regulated by state and federal governments, Indonesian mosques have a higher degree of autonomy in the management of their activities and in the upkeep of the buildings and other facilities. Nevertheless, a close and objective scrutiny of mosques in Muslim Southeast Asia would enable us to uncover the strong sense of Muslim cosmopolitanism inherent within them.

Mosques and Aesthetic Cosmopolitanism

Mosques across Muslim Southeast Asia display the cosmopolitan character of the Muslim communities that worship in them through their hybrid architectural forms. That mosques in the region are architecturally cosmopolitan should not come as a surprise, given that there is no clearly defined template or doctrine in Islam regarding mosque-building. Since the era of the Prophet Muhammad in the sixth century, Muslims have enjoyed the freedom of building mosques in a manner that blended the attraction of the natural surroundings with the imagination of the architects and builders.[12] Mosques in Muslim Southeast Asia have lived up to this tradition for many centuries. In point of fact, the majority of mosques in the region exhibit the multicultural make-up and interreligious landscapes that surround them. Put differently, the aesthetics of the mosques bear evidence of a synthesis of forms, motifs and sensory effects. The 'aesthetic cosmopolitanism', as Nikos Papastergiadis rightly stressed, 'does not simply refer to the aesthetic representations of cosmopolitanism, but to a cosmopolitan worldview that is produced through aesthetics'.[13]

Aesthetic cosmopolitanism in Southeast Asian mosques can be discerned from their architectural complexion. Many mosques in the region amalgamate the traditions of different religions while integrating a variety of styles and forms that are seemingly foreign to the Malay world. Certainly, it has long been common for 'non-Malay' and even outwardly 'non-Muslim' elements to be incorporated into the making of mosques. These elements have remained untouched to the present day. What is the explanation for this? Roger Joseph argues convincingly that the space, both inside and outside the mosque, communicates a system of relationships of individuals to society, to each other, and to themselves. If, however, the structure of mosque space is a social code embedded in the cultural experience of various ethnic and historical communities, we should not expect any absolute homogeneity of cognitive or aesthetic expression.[14]

Mosques in Muslim Southeast Asia, from such a perspective, display a high degree of heterogeneity, as opposed to homogeneity, of aesthetic expression because they have been built in ways that are sensitive to the multicultural spirit of the local Muslim societies that have unremittingly celebrated syncretism and diversity in their expressions of Islam.[15]

The best illustration of this is Beijing Mosque (Masjid Beijing, also known as the 'Sultan Ismail Petra Silver Jubilee Mosque') at Kota Bharu, Kelantan. Inaugurated in 2010, the mosque was envisioned as a 'multicultural mosque that would reflect the diverse cultural influences in the Malay world – ranging from Chinese, Indian, Siamese, Malay and other sources'.[16] The mosque frontage delivers even more than its creators had promised. At first glance, Beijing Mosque looks like any ordinary Chinese temple, featuring sloping roofs with upturned corners, a symmetrical floor plan and ornamental designs, and a big courtyard in the centre of the mosque compound. Overall, Beijing Mosque is almost a replica of many mosques in China today. What is most striking about the mosque is that it is constructed in a Malay state purportedly known for its Malay-Islamic conservatism. The construction of Beijing Mosque shows that Muslim cosmopolitanism, in both architectural form and daily life, has a secure place in Kelantan. Another, more intriguing, example of aesthetic cosmopolitanism is Hajjah Fatimah Mosque in Singapore. Built in 1846 by (and named after) a successful Bugis businesswoman, the mosque combines Eastern and Western designs as well as Islamic and Christian architectural forms. The mosque's minaret is a duplicate of the church spire of the century-old St Andrew's Cathedral located some kilometres from it. Slightly slanted, the minaret has been dubbed the Singaporean version of Italy's Leaning Tower of Pisa. Chinese-style windows and grilles are also part of the mosque's external design, along with Malay traditional woodcarvings and the huge dome that is commonly found in many mosques in the region. Even after several major renovation works, the mosque still

maintains its hybrid appearance. Hajjah Fatimah Mosque has been designated as a national monument.[17]

Chinese influence on mosque architecture in the Malay world deserves
further elaboration here. Certainly, Chinese motifs have had an imprint on
the aesthetics of mosques for many centuries. Mohamad Tajuddin's study of
the architectural heritage of the Malay world cements this enduring legacy.
He describes Kampung Hulu Mosque in Malacca City 'as one of the best
examples of a well to do hybrid traditional Malay-Chinese architectural influence'.[18] In recent years, Al-Azim Mosque, built in Malacca in 1991, 'combines Chinese culture with vernacular architecture'.[19]

This easy acceptance of the architectural forms of other traditions was
born of the Sufistic and inclusive nature of Islam in Muslim Southeast Asia,
where forms seen as congruent with the Islamic spirit have been embraced
by mosque designers and builders since the coming of Islam through to the
early modern period. Southeast Asian mosques have also integrated Hindu
elements, which reflects continuity with the region's pre-Islamic past. A great
number of mosques on the island of Java maintained the *meru* (the Hindu
sacred mountain) structure and many Hindu motifs until the eighteenth
century (see Figure 2.2). Most prominent among these syncretic mosques
is Menara Kudus Mosque (Masjid Menara Kudus, also known as 'Al-Aqsha
Mosque').[20]

Another layer of cosmopolitanism lies in the fusion of modern and premodern, of vernacular as well as imported architectural traditions, projecting
an image of both adaptation and synthesis. This fusion of forms and styles
shows not only progress, but also the ability to preserve aspects of the Malay
past that remain relevant in the reconstruction of Islam in a postcolonial
and multicultural world. To quote Kishwar Rizvi, 'Architecture serves as
the physical embodiment of this mobility of meaning; the mosque is thus
simultaneously a memorial to the past and an aspiration toward what is to
come'.[21] This is illustrated by the aesthetics of the National Mosque (Masjid
Negara) in Kuala Lumpur. Built in 1965 as part of the ambition of Malaysia's
first prime minister, Tunku Abdul Rahman, to forge a national identity via
architectural splendour, the National Mosque is a mixture of the old and the
new. Its main prayer hall mirrors that of a traditional Malay house through
the use of an umbrella-shaped roof and concrete stilts. This facade of tradi-

Figure 2.2   Menara Kudus Mosque with its distinctive *meru* structure.

tionalism is counterbalanced by a 73 metre-tall minaret, which looks like an antenna rather than a typical minaret found in the Middle East. The mosque, as one scholar notes, represents the 'spirit of the times' and 'true Malaysian identity'.[22] It appeals to contemporary tastes just as its design harks back to the remote history of the Malay world. The National Mosque was the first mosque in Malaysia – and probably the first mosque in Southeast Asia as well – to synthesise vernacular and modernist architecture.[23] Other mosques in Malaysia followed suit, such as Negeri Sembilan State Mosque that blends Minangkabau and modernist architectural designs.

It took the Indonesians a few more decades before they were able to make visible the mingling of modernist and traditionalist architectural forms in their mosques. From the 1950s until the 1970s, mosques in Indonesia largely gravitated towards the Middle Eastern forms. Istiqlal Mosque (Masjid Istiqlal) in Jakarta is an exemplar of this trend that was born of the Indonesian leaders' desire to win over Islamic groups in the country that were influenced by developments in the Middle East. Mosque design, therefore, served as

Figure 2.3   Grand Mosque of Central Java, Indonesia.

a symbol of the government's commitment to 'Islam as the basis of the Indonesian identity and Islam as an important constituent of Indonesian unity'.[24]

By the early 1980s, the Indonesia Institute of Architects called for a rethinking of Indonesian religious architecture in order to imbue it with vernacular elements. From then on, Indonesian mosques featured both modern and traditional architectural influences. A local Indonesian historian described this transformation as a movement from 'architectural homogeneity' to 'architectural hybridity'.[25] The University of Gadjah Mada Campus Mosque makes this apparent with its arabesque and modernist patterns interlaced with a roof and other structures that are similar to the historical Agung Demak Mosque.[26] Another example is the Grand Mosque of Central Java (Masjid Agung Jawa Tengah) that embodies a bricolage of local Javanese and modernist Middle Eastern forms (see Figure 2.3). Such architectural hybridity can also be seen in the case of mosques in Singapore such as the Darul Aman in Changi Road, which was designed and built by the government's Housing and Development Board (HDB) with an elaborately Malay architectural character. From the outside, the mosque looks like a traditional palace, flanked by the most contemporary and state-of-the-art facilities. The mosque represents the Singapore state's creative experimentation of merging regional and international architectural flavour as the country intensifies its movement towards high-technological modernity.[27]

Sacred Tolerance

On 27 March 1998, fighting broke out between local Malays and Indians at Jalan Patani in Penang. According to sensational media coverage, the mayhem was provoked by reports of plans by the local Hindus to extend the site of the Raja-Raja Madurai Veeran Temple, which is located in close proximity to a historical mosque, Masjid Jamek Kampung Rawa. Muslim worshippers marched from the mosque to the temple to protest the plans to expand the temple without prior approval from the state authorities. As tensions flared between protesters from both religious communities, 600 law enforcement personnel were called and 150 arrests were made within a single day. A local politician couched this incident as 'the latest in a series of blows to Malaysia's international image as a model multi-racial, multi-religious and multi-cultural nation which is peaceful, tolerant, modern and progressive'.[28] The reality of the situation was somewhat different.

While the brief confrontation had destabilised, albeit briefly, the relationship between worshippers at the mosque and those at the temple, the matter was resolved so quickly that using this incident as evidence that Muslims and Hindus barely tolerate one another would miss the larger fact of peaceful coexistence between them. If we train our eyes to observe places where mosques are located near temples, churches, synagogues or other sacred sites, we realise that Muslim Southeast Asia is replete with examples of where amity and harmony between worshippers of different religious sites are actually lived and upheld. This assertion is not made to downplay instances when radicals from different religious groups have obstructed access to religious places, picked fights with worshippers of other faiths or even gone to the extent of destroying religious sites. Rather, it is to say that, as tragic as such incidents are, they do not constitute the predominant conduct of either Muslims or non-Muslims in Southeast Asia, who generally value peaceful coexistence.

I term this peaceful coexistence between mosques and other religious sites, and between Muslims and non-Muslims, 'sacred tolerance'. It is a condition where devotees of religious sites maintain the uniqueness and sacredness of their places of worship without infringing upon the rights of others who do not subscribe to their beliefs. Sacred tolerance is evinced through the sharing of spaces within and outside specific religious sites. Adherents of different religions draw upon each other's spaces to ensure that their rites and rituals can be practised easily and openly without inhibition. Furthermore, what makes sacred tolerance possible is the process of adaptation undertaken by Muslims and non-Muslims towards ensuring amity. Through the vehicle of mosques, Muslim cosmopolitans assist and support other communities of believers during festive occasions and, if necessary, during moments of crisis.

Sacred tolerance has been a feature in the history of Islam since mosques were instituted. The mosque began as an inclusive space where Muslims and even non-Muslims of all ages, sexes and backgrounds could come together for purposes of devotion, for social gatherings and for planning sessions for all sorts of activities including war and reconciliation. During the time of the Prophet Muhammad, there was a famous incident when a non-Muslim Bedouin came into the mosque and urinated within the compound. The Muslims were upset and ready to teach the man a lesson in basic manners, but the Prophet stopped them. Rather than approve his companions' plans to drive the man away for this unrefined behaviour, the Prophet said, 'do not interrupt his urination'. The Prophet then poured water over the spot where the Bedouin had urinated. The Bedouin watched and was impressed with the message that the Prophet had preached; a message of forbearance and wisdom is reflected most vividly by this famous incident which occurred in a mosque.[29] The Prophet's actions set the example for Muslims in the generations to come regarding the inclusive nature of mosques. A mosque should be not only a domain where believers bring themselves closer to God and to their community, but a site where piety can be shared and appreciated by those who have yet to enter the fold of Islam.

Mosques in the Malay world are inheritors of this spirit of openness and tolerance. The acceptance of non-Muslims into mosque compounds is becoming increasingly common, to the extent that, in recent years, it has become a source of concern among some congregants. Religious scholars and teachers have been asked whether non-Muslims should be allowed to enter mosques. The standard answers given by the Muslim learned class is that not only is it permissible, but in fact it should be encouraged so as to inform non-Muslims about the role of mosques and the vision of Islam. Dr Mohd Asri Zainal Abidin ('Maza') writes about this at some length:

> Our mosques ought to function like the mosques during the time of the Prophet (peace be upon him). Non-Muslims were permitted to listen to lectures or religious talks, or to seek financial assistance for those among them who were in need. Mosques should be opened to non-Muslims to know Islam, to be present to witness Muslim devotions and to obtain reliable information about Islam. This was the case during the time of the Prophet (peace be upon him). Muslim and non-Muslim delegates from various places met the Prophet (peace be upon him) in the mosque or they sat to observe Islamic rites in the mosque, the closed-minded will eventually become active and participative.[30]

Dr Maza's explanations were prompted by some in Muslim Southeast Asia being troubled by the presence of non-Muslims in the mosques. This is to be expected, given that there are legal opinions that bar non-Muslims from mosques because of their perceived impurity (*najis*),[31] but only a minority of Muslim jurists actually hold this opinion. In reality, there is a widespread tolerance and acceptance of the 'other' in many mosque activities, displayed in Muslim Southeast Asia in various ways. One way this is shown is through the annual religious functions and festivals and a good example of this is during the breaking of the fast during Ramadan. In July 2014, some seventy non-Muslim tourists joined Muslims in a breaking of the fast event at Putra Mosque in Kuala Lumpur. Co-organised by the Muslim Youth Movement of Malaysia and the Islamic Tourism Centre, the session included talks about Islam and the significance of fasting. The non-Muslims also joined in the congregational prayers to have a first-hand experience of Muslim devotions.[32] The breaking of the fast with non-Muslims has now become a yearly ritual in mosques across the region. Ministers and other prominent non-Muslim community leaders are often present during these events as part of their efforts to gain the support of the Muslim community.[33]

Another way in which mosques are open to non-Muslims is through impromptu visits. These are basically walk-ins by non-Muslims who are in search of some form of assistance or those who wish to know more about the mosque and its functions. Many mosques in the Malay world accommodate such impromptu visits. Raya Baiturrahman Mosque in Banda Aceh is one such mosque which allows non-Muslims to drop by at any moment they wish, provided the mosque is not closed for the night or for renovation works. Certainly, the mosque is one of Aceh's major post-tsunami tourist destinations.[34] Long dresses and pants are also prepared for non-Muslims to wear when they enter the mosque.

In the Malay world, non-Muslims can also enter mosques through institutionalised arrangements. These are structures that are established by mosques to attract non-Muslims to visit regularly and may come in two forms: outreach programmes and visual displays. Outreach programmes include dialogues, discussions and the sharing of perspectives on issues affecting Muslims and non-Muslims in general. In Singapore, outreach programmes have been one of the core activities of mosques since the September 11 attacks. At An-Nahdah Mosque in Singapore, for example, the Harmony Centre was established in October 2006. It is basically a space within the mosque where visitors can learn about Islam and Muslim civilisations. Interfaith dialogues are also organised between the major religious groups in the country, which include Christianity, Buddhism, Hinduism, Sikhism and Baha'ism. The implicit aim of this centre, as Eugene Tan observes, is to encourage Muslim youths to steer away from radical ideologies.[35] More than that, underlying many of the Harmony Centre's activities is the will on the part of the Muslim community to combat Islamophobia and misconceptions about the religion and its adherents.

In Indonesia, institutionalised structures come in the form of converting parts of the mosque compound into business and educational hubs. Mosques in Semarang and Bandung are equipped with exhibition halls, meeting and conference rooms, libraries and cafeterias for anyone to lease and utilise. To attract non-Muslims into the mosques, the architecture of the mosques has been designed to mirror the modern buildings that surround them. The Grand Mosque of Central Java in Semarang is one such mosque. As a mammoth complex that can accommodate about 10,000 people, it is 'also an urban oasis for sociocultural, business and leisure activities. It comprises a 400-seat convention centre, meeting rooms, rental offices, a food court, a 23-suite hotel, shops and a sightseeing tower'.[36]

While the outreach programmes in Singaporean and Malaysian mosques are usually initiated and undoubtedly monitored by the state, in Indonesia, after the fall of Suharto in 1998, mosque committees demonstrated much freedom and agency on the part of the masses in bridging the divide between Muslims and non-Muslims. Cheng Ho Mosque, built by the minority Chinese Muslim community of Java in 2002, provides a revealing model. The architecture of the mosque exhibits the aesthetic cosmopolitanism that we have discussed earlier, in that it is an amalgamation of traditional Chinese and modern styles. In fact, the mosque looks exactly like a Buddhist temple. Managed by the Persatuan Islam Tionghoa Indonesia (PITI, 'Organisation of Indonesian Chinese Muslims'), the mosque committee sees the non-Muslim Chinese as its primary group of potential converts. Islam classes are organised for Chinese converts and non-Muslims as well.

The mosque also provides financial and social assistance for needy Chinese. It arranges events with non-Muslim organisations for purposes of education, interfaith understanding, economic ventures and minority affairs. Owing to its proactive and cosmopolitan outreach programmes, the mosque receives financial support from the non-Muslim Chinese. The deputy governor of East Java referred to the mosque as 'a unison of two cultures, between Chinese and Islam . . . This is a place of worship that symbolizes harmony, love and togetherness despite race or language'.[37] The mosque is an avenue through which a localised understanding of 'Chineseness' is constructed in a way that makes it different from the rest of the ethnic Chinese in Southeast Asia.[38]

The activities of Cheng Ho Mosque have been replicated by other mosques in Indonesia, such as those in Surabaya, Jember, Pandaan Pasuruan, Malang, Purbalingga, Kalimantan, Jakarta and Palembang Jakabaring.[39] These mosques have become instruments by which anti-Chinese sentiments among the native Indonesians can be assuaged. Such a project is especially pertinent following the fall of the Suharto regime in 1998 and the anti-Chinese riots which resulted in close to a thousand deaths and the raping of Chinese women in various parts of Indonesia. The riots were a consequence of many decades of resentment against Chinese dominance of the economy; it was essentially a class war more than a war between ethnic and religious communities. In this context, by building these mosques and serving the locals through its many programmes, what the Chinese Muslim community has done is project its own unique identity while showing that religious sites are also cosmopolitan spaces.[40]

Memorials and displays constitute another medium that Muslims in Southeast Asia use to attract non-Muslims to the mosques. In so doing, mosques fulfil a dual function, serving as places of worship and as repositories of historical information. Mosques perform the role of protectors and communicators of the living memories of the people who built these mosques and the communities that grew around these sites.[41] Ba'alawi Mosque at Lewis Road in Singapore is known for its utilisation of memorials and displays. Erected by Arab philanthropists in 1952, the mosque's regular congregants are Muslims from all walks of life in Singapore. The imam (leader) of the mosque, Habib Hassan, has been active in organising interfaith discussions with other religious leaders in the country, aside from welcoming international guests.[42] The mosque uses the spaces within it to promote Islamic heritage by displaying, for example, different versions of the Qur'an through the ages or the types of headgear worn by Muslims in different countries. Non-Muslim visitors are given insights into a slice of local and global Islamic histories through such displays.

Similarly, the visual displays at Sultan Mosque at Kampung Glam in Singapore have generated a lot of interest among non-Muslims. Rebuilt in the late 1920s in the Indo-Saracenic style on a site where a mosque had once stood since 1824, the Sultan Mosque is an illustrative sample of Western neoclassical styles fused with Persian, Turkish and Moorish architecture.[43] The mosque is a must-go place for non-Muslim tourists, who can view displays about Islam as a global faith. The displays provide detailed explanations about sacred scriptures in Islam, the value of prayer and spirituality, family life and the important position of women in Islam. To explain the main thrusts of these displays, staff members of the mosque have also learnt Japanese and Chinese in order to interact with the overwhelming numbers of visitors from Japan and China. The impression given by these displays is that Sultan Mosque serves as a religious site and also as a space that reflects the cosmopolitan nature of Singapore. The mosque thus expresses the universalist nature of Islam to non-Muslims.[44]

The sacred tolerance of mosques is also made visible through the sharing of common spaces with other religious institutions. Such is the case with An-Naim Mosque in Sarawak, which was built less than a hundred metres from Good Shepherd Church. The mosque and the church share their car parks on specific days. The church allows Muslim congregants to use its car park every Friday for their weekly prayers. The mosque, in turn, opens its car park for churchgoers on Sunday. Both mosque and church worshippers have been breaking fasts together annually during the month of Ramadan for the past fifty years. The church reciprocates in kind by inviting Muslims to the church for dinner during Christmas. Commenting on such mutual reciprocity, the imam of An-Naim Mosque, Imam Mohd Zulkifli, said, 'It has become a way of life for us to share car parks and meet for gatherings. To us, Muslims and Christians are one big family'.[45]

The same spirit of tolerance is experienced daily at the famous UNESCO Heritage Site, Malacca City. Along Jalan Tukang Besi (famously known as 'Harmony Street') are three places of worship sharing a common space: the Muslim Kampung Kling Mosque, the Hindu Sri Poyyatha Vinagar Moorthi Temple and the Buddhist Cheng Hoon Teng Temple. That there have been no tensions at all between these three religious institutions is telling of how tolerant and respectful they have been towards one another. A well-known Southeast Asian travel blogger captures the ambience well:

In the afternoon, the Muezzin's call of Adhan is blaring from the Kampung Kling Mosque reminding the Muslims to do their Zuhur midday prayer. Hearing the Adhan sound, a Makcik selling key chains and souvenirs at a nearby shop turns off her radio from playing Malay pop music until the Adhan calling is over. None of the people around the mosque seem to be bothered by the Adhan even though the mosque is surrounded by many tiny Chinese art shops and food stalls. Just the way the hostel occupants and I remain undisturbed by the Hindus Morning Prayer chant. Here, the religions and cultures have been co-existed side by side for centuries. This is what makes Malacca [the English rendering of Melaka] so unique in many visitors' eyes as well as mine. A pair of doves hovers over my head then both perch on the edge of the pond looking for fresh water to quench their thirst. Peaceful positive vibes are oozing in the air as I leave the idyllic Harmony Street down to the Dutch Square. Recalling what an Encik (old

Chinese woman) said to me, 'we don't ask each other about one's race and religion. But what we do always ask each other is "have you eaten?"' Not only preserving their historical sites, multi cultures and religions, Malacca most vitally also preserves its people to keep their lives eternally beating in harmony alongside The Malacca River.[46]

Nowhere is such cosmopolitan temperance more visible than at Jalan Gatot Subroto, Surakarta, in Indonesia. Al-Hikmah Mosque shares not only the same space as Joyodiningratan Church, but also the same mailing address. When asked how the church and the mosque could coexist in such a manner, a local pastor remarked, 'we [the church and the mosque] have to live together or learn to live together as we are born to be together . . . we are only two meters apart . . . we have made every effort to establish a mutually beneficial partnership'.[47] He admitted that there have been episodes of tension, but, by and large, both religious groups get along well together. Their main instrument for sustaining a close relationship is through acts of reciprocity and tolerance. The mosque turns off the speakers used for the call to prayer (*adzan*) when the church organises events that would be disturbed by amplified prayers. The church, in return, cancels its morning service should it coincide with Muslim festive holidays (such as Eidul Fitri and Eidul Adha) to avoid congestion and also to respect Muslim sensibilities in regard to dress codes on religious days.[48]

Elsewhere in Indonesia, Bakti Mosque in Medan stands right next to the Protestant Church of Indonesia at Simpang. The two religious institutions have been getting along so well that youths of both religions frequent each other's social events. On Fridays, the church organises events to coincide with the Muslim prayers, and vice versa on Sundays. Correspondingly, at Jalan Enggano, No. 52 Tanjung Priok, Jakarta, Al-Muqarrabin Mosque shares the same wall as the Protestant Church of Mahanaim. Both mosque and church volunteers assist each other at their religious events. This shared cooperation – or perhaps it is best described as 'sacred tolerance' – has endured through more than half a century of social change and modernisation in Indonesia.[49]

Women in Mosques

Women have been active in mosques for most of Islamic history. Marion Holmes Katz in her comprehensive historical and comparative study of women in mosques argues that, even though many Muslim legal scholars have discouraged women from playing prominent roles in mosques, such legal pronouncements have usually been ignored and breached by Muslim women for the past millennium. From the sixteenth century onwards, revisionist legal interpretations in Egypt have argued that women should be encouraged to be active in the mosques as a means of contributing to mainstream society. Even the most conservative group within Islam, the Salafis, adopted the position that 'it is permissible for a woman to attend prayers in the mosque as long as she adheres to shar'i [legal] standards of modesty and gender segregation; her husband may not forbid her from doing so, provided that she fulfills these conditions; nevertheless, it is more meritorious for her to pray at home'.[50]

While the presence of women is felt in most mosques across the Muslim world, there have been instances of 'outright exclusion of women from mosques; in others they were relegated to separate compartments or balconies, a feature commonly found in *masjid* design today'.[51] Muslim Southeast Asia belongs to the latter category. In Java, special spaces reserved for women are called *pawestren* or *pangwadonan*, which can be loosely translated as 'women's prayer spaces'. But this does not signify exclusion or marginalisation. Women's prayer spaces were built separately from the main prayer hall to ease the movement of the womenfolk and to ensure their privacy. Additionally, such adjunct spaces were built to allow women during their menses to still attend activities in the mosques. Hence, unlike mosques in other parts of the Muslim world, as seen in the case of Cape Town in South Africa where women have struggled for their own autonomous spaces and for more involvement in the running of mosques, there are no cases of 'gender jihad' in Southeast Asian mosques.[52] Women in Muslim Southeast Asia have enjoyed relative freedom of access to most mosques. In isolated cases when mosques do restrict women, it is largely attributed to a gender bias that many foreign communities have brought into the management of local mosques. Muslims from parts of South Asia are most strict about women's freedom within mosques. Different from what is commonly found in South Asia, gender justice rather than 'gender jihad' demarcates how mosques in Southeast Asia function.[53]

But, how have women made their presence felt in Southeast Asian mosques? They are most obvious as spectators and recipients of Islamic knowledge. Julian Millie found that women in West Java 'attend a more diverse range of preaching events than men and do so in greater numbers'.[54] While no similar studies on women's participation in mosques have been done in Malaysia and Singapore, my own fieldwork points to a similar trend found in Indonesia. Women often surpass men in terms of attendance of lectures, classes and study groups (which are called *majelis taklim* or *majlis ta'lim* in Malay). The special spaces made available to women enable them to attend many of these preaching events and classes without much prohibition. These women are not passive recipients of knowledge, nor are they merely passing time in the mosques. Rather, as many studies have shown, women who attend study circles and lectures in mosques tend to become purveyors of reformist ideas and act as mediators in defence of conservatism and the preservation of many facets of Islam within their own families.[55]

Southeast Asian Muslim women also serve as *muballighat* (preachers), teaching classes in mosques about Islamic law (*fiqh*), creed (*aqidah*), morals (*akhlaq*), spirituality (*tasawwuf*), Islamic history and Qur'anic reading and exegesis.[56] These preachers deliver lectures that address major problems affecting Muslims locally and globally. Such events attract large groups, both in village and urban mosques. In Malaysia, for example, female preachers sometimes enjoy a larger following in mosques than their male counterparts. Three preachers who are especially well known in contemporary Malaysia are Dr Sharifah Hayati Syed Ismail, Siti Nor Bahyah Mahamood and Dr Fatma al-Zahra. Similarly in Indonesia, two female preachers, Sharifah Halimah Alaydrus and Sharifah Khadijah Al-Junayd, have become authoritative in both the local and international Muslim arenas. Their Hadhrami lineage, which traces their ancestry back to the family of the Prophet Muhammad, augments the prominence that they enjoy in mosques.[57]

Women work as counsellors, teachers and office workers in mosques and many have become activists and volunteers outside their working hours. Most if not all mosques in Singapore have women's sections that organise weekly classes, forums, funfairs and fitness sessions for women living near the mosques. The active involvement of women is made possible by their presence on mosque executive committees, to the extent that there have been protracted debates over whether women could become chairs of mosque committees. Although some voices within the Singaporean Muslim community were uncomfortable with the idea of women taking the topmost positions on mosque committees, many local Muslim scholars and teachers opined that Islam does not prohibit women from taking up such positions.[58] Still, the small number of women taking up chairmanships in mosques leaves much to be desired. Certainly, there is a remote possibility for the future establishment of women-only mosques in Southeast Asia, like those in China.[59] This has little to do with the sexism that exists within the Malay community. Rather, it is due mainly to the long-held culture among both Muslim men and women of accepting men as leaders in sacred institutions such as mosques.

The issue of Friday prayers deserves at least a brief mention here. Although women in Muslim Southeast Asia are generally discouraged from attending the weekly Friday prayers, because this is regarded as obligatory only for Muslim men, they are allowed to do so, and in some places are even encouraged to. The Gayo society in Aceh offers an illustrative example. According to John Bowen:

> More than any other single event, the Friday service in the Takèngën mosque structures the week's activities for men and women living in nearby villages . . . Women and especially men begin to drift in to the Takèngën mosque during the morning. Men sit in the front portion of the mosque; women gather halfway back, behind a light sheet draped over a rope . . . The mosque attracts about fifteen hundred men and about two hundred women on most Fridays.[60]

In sum, there are no restrictions on women's attendance during Friday prayers in mosques in Muslim Southeast Asia as long as space permits. Most of the Muslim women in Singapore that I have spoken to prefer not to attend these Friday prayers, not because they are discouraged from doing so, but because they feel that, since men are obligated to attend the Friday prayers, they should be given the space and opportunity to pray in the mosques on Fridays when space is limited.

Conclusion

Mosques in Muslim Southeast Asia have long functioned as cosmopolitan spaces where Muslims can connect with the divine and intermingle with their co-religionists, and where non-Muslims can equally benefit from the amenities and services offered by the mosques to the community at large. However, the mosque's reputation as a cosmopolitan space goes further than that. Cosmopolitanism can also be found in the mosques' outward manifestations, in that they are built and designed in styles and forms that make them appealing to the eyes of believers and non-believers alike. These designs have drawn upon the traditions of East and West, as well as a combination of modern, local and global ideas about the creation of iconic buildings. But, that is not all. Within the mosque compounds, we witness gender cosmopolitanism, as seen from the equal access given to men and women in using the facilities and in spreading their own understandings of Islam. By virtue of the fact that women play critical roles in mosques across Muslim Southeast Asia, these religious spaces have become platforms where gender parity and justice are upheld. Mosques, therefore, have become microcosms of the reforms happening in gender relations in Southeast Asian Muslim societies.

It is astonishing, therefore, that, even after more than seven centuries of instrumental existence, mosques in Muslim Southeast Asia have escaped the attention of researchers in their analyses of cosmopolitan sites. A plausible reason for this has to do with the perception that mosques are generally exclusive to Muslims and that conservatives and fundamentalists have jealously guarded this exclusivity.[61] While this perception of mosques may be true in exceptional cases, it does not reflect the general texture of social relations within the mosques, or even the external appearances of these places of worship. Mosques are cosmopolitan spaces and scrutinising them in this manner enables us to reconsider these and other sacred places in Islam as sites where both Muslims and non-Muslims can derive much personal and spiritual inspiration.

Notes

1. Roemer van Toorn, 'Counteracting the Clash of Cultures: Mosque Architecture as an Emancipating Factory', in Ergün Erkoçu and Cihan Buğdacı, *The Mosque:*

Political, Architectural and Social Transformations (Rotterdam: Nai Publishers, 2009), p. 112.

2. Abidin Kusno, *The Appearances of Memory: Mnemonic Practices of Architecture and Urban Form in Indonesia* (Durham, NC: Duke University Press, 2010), p. 216.

3. Djohan Hanafiah, *Masjid Agung Palembang: Sejarah dan Masa Depannya* (Jakarta: CV Haji Masagung, 1988), pp. 50–2.

4. Thomas Metcalf, *An Imperial Vision: Indian Architecture and Britain's Raj* (Berkeley: University of California Press, 1989), p. 58.

5. Abdul Halim Nasir, *Mosque Architecture in the Malay World* (Bangi, Malaysia: Penerbit UKM, 2004), p. 99.

6. See Majlis Ugama Islam Singapura, 'Mosque Directory', <http://www.mosque.sg/mosque-directory.html> (last accessed 3 March 2016).

7. Ross King, *Kuala Lumpur and Putra Jaya: Negotiating Urban Space in Malaysia* (Singapore: NUS Press, 2008), p. 124, and Kusno, *Appearances of Memory*, p. 220.

8. Rodolphe de Koninck, Julie Drolet and Marc Girard, *Singapore: An Atlas of Perpetual Territorial Transformation* (Singapore: NUS Press, 2008), p. 66.

9. By 'Arab world', I am referring to the countries of the modern-day Middle East and North Africa that utilise the Arabic language as a lingua franca.

10. Kishwar Rizvi, *The Transnational Mosque: Achitecture and Historical Memory in the Contemporary Middle East* (Chapel Hill: University of North Carolina Press, 2015), p. 5.

11. A. Ghafar Ahmad, 'The Architectural Styles of Mosques in Malaysia: From Vernacular to Modern Structures', in Muhammad ibn Abdullah ibn Salih et al. (eds), *Proceedings of the Symposium on Mosque Architecture: The Historic and Urban Developments of Mosque Architecture*, vol. 2 (Saudi Arabia: King Saud University, 1999), pp. 147–63.

12. Seyyed Hossein Nasr, *Islam: Religion, History and Civilization* (San Francisco: Harper, 2003), p. 94.

13. Nikos Papastergiadis, *Cosmopolitanism and Culture* (Cambridge: Polity Press, 2012), p. 90.

14. Roger Joseph, 'The Semiotics of the Islamic Mosque', *Arab Studies Quarterly*, 3, 3 (1981), p. 288.

15. David Snellgrove, 'Syncretism as a Main Feature of Indonesian Culture, As Seen by One More Used to Another Kind of Civilization', *Indonesian Circle*, 20, 56 (1991), pp. 24–48.

16. Farish A. Noor, 'Kelantan's Multicultural Mosque Laudable', Malaysiakini, 8 November 2000, <http://www.malaysiakini.com/news/66> (last accessed 5 February 2016).

17. Lily Kong and Brenda S.A. Yeoh, *The Politics of Landscapes in Singapore: Constructions of 'Nation'* (New York: Syracuse University Press, 2003), p. 85.

18. Mohamad Tajudin Mohamad Rasdi, *The Architectural Heritage of the Malay World* (Skudai, Malaysia: Penerbit UTM, 2000), p. 68.

19. Wael A. Yousef Mousa, *Modern Mosques in Malaysia: Between Regionalism and Eclecticism* (Penang, Malaysia: Universiti Sains Malaysia Press, 2014), p. 142.

20. H. J. de Graaf, 'The Origins of the Javanese Mosque', *Journal of Southeast Asian History*, 4, 1 (1963), pp. 1–5, and Bagoes Wiryomartono, 'A Historical View of Mosque Architecture in Indonesia', *The Asia-Pacific Journal of Anthropology*, 10, 1 (2009), pp. 33–45.

21. Rizvi, *The Transnational Mosque*, p. 4.

22. Mohamad Tajudin Mohamad Rasdi, *Malaysian Architecture: Crisis Within* (Kuala Lumpur: Utusan Publications, 2005), p. 27.

23. Hassan-Uddin Khan, 'An Overview of Contemporary Mosques', in Martin Frishman and Hassan-Uddin Khan (eds), *The Mosque* (Cairo: American University in Cairo Press, 1997), p. 265.

24. Gerard M. Macdonald, 'Indonesia *Medan Merdeka:* National Identity and the Built Environment', *Antipode*, 27, 3 (1995), pp. 270–93.

25. Wiryomartono, 'Historical View', p. 43.

26. Pudji Pratitis Wismantara, 'The Dynamics of the Form of Nusantara Mosque: Architectural Homogeneity Pmbol of pa, 'Cheng Ho Mosque, a hanld seem to be the better one to have. same place, i.e. the annual report, but this link showvis a vis Architectural Hybridity', *Journal of Islamic Architecture*, 2, 1 (2012), pp. 21–7.

27. Tay Kheng Soon, 'Architecture of Rapid Transformation', in Kernial Singh Sandhu and Paul Wheatley (eds), *Management of Success: The Moulding of Modern Singapore* (Singapore: ISEAS, 1989), p. 867.

28. Lim Kit Siang, 'Media Statement', Indian-Malaysian Online, 31 March 1998, <http://www.indianmalaysian.com/demolition.htm> (last accessed 6 February 2016) and Editorial, 'Temple-Next-To-Mosque Issue Settled, Says Anwar', *Utusan Malaysia*, 28 March 1998.

29. Muhammad bin Ismail al-Bukhari, *Translation of the Meanings of 'Sahih al-Bukhari'*, translated by Muhammad Muhsin Khan (Chicago: Kazi Publications, 1997), p. 41.

30. Mohd Asri Zainal Abidin, *Mengemudi Bahtera Perubahan Minda* (Kuala Lumpur: Utusan Publications, 2008), p. 82.

31. Ahmed El Shamsy, *The Canonization of Islamic Law: A Social and Intellectual History* (Cambridge: Cambridge University Press, 2013), p. 109.

32. Zainarida Emilia Zaidi, '70 pelancong bukan Islam sertai majlis berbuka puasa', My Putrajaya News, 17 July 2014, <http://myputrajayanews.com/v2/70-pelancong-bukan-islam-sertai-majlis-berbuka-puasa/> (last accessed 8 February 2016).

33. Lim Yan Liang, 'Ministers Join 800 Breaking Fast at Mosque', *The Straits Times*, 23 June 2015.

34. Sue Kenny et al., 'Deconstructing Aceh's Reconstruction', in Sue Kenny, Matthew Clarke, Ismet Fanany and Damien Kingsbury (eds), *Post-Disaster Reconstruction: Lessons from Aceh* (London: Earthscan, 2010), p. 13.

35. Eugene K. B. Tan, 'Norming "Moderation" in an "Iconic Target": Public Policy and the Regulation of Anxieties in Singapore', *Terrorism and Political Violence*, 19, 4 (2007), p. 453.

36. Wiryomartono, 'Historical View', pp. 43–4.

37. Indra Harsaputra, 'Cheng Ho Mosque, A Symbol of Peace', *The Jakarta Post*, 28 July 2013.

38. Chiou Syuan-yuan, 'Building Traditions for Bridging Differences: Islamic Imaginary Homelands of Chinese-Indonesian Muslims in East Java', in Chan Kwok Bun, Jan W. Walls and David Hayward (eds), *East-West Identities: Globalization, Localization, and Hybridization* (Leiden: Brill, 2007), p. 276.

39. Choirul Mahfud, 'The Role of the Cheng Ho Mosque: The New Silk Road, Indonesia–China Relations in Islamic Cultural Identity', *Journal of Indonesian Islam*, 8, 1 (2014), p. 27.

40. Hew Wai Weng, 'Cosmopolitan Islam and Inclusive Chineseness: Chinese-style Mosques in Indonesia', in Chiara Formichi (ed.), *Religious Pluralism, State and Society in Asia* (London: Routledge, 2013), p. 175.

41. Robert Hodge and Wilfred D'Souza, 'Museums as a Communicator: A Semiotic Analysis of the Western Australian Museum Aboriginal Gallery, Perth', in Eilean Hooper-Greenhill (ed.), *The Educational Role of the Museum* (London: Routledge, 1999), p. 53.

42. Mona Abaza, 'A Mosque of Arab Origin in Singapore: History, Functions and Networks', *Archipel*, 57 (1993), pp. 61–83.

43. Ten Leu-Jiun, 'The Invention of a Tradition: Indo-Saracenic Domes on Mosques in Singapore', *Biblioasia*, 9, 1 (2013), p. 17.

44. Ismail, 'Ramadan and the Bussorah Street', pp. 243–56.
45. Foreign Desk, 'Muslims, Christians Hold Joint Break Fast Event at Adjoining Mosque, Church in Sarawak's Miri', *The Straits Times*, 4 July 2015.
46. Novani Nugrahani, 'Walking a Harmonious Life on Harmony Street', PsychoParadiso [blog], 10 September 2013, <http://psychoparadiso. com/2013/09/10/walking-a-harmonious-life-on-harmony-street/> (last accessed 7 February 2016).
47. Quoted in Myengkyo Seo, *State Management of Religion in Indonesia* (London: Routledge, 2013), p. 80.
48. Seo, *State Management of Religion*, p. 80.
49. UCAN Indonesia, 'Gereja dan masjid sebagai symbol toleransi', 22 July 2013, <http://indonesia.ucanews.com/2013/07/22/gereja-dan-masjid-sebagai-simbol-toleransi/> (last accessed 7 February 2016) and Editorial, 'Bersebelahan dengan Masjid, Ini Cara Gereja Mahanaim Atur Kebaktian Natal', *Tribun Pekanbaru*, 25 December 2015, <http://pekanbaru.tribunnews.com/2015/12/25/sebela han-dengan-masjid-ini-cara-gereja-mahanaim-atur-kebaktian-natal> (last accessed 7 February 2015).
50. Marion Holmes Katz, *Women in the Mosque: A History of Legal Thought and Social Practice* (New York: Columbia University Press, 2014), p. 279.
51. Hussein Keshani, 'Architecture and Community', in Amyn B. Sajoo (ed.), *A Companion to Muslim Cultures* (London: I. B. Tauris, 2012), p. 128.
52. Uta Christina Lehmann, 'Women's Rights to Mosque Space: Access and Participation in Cape Town Mosques', in Masooda Bano (ed.), *Women, Leadership and Mosques: Contemporary Changes in Leadership* (Leiden: Brill, 2012), pp. 481–506.
53. Pieternella van Doorn-Harder, *Women Shaping Islam: Indonesian Women Reading the Qur'an* (Urbana: University of Illinois Press, 2006), p. 79, and Kartum Setiawan, *Masjid-masjid Bersejarah di Jakarta* (Jakarta: Penerbit Erlangga, 2011), pp. 30–1.
54. Julian Millie, 'Islamic Preaching and Women's Spectatorship in West Java', *The Australian Journal of Anthropology*, 22, 2, (2011), p. 151.
55. Philip Winn, 'Majelis Taklim and Gendered Religious Practice in Northern Ambon', *Intersections: Gender and Sexuality in Asia and the Pacific*, 30 (2012), <http://intersections.anu.edu.au/issue30/winn.htm> (last accessed 9 February 2016).
56. van Doorn-Harder, *Women Shaping Islam*, p. 9.

57. Eva F. Nisa, 'Female Voices on Jakarta Da'wa Stage', *Review of Indonesian and Malaysian Affairs (RIMA)*, 46, 1 (2012), pp. 55–81.

58. Haniff Hassan, 'Islam tidak melarang wanita menjadi pengerusi masjid', *Berita Harian*, 8 October 2011.

59. Maria Jaschok and Shui Jingjun, *The History of Women's Mosques in Chinese Islam: A Mosque of Their Own* (Richmond: Curzon Press, 2000).

60. John R. Bowen, *Muslims through Discourse: Religion and Ritual in Gayo Society* (Princeton, NJ: Princeton University Press, 1993), p. 296.

61. François Raillon, 'The Return of the Pancasila: Secular vs Islamic Norms, Another Look at the Struggle for State Dominance in Indonesia', Michel Picard and Rémy Madinier (eds), *The Politics of Religion in Indonesia: Syncretism, Orthodoxy, and Religious Contention in Java and Bali* (London: Routledge, 2011), p. 98.

3

BLOGGING MUSLIM COSMOPOLITANISM

Beyond the lived worlds of ordinary Muslims in Southeast Asia, the digital world is one of the most conspicuous places where Muslim cosmopolitanism is talked about, discerned and internalised. Unending discussions over what it means to be a Muslim and, at the same time, a citizen of the world occupy the pages of Facebook, Twitter, YouTube and Instagram, just as these deliberations are ever-present in blogs and other social media platforms. A cursory survey of the Muslim digital universe reveals efforts by lay and learned Muslims to assist communities in need, as well as voices calling for justice and equality for those who have been marginalised by states and societies alike. So powerful have the internet and social media become in Southeast Asia that they have been portrayed as 'not just tools for reasoned decision-making, but sites of political contest, or *media activism*'.[1]

Blogs are among the social media platforms that have been at the centre stage of various forms of activism. From 2008 to 2015, Southeast Asian states introduced new laws to regulate digital media and filed more than a dozen legal suits and arrest warrants against bloggers. In 2008, a Malaysian blogger, Raja Petra Kamarudin, was put on trial for sedition for blog postings that the Malaysian government alleged could spark racial tensions.[2] In June 2012, Alexander Aan was sentenced to two and half years in prison for posting blasphemous pictures and insulting Islam on Facebook. These materials were shared and discussed widely in the blogosphere and other social media platforms, which prompted the Indonesian government to arrest him. Commenting on the issue, the 'Father of Indonesian Bloggers' (Bapak Blogger Indonesia) said, 'It's funny – we say we have freedom of expression, but it's only up to a certain point . . . Atheism is a no-no, it seems'.[3] The most recent case involved a sixteen-year-old Singaporean teenager, Amos Yee, who was jailed for fifty days for making insensitive remarks about Christianity and uploading obscene pictures to his blog.[4]

This chapter analyses how virtual spaces such as blogs have become places where Muslim cosmopolitanism is discursively planted. My focus is on blogs created by Muslims that have become spaces for a whole range of netizens to partake in discussions about pertinent issues, thereby gaining understanding and clarity about what Islam stands for towards the betterment of humanity. My emphasis is on discussions aimed at bridging ties between people of varying persuasions, in order that they eventually appreciate the universalist and inclusivist proclivities in Islam. As a whole, this supports Bruce Lawrence's declaration that the 'information age portends a new era for Muslim cosmopolitanism'.[5]

Before proceeding, it is important here to outline the digital trends in Southeast Asia over the last few decades. Studies of internet penetration in Singapore, Malaysia and Indonesia reveal fascinating developments. Singapore had the highest penetration (78.5 per cent) in the year 2013, followed by Malaysia (66 per cent) and Indonesia (28.3 per cent).[6] Smartphone usage has also grown exponentially since its introduction in the early years of the twenty-first century, to the extent that most ordinary Southeast Asian Muslims living in the cities have owned at least two mobile phones in the past five years. These portable communication technologies provide Muslims with easy access to the digital world while making it simpler for them to share ideas with a larger audience at the touch of a button. Blogs are among the most popular springboards for sharing ideas and knowledge.

Dubbed 'internet sensations', especially between 2004 and 2011, the number, influence and reach of blogs have barely decreased in recent years. The Muslim blogosphere has expanded so greatly that it has become one of the sources of Islamic knowledge and information for Southeast Asian Muslims.[7] Gary Bunt, a leading expert on Muslim activism in the digital world, observes: 'In short, blogging is a dynamic and rapidly evolving sector in cyberspace that has been drawn upon by iMuslims of all political and religious persuasions'.[8] He goes further to suggest that,

> in the final analysis, bloggers may not be writing about Islam or define themselves as Muslim, but they may still influence how the Islamic blogosphere is perceived. This may incorporate intra-Muslim perspectives, with blogger and reader learning about their peers through their online articulation.[9]

With the availability of blogging platforms such as Blogger.com, LiveJournal.com, Wordpress.com and Multiply.com, more Southeast Asian Muslims are turning to blogs to document their daily thoughts and reflections as well as to advocate for specific issues and concerns that affect them. In 2007, Jakarta, the capital city of Indonesia, gained fame as one of the world's top thirty blogging cities. Merely five years later, it was reported that Bahasa Indonesia (the Indonesian language) had become one of the most widely used languages in the blogosphere other than English. The allure and growth of blogging in Indonesia mirror similar developments in Singapore and Malaysia.[10] Most bloggers are young Muslims from ten to forty years of age. Even the elderly have now caught blogging fever, as is seen in the ninety-year-old former prime minister of Malaysia, Mahathir Mohamad, who writes regularly on his blog Dr. Mahathir Mohamad: Blogging to Unblock (http://chedet.cc).

Who are the consumers of these blogs? A recent study on blogging in Malaysia found that the people who read and share blogs the most are youths from the age of nineteen to twenty-three years. They usually have secondary education and above, are internet-savvy and fluent in both English and the Malay-Indonesian languages. They regard blogs as alternative sources of news and information to those in the mainstream media and other published sources. Most bloggers are, undoubtedly, cynical about the news reported by government-controlled media channels.[11] They share alternative news items gleaned from various blogs and independent websites and engage in 'contentious journalism' that challenges, subverts and questions the dominant ideologies and media narratives churned out by Southeast Asian states.[12]

Southeast Asian Muslims spend much of their energy on three kinds of blogs. The first is a personal or diary-style blog, which Muslim bloggers use to document life's travails and tribulations. Such blogs are most popular among Southeast Asian Muslims, but they usually have short lifespans, sometimes of only a few months. The second type of blog includes topic-driven blogs where bloggers centre their postings around specific themes that are urgent and require immediate response. These blogs usually enjoy longer existences, especially when the postings receive overwhelming responses from netizens. The third and least popular kind of blog in the Southeast Asian context is what has been termed 'filter blogging'. Filter bloggers provide commentaries on different websites as a way of directing their readers' attention to particular topics or areas of interest. I focus on personal and topic-driven blogs in this chapter.[13] These two types of blogs are not mutually exclusive; in fact, personal blogs can sometimes be topic-driven and vice versa.

The blogs that I will discuss have been chosen based on a few criteria. The most vital is that they should touch on issues surrounding Muslim cosmopolitanism. These blogs present Muslim inclusivist views about Islam, Muslims and their encounters with non-Muslims, as well as how they have dealt with being a part of multicultural and multireligious societies. The second criterion is the impact and popularity of these Muslim blogs. They should be viewed, followed, shared and commented upon by thousands of netizens in blogs in Muslim Southeast Asia and beyond. For example, AngelPakaiGucci (http://angelwearsgucci.blogspot.sg) has more than 8,000 followers and is viewed daily by netizens from as far as Australia, Europe and the United States of America.

Above all, I have chosen blogs that are still active. There are many blogs with wide readerships that have become dormant but remain online. This is regarded as normal, because most blogs are often motivated 'by an initial burst of blogging enthuasism'.[14] By concentrating on those blogs that are alive and active, I seek to show that issues pertaining to Muslim cosmopolitanism are not merely matters of fad and fashion for these bloggers. They display strong inclinations towards cosmopolitan visions, which they write about in their own unique ways. Of course, not all of these bloggers have been cosmopolitans throughout their lives, as seen later in the case of Mahathir Mohamad. Some may have espoused Muslim cosmopolitanism as a consequence of their encounters with new ideas and personalities. Others may have been drawn into the cosmopolitan frame of reference by way of self-introspection and confrontation with their own personal biases, political exclusivism and social prejudices. Taken together, these blogs represent Islam as an embracing world faith in the virtual public sphere.

Recasting the Image of Muslims

One of the issues most widely debated in Southeast Asia since the 1970s has been on the nature or character of Muslims. The long-held image that Muslims in the region are best characterised as soft, tolerant, peaceful and smiling does not seem to hold water. In its place is the notion that Muslims in the region are blinkered, bigoted and judgemental. New terminologies such as 'radical Islam', 'political Islam' and 'Islamic terror' litter many of the news headlines published in the last four decades. These concepts and the presumption that Southeast Asia is the second front in the 'war on terror' and a region vulnerable to radical Muslims have gained deep resonance in academic discussions, so much so that it has now become difficult to differentiate between expert analyses and fantasy guided by analytical myopia and unfounded fear.[15]

Presumptions about 'rising Muslim fundamentalism' are fortified by episodes of violence across Southeast Asia. From the Bali bombings to ethnic conflicts in Madura to debates over the use of the word 'Allah' by non-Muslims in Malaysia and the uncovering of terror plots in Singapore, each of these episodes has magnified the idea that Southeast Asian Islam is no longer what it used to be. Not only have Southeast Asian Muslims become more belligerent, they are now undergoing 'Arab colonisation'.[16] The victims of such a process have tended to be non-Muslim minorities and women, so it would seem.

Muslim bloggers are acutely aware of these negative and exaggerated images of Southeast Asian Islam. While some may be pushed into extremism because of this sensationalised antagonism against Islam, many bloggers have opted for another form of reaction, which Andrew Rippin describes as providing 'a renewed expression of faith', to address the problem of Islamophobia.[17] Their responses to these characterisations reveal an understanding of what Islam stands for and of what Islam in the region has to offer in order for it to remain relevant to the lives of Muslims and also non-Muslims. Rather than exhibiting a reactive posture towards the proponents of adverse images of

Southeast Asian Islam, many influential Muslim bloggers have gone a step further to present Islam in a positive and cosmopolitan way. Or, to put it in the manner preferred by former premier of Malaysia Mahathir Mohamad, they delve into the craft of 'blogging to unblock'[18] other perspectives of Islam that have been drowned by extreme negativities.

Muslim bloggers have to deal with the problem of Islamophobia, which, as Andrew J. Shycock has incisively noted, is 'not located in fear alone, or in hate; nor is it found in the designation of enemies as such . . . What is problematic about Islamophobia is its essentializing and universalizing quality, which casts Islam itself and all Muslims as real or potential enemies'.[19] Among such bloggers is a Malaysian scholar-activist, Zulkifli Hasan. A senior lecturer at the Faculty of Shari'ah and Law at the Islamic Science University of Malaysia, Zulkifli is also an active member of civil society movements. He commands a large internet following because of his deep involvement as one of the leaders of Angkatan Belia Islam SeMalaysia (ABIM, 'Muslim Youth Movement of Malaysia'), which prides itself in having thousands of members in Malaysia and many parts of the world. His posting 'Understanding the Issue of Islamophobia: Between Perceptions and Realities' has attracted the attention of many local readers such that it is among the most visited and shared pages on his site. In this long posting, laced with references, Zulkifli examines the devastating impact of the September 11 attacks upon the Muslim world in general and Malaysia in particular. One of the negative effects of that atrocity has been a magnification of negative images of Islam and the growth of non-Muslim fears towards the religion. Muslims have been cast as 'fundamentalists' and 'fanatics'. Irresponsible media, the weaknesses of Muslim institutions, the lack of political will on the part of Muslims in combating negative perceptions and wrongful misunderstandings of Islam are among the factors that have aided in the spread of Islamophobia in Malaysia.[20]

Zulkifli does not stop at outlining why and how Islamophobia came about and became widespread in Malaysia. He offers some solutions which attest to his receptiveness towards Muslim cosmopolitanism. He argues that among the best ways to surmount Islamophobia is to work together with various parties to present what has been known as the moderate path in Islam (*al-wasatiyyah*). Here Zulkifli shares common ideational ground with another

Muslim intellectual based in Malaysia, Mohammad Hashim Kamali. In his book entitled *The Middle Path of Moderation in Islam*, Mohammad stresses that Islamophobia 'can only be addressed by parallel efforts to call attention to the often neglected peace-like, humanitarian, and compassionate teachings of Islam and its advocacy of moderation in human relations'.[21] Zulkifli echoes Mohammad's ideas by urging for more dialogue to be held between Muslims and non-Muslims to explain Islam and to highlight erroneous suppositions about the religion. In his appreciation, he writes:

> There is a dearth of dialogue and academic discussions about Islamophobia including aspects of religious tolerance in Malaysia. If there are any, such dialogues are initiated by specific groups and do not reach the grassroots. Given that Islamophobia is not a central concern of most politicians and no initiatives have been made to overcome it, Islamophobia will continue to grow and eventually have a significant impact on Muslims.[22]

Islamophobia, Zulkifli argues, can be eradicated through close cooperation between Muslims and various mainstream institutions, such as schools. The government must also work hand in hand with civil society groups to explain the true nature of Islam as a religion of peace. Zulkifli ends his post with the hope that Muslims will strive harder to explain Islam in ways that will present a true picture of the religion.[23]

While Zulkifli's take on Islamophobia is rather academic in nature with a tinge of advocacy, another influential Indonesian blogger, Kang Arul, writes in a more populist way. He throws into sharp relief the media bias towards Islam in Indonesia by highlighting that episodes of violence and conflicts in Southeast Asia have been given inordinate attention at the expense of peace and harmony between communities in the realm of everyday life. The media is largely responsible for covering up the truth about Muslim lives and activities and for airing issues that sanction Western bias towards Islam. Kang Arul reiterates the point made by Edward Said in his classic *Covering Islam*, that 'bad news' in Muslim societies is regarded as 'good news' for Islamophobic journalists.[24] Kang Arul notes the example of media coverage about conservative Islamic groups and activists in Indonesia. Everything that has been written and said about such groups by the media is largely deleterious, so much so that readers can see nothing that is good about them. Kang Arul drives the point home by concluding that the media in Southeast Asia has the effect of 'obscuring memories' (*menyelimuti memori*) and that in the end we are showered with images of Islam that can only be recognised through terms like 'violence', 'vigilante', 'jihad' or 'intolerant'.[25]

The task of presenting Islam in a more balanced way has been fulfilled by an Indonesian blog, Islam Indah (http://tamanjati.blogspot.sg). Established by a blogger by the name of 'Jusman' and viewed by more than 100,000 netizens, the blog focuses solely on 'spreading the beauty of Islam' (*menyebarkan keindahan Islam*). Among its most popular postings is 'Hubungan Umat Islam dengan Pengikut Agama Lain' (The Relationship between Muslims and the Followers of Other Religions). In this posting, Jusman explains that Islam encourages its followers to forge close ties and working relationships with non-Muslims. This spirit of cooperation is especially necessary to uphold justice (*adil*) in society. Jusman goes on to stress that the Qur'an supports the view that there should be no conflict between Muslims and non-Muslims other than in instances when justice has been violated. 'Islam,' Jusman adds, 'teaches love, care and good deeds that are universal in nature, because Islam is a mercy for all mankind, hence hatred and animosity are alien to the spirit of mercy [in Islam]. How can this mercy be achieved if Muslims limit the scope of it, excluding the non-Muslims?'[26]

Jusman's interpretation of Islam based on the Qur'anic injunctions of justice, love and mercy for all mankind, rather than just for Muslims, reveals an open-minded and universalist approach to Islam that is contrary to an ethnocentric interpretation. From his standpoint as a Muslim based in the Muslim-majority country of Indonesia, non-Muslims have rights of their own. These rights ought to be protected in order that non-Muslims contribute alongside Muslims to the betterment of society. Reading Jusman's posting calls attention to Clinton Bennett's enumeration of different Muslim approaches to non-Muslim rights, which has implications for how Islam is viewed in the contemporary world. Jusman belongs to what Bennett calls the 'centre right' approach to non-Muslim rights, one that 'can fully accommodate minority and human rights'.[27]

Not all of the bloggers have tackled the issue of Islamophobia and misperceptions of Islam directly. Some bloggers address negative representations of Islam obliquely through the use of historical analogies and personal travelogues. This is evinced in the case of a celebrated Malaysian Muslim scholar, Dr Mohd Asri bin Zainul Abidin, more commonly known as 'Dr Maza'. His blog drmaza.com is probably among the most frequently visited of the sites created by clerics in contemporary Malaysia. He has, to date, clocked more than 18 million viewers and his postings have gone viral on a variety of social media platforms such as Facebook and Twitter. His criticisms of the conservative *ulama* (Muslim scholars) and also of liberal Muslims in Southeast Asia has earned him the label of 'reformist clergy', whose main goal is to provide fresh interpretations of Islam in a globalising world.[28]

One of the objectives of Dr Maza's blog is to encourage the spirit of toleration among Southeast Asian Muslims. He draws his readers' attention to the legacies of Islamic Spain, about which he had learnt more deeply during his visit to the historic Muslim cities of Seville, Cordoba and Granada in May 2012. Dr Maza draws his readers' attention not to the ruins of these emblematic cities, but to the spirit that was left behind and yet forgotten by modern-day Muslims. He writes: 'Whatever it is, in the history of Muslim Spain, the Islamic polities have successfully exhibited a high spirit of tolerance between peoples of different faiths'.[29] Tolerance, Dr Maza adds, gained Muslims the respect of Jews and Christians, whose religious beliefs flourished and were, moreover, fostered under Islamic rule in Spain from the eighth to the fifteenth century. It was this spirit of tolerance rather than hostility that made Islam a powerful religion during the Middle Ages. Dr Maza laments that such tolerance has dissipated, especially in Muslim societies, at the present moment. He criticises his fellow Muslims in Malaysia for their superficial practice of Islam and for exploiting the religion to suit their political agendas. The image of Islam has been tarnished by the Malay Muslims themselves. Muslims in Southeast Asia, from Dr Maza's vantage point, must turn back towards the true essence of Islam by upholding the equality, social justice and tolerance that were epitomised in the heyday of Islamic Spain.[30]

Dr Maza's use of history as a tool to reform Muslim thinking about their faith and to address wrongful perceptions of Islam resonates with the writings of prominent Southeast Asian Muslim scholar Haji Abdul Malik bin Abdul Karim Amrullah (1908–81), also known as 'Hamka', whom Dr Maza greatly admires. Hamka wrote 'reformist histories' which fulfilled the practical function of reforming the minds of ordinary Southeast Asian Muslims. Like Dr Maza, Hamka did not merely narrate facts; instead, he used historical facts to challenge conventional and commonplace assumptions about Islam in order to bring about changes in the everyday life and in ways of thinking among Muslims and non-Muslims. History has thus been utilised to inspire present-day Muslims to revive the legacy of tolerance and to inform non-Muslims about the contributions of this world faith to the making of human civilisations.[31]

Dealing with Intrareligious Differences

Differences in interpreting what Islam is and how it should be practised have characterised Southeast Asian Islam since the era of the region's Islamisation from the thirteenth to the sixteenth century. In the twentieth and early twenty-first centuries, such differences have taken on new forms seen in the conflicts between Sufis and Salafis, between liberals and conservatives and between secularly educated Muslims versus those trained in religious seminaries. Aside from serving as a medium for easy interaction and mutual understanding, the rise of the digital age and the networked society has made these differences apparent as each group capitalises on the internet to further its interests and agendas.[32]

The bloggers under examination here are Muslims who have sought to bridge the religious differences that have arisen among their co-religionists. For all of these bloggers, the Muslim world is currently threatened with so many issues that it is necessary for Muslims to transcend the petty partisan issues that have torn Muslim societies and communities asunder. I have divided these bloggers into a few categories: those who engage in jurisprudential differences, those who write about sectarian divisions and those bloggers who touch upon the disputes between nominal and practising Muslims which have had serious implications for trust and harmony within the Muslim community.

Unlike in the parts of the Muslim world where Islamic jurisprudential differences have, on some occasions, led to extreme persecution of fellow Muslims, in Southeast Asia such differences have been handled in an urbane fashion. Consider, for example, the disputes between the Kaum Muda (Young Faction) and the Kaum Tua (Old Faction) in colonial Southeast Asia in the twentieth century. Decades of disagreement and disputations between them led to groups marginalising one another and denying access to various avenues of religious preaching. Probably the most violent religious persecution suffered by a given Muslim group was the case of the Muhammadiyah movement in Singapore. Faeces were thrown at adherents for propagating modernist interpretations of Islamic laws.[33]

Still, even though Southeast Asian Muslims have generally been better at dealing with jurisprudential differences, the reality is such that these differences have led to families breaking apart, Muslims refusing to pray and mingle with each other in mosques and endless arguments over *furu'* (non-fundamental) issues in the public sphere.[34] Dr Zaharuddin Abdul Rahman is one Muslim blogger who has responded cogently to these jurisprudential differences. Author of no less than eighteen books and a senior lecturer at the International Islamic University of Malaysia, Zaharuddin is a well-known figure throughout Muslim Southeast Asia for his public talks on Islamic finance and contemporary Islamic issues. Two of his books are best-sellers in Malaysia and Singapore. As a scholar trained in different schools of Islamic law during his studies in Jordan and the United Kingdom, Zaharuddin approached the issue of jurisprudential differences by bringing to light the factors that led to the arrest of Dr Maza (whom we have encountered earlier) over charges that he was promoting Wahhabism in Malaysia.

To Zaharuddin, such moves by a religious body in Malaysia clearly demonstrates a lack of tolerance and understanding of the variety of religious opinions within Islam. Instead of dealing with practices that they are not familiar with or which they are opposed to in a reasoned manner, the religious authorities have resorted to using labels such as 'Wahhabi' as a convenient tool to safeguard the faith of ordinary Muslims.[35] The use of the 'Wahhabi threat' by religious authorities, the government and the media to silence, demonise and eventually proscribe Muslim preachers is not peculiar to Malaysia or Southeast Asia. In Russia and Central Asia, the Wahhabi threat is used by state agencies and the media to downplay chronic problems in society, such as corruption, poverty, unemployment and the collusion between religious scholars and authoritarian states. The Wahhabi threat also serves as a bogeyman to frighten ordinary Muslims with the prospect of falling into heterodoxy should they let Islam be shaped by grass-roots movements rather than by quasi-state agencies.[36] What, then, is the way out of such scares and schisms?

Zaharuddin proposes that Muslims develop a research culture rather than rely on second-hand news and uncritical judgements. They should explore thoroughly the different strands of opinions in Islam and understand that the correct opinions and worldviews are those supported by the Qur'an and the Hadith (sayings of the Prophet). He counsels religious leaders and ordinary Muslims to avoid being easily swayed by the machinations of 'agitators of conflict' (*tekong-tekong gaduh*). They should avoid being confrontational in the face of jurisprudential issues, be respectful when discussing contentious topics and focus on issues that would unite the community.[37]

Another influential blogger who extends Zaharuddin's line of reasoning is known by his pseudonym, AngelPakaiGucci (Angel Wears Gucci). His site is probably the most popular Muslim blog in Malaysia today, attracting comments from netizens daily (see Figure 3.1). He maintains the interest of his followers by writing on Muslim issues that affect them at personal, familial and societal levels. Jokes and narratives are woven into his postings to add colour to his discussions on some of the serious challenges confronting Muslims. He addresses the problem of jurisprudential differences by telling a story about Muslims arguing over religious matters without realising that their arguments are shaped by their prejudicial attitudes. Muslims are quick to find fault with their co-religionists because they do not put much effort into finding out why some people have certain practices that are different from what they are accustomed to. The strange and the unknown are therefore assumed to be backward. Jurisprudential differences are made worse by lies, gossip and smear campaigns that often come with disputations between different Muslim groups. The best way to transcend such unnecessary infighting among Muslims, according to AngelPakaiGucci, is to study the examples of the Muslim scholars of the past who respected each other's differing viewpoints. Muslims must keep an 'open heart' (*berlapang dada*). They must be active in finding out more about religious practices that appear to be strange and to suspend judgement until provided with all the necessary information about what others do. He writes in a melodramatic way: 'Have an open heart, because that is starting point of brotherhood. If having an open heart proves to be too difficult for us to put into practice, what then is left of our brotherhood?'.[38]

Figure 3.1   A screenshot of the AngelPakaiGucci blog.

Aside from jurisprudential differences, sectarian divisions do exist within pockets of Southeast Asian Muslim communities. Divisions between the majority Sunni Muslims and the minority Shi'ites have become so pronounced in recent years that it has led to episodes of social exclusion and rhetorical violence.[39] This was not the case in the past because Sunnis and Shi'ites have lived rather peacefully together for many generations, influencing many of the rituals and doctrines of Southeast Asian Muslims.[40] With the rise of Iran as an assertive Shi'ite state since the early 1980s and the dawning of anti-Shi'ite movements in the Middle East, the image of Shi'ism in Southeast Asia as a benign sect in Islam has morphed into that of a menacing cult that threatens the piety of the Sunni majority. In Singapore, Shi'ites are allowed to practise their beliefs and establish their institutions, but any attempts to propagate their beliefs to the local Muslim community swiftly invites displeasure from the Sunni religious elites.[41] The situation is radically different in Malaysia where Shi'ism is banned by the state religious agencies and Shi'ite gatherings and events are constantly raided by religious officials, who are always on high alert to the spread of the ideology.[42] Although Shi'ism is not banned in Indonesia, Shi'ites have been subjected to persecution and harassment for their beliefs.

The shifts in Sunni–Shi'ite relations in Southeast Asia have prompted Muslim bloggers to write about bridging the differences between the two groups. A cursory survey of blogs on Sunni–Shi'ite sectarianism reveals a high degree of intolerance among a small segment of Muslims from both ideological persuasions. However, the majority of Muslim bloggers advocate peaceful coexistence between the two groups. Among such conciliatory voices is the former prime minister of Malaysia, Mahathir Mohamad. Since his retirement from politics, Mahathir has gained a reputation for being a most vehement critic of the Malaysian government and UMNO (United Malays National Organisation) under the leadership of Najib Tun Razak. His new-found role as a shaper of public opinion in Malaysia and the most read blogger in the country has even earned him the respect of his former adversaries.[43] One blog posting that has made him especially popular among cosmopolitan Muslims is on Sunni–Shi'ite reconciliation in the Southeast Asian region.

In a blog post entitled 'Sunni and Syiah' written on August 2013, Mahathir recalls the unceasing history of Sunni–Shi'ite conflict, which has lately reached a level of extreme violence and is waged in mosques across the Arab world and South Asia. This protracted animosity has benefited none other than the enemies of Islam. Mahathir points out that such bloody skirmishes are not found in Malaysia because Muslims in the country adhere to the Shafi'ite school of jurisprudence, which has shaped their approach to the Shi'ites. Although Malaysian Muslims recognise the ideological differences between Sunnis and Shi'ites, they are willing to respect the Shi'ites. But, this proclivity has changed over the past decades because of the aggressive missionising efforts of the Shi'ites. Left unchecked, Mahathir foresees a lethal clash between the two schools of thought which will threaten the peace and harmony of the country. Mahathir's solution to this challenge points to his implicit adoption of the 'pragmatic cosmopolitan virtue, i.e. respect and care for "others" as a precondition of tolerance and possible harmony in an epoch of diversity and social vulnerability induced by global risks'.[44] Mahathir highlights the risks that come with the global spread of Shi'ism. He is certainly aware that the global 'Shi'a revival', as one scholar calls it, is at full steam.[45] For Sunnis and Shi'ites to coexist peaceably in Malaysia, Mahathir suggests a pragmatic approach rather than an idealistic solution: Shi'ites should not spread their beliefs to the majority Sunni Muslims. That way, Mahathir stresses, 'hostility will not arise and society remains calm'.[46] One element that is left unsaid in Mahathir's posting is the imposition of restrictions on the Malaysian Shi'ites' public display of their beliefs. Hence, although Mahathir embraces some forms of Muslim cosmopolitanism when it comes to transcending the Sunni–Shi'ite schism, he leans more heavily towards maintaining the status quo as defined by the Sunni majority instead of allowing for the complete freedom for the Shi'ites in Southeast Asia.

Mahathir's pragmatism is not necessarily shared by other Southeast Asian Muslims. The famed Indonesian freelance journalist and social activist, Satrio Arismunandar, takes on a live and let live slant to the question of sectarian differences in Islam, especially in the case of the highly charged issue of the Sunni–Shi'ite schism. In his blog posting entitled 'Saya Bukan Penganut Syiah, Tetapi Saya Tidak Merasa Terancam Berhubungan dengan Muslim Syiah atau Penganut Apa pun' (I Am Not Syiah, But I Do Not Feel Threatened by Having Relationships with Shi'ites or Persons of Any Religious Persuasion), he shared his thoughts about his friends' bids to convince him about the waywardness of Shi'ite ideology. He registers his respect for their efforts but contends that there was nothing wrong with befriending Shi'ites. Satrio attributes his stance to the Sufistic tradition to which he faithfully adheres and to his wide travels as a journalist. Indeed, Sufism in Southeast Asia has been coloured by many aspects of Shi'ite thought and belief since Islam first arrived in the region. Even today, Malay religious practices and devotional tracts are still strewn with references to the Persian Shi'ite figures who are said to have inspired the Sufis to spread Islam in Southeast Asia.[47]

Satrio regards himself as a beneficiary of that long tradition. He differentiates between the Sunni–Shi'ite conflict at the state level and at the level of ordinary life. He advocates what Asef Bayat terms 'everyday cosmopolitanism', which is 'the idea and practice of transcending self – at the various levels of individual, family, tribe, religion, ethnicity, community, and nation – to associate with agonistic others in everyday life'.[48] To realise this, according to Satrio, Muslims should decouple the political struggles between Sunnis and Shi'ites to focus on the values and practices that these two groups share and which would allow them to live together and interact easily.[49]

Likewise, Muslim bloggers have touched upon the disputes between nominal and practising Muslims, or the struggle between 'shariah-minded Muslims' and 'cultural Muslims'. A Singaporean blogger, Alia Abdullah, whose site has been visited by close to 200,000 netizens, tackles lengthy debates in the blogosphere about this division within the Muslim community. She rebukes Muslims who are 'mean' and 'harsh' towards other Muslims whom they view as nominal in their practice of Islam. For Alia, the best form of invitation to the right way is through patience, kindness and generosity. Alia encourages Muslims of all backgrounds to enter into cultured conversations with one another and not to distance themselves for the sheer fact of their degrees of adherence to Islam. This is personified in the life of the Prophet Muhammad. He succeeded in transforming his community by way of good manners and inspired those who were lax in their devotions to reform themselves.

Alia's central contention is, therefore, a potent one: both doctrinal and cultural Muslims must recognise that they have something to learn from one another. Both must engage in self-criticism before criticising others. Alia asks, 'How about us? When we give advice, do we also ensure that we ourselves are setting a good example? Do we really practise what we preach? When someone needs guidance, do we listen with empathy, compassion and understanding or do we listen to rebut, ridicule and criticise?'.[50] The form of cosmopolitanism that is needed, then, is a 'self-reproaching cosmopolitanism' where diverse ways of manifesting Islam are respected. And yet, all groups of Muslims are free to inform one another about their convictions without imposing their views on following a better way of life in line with the precepts of Islam.

Promoting Online Ethics

The question of ethics in the virtual space, or 'online ethics', preoccupies many of the discussions among Muslim bloggers. This should come as no surprise, given that digital media is littered with problems involving transgressions of people's privacy and rights. Rancorous arguments over issues regarding Muslim faith and piety dominate many online forums and discussion groups. Peter Mandaville confirms this by stating that, since first being introduced in the 1990s, the internet has become a double-edged sword for the transnational Muslim community. It has opened up more room for those who are not formally trained in theology or other Islamic disciplines to actively participate in discussions about Islam and Muslims. Conversely,

Figure 3.2   A screenshot of the AbahYasir.com blog.

the internet is rapidly becoming a combative arena where Muslims can con-demn, criticise and castigate their co-religionists and people of other faiths. The internet has become a place where Muslims do more than preach and missionise; they spend long man hours to demolish points of views that are contrary to their own.[51]

Muslim bloggers in Southeast Asia have reacted to these tussles on the internet in ways that, at first blush, appear to be prescriptive and reactive. However, a more nuanced reading of these blogs shows that bloggers are actually offering compelling solutions to the religious infighting by drawing from the sources of Islam as well as from sources of ethical wisdom to bolster their positions. One such blogger is Abah Yasir (see Figure 3.2), also called 'Ustaz Yusri Yubhi' outside the blogosphere. Yusri earned a degree in shariah law from Al-Azhar University in Egypt and he is now active in community work such as the Religious Rehabilitation Group (RRG), a voluntary organi-sation established by religious scholars and teachers to provide counselling for those who have been detained for their involvement in terrorist-related activities.[52] Yusri is cognizant of the fact that the internet has become a bat-tleground between Muslims. As is the case with most Muslim counsellors in Singapore, Yusri recognises that young Muslims especially are turning to the internet for religious guidance as well as other faith-related activities (see Figure 3.3 above).

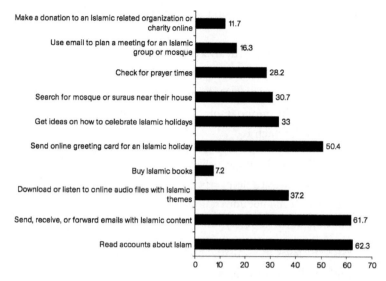

Figure 3.3   Various forms of activity in which Singaporean Muslims are engaged online. Source: Shirley S. Ho, Waipeng Lee and Shahiraa Sahul Hameed, 'Muslim Surfers on the Internet: Using the Theory of Planned Behaviour to Examine the Factors Influencing Engagement in Online Religious Activities', *New Media and Society*, 10, 1 (2008), pp. 93–113.

Moreover, recent studies show that youths in general can be cosmopolitan in their participation in digital media. Nevertheless, the voices of cosmopolitanism can sometimes be eclipsed by online postings of youths with 'deeply individualistic, dismissive, and even downright callous mindsets'.[35] To encourage reasoned and civil discussions among young Muslims online, Yusri wrote a blog posting called 'Adab-adab di Alam Maya' (Ethics on the Internet). This posting was adapted from a series of discussions he had with religious teachers in Singapore. Yusri divided his postings into a set of dos and don'ts. Muslims should respect the views of their online friends in the same manner that they hold in high regard the opinions of their friends in real life. Language usage is also important for maintaining a degree of civility. Sarcasm, vulgarities, insults, bullying tactics and *ad hominem* attacks should be eschewed. All claims made online and any sharing of information must be based on in-depth research. The views of others should be cited properly, news about anyone should be verified and materials drawn from religious texts should be referenced. He encourages his readers to avoid anonymity and to have a real online profile to exhibit a sense of accountability for any views that they choose to express.

Yusri hopes that Muslims will always think well of others and not assume an arrogant and accusatory attitude towards online contacts or try to force their ideals upon everyone else without being sensitive to the feelings of others. Charles Ess, in his monograph on digital media ethics, calls this 'epistemological humility', which is

> humility regarding our language, beliefs, norms, and practices. That is, we are more likely to *know* at a deep, experiential level that these basic cultural elements are *limited* and not universally shared. Hence, we cannot (naïvely) assume our ways 'work' for everyone else.[54]

However, Yusri believes that being humble, thinking well of others and maintaining a friendly posture does not warrant unrestricted communication between men and women through online platforms. A religious teacher by training, Yusri makes it clear that male–female conversational relationships must be regulated within the framework of rules that Islam has stipulated.[55] In other words, he encourages respect for Islamic boundaries in a virtual world and entreats Muslims to be attentive to cosmopolitan ethics in the virtual world.

Another trending blogger who reiterates some of the concerns raised by Yusri is Nasrudin Hassan Tantawi. He enjoins Muslim bloggers to be wary of the implications of what they write. Whether bloggers realise it or not, their writings may eventually shape public perceptions towards them and towards the issues that they are writing about. Nasrudin calls for wisdom and discernment whenever Muslims write about issues regarding faith and piety on the internet. To him, Islam has provided basic ethical codes (*adab*) which all Muslims should follow, whether online or offline. Failure to comply with such codes will have negative consequences, such as damaging discourses and various forms of character assassination on the internet.[56]

Conclusion

Both Yusri and Nasrudin are archetypes of cosmopolitan Muslim bloggers who strive to build bridges between Muslims and non-Muslims rather than merely try to demolish the viewpoints of others. Their cosmopolitan outlook gives added weight to the postulation that cosmopolitanism can take root in the virtual world, a form of cosmopolitanism that has been conveniently labelled by some scholars as 'virtual cosmopolitanism'. As Bree McEwan and Miriam Sobre-Denton have indicated, 'social media facilitates virtual spaces where individuals can co-construct third cultures, develop cosmopolitanism, and transfer cultural and social capital'.[57] The third culture that the Muslim bloggers in Southeast Asia have developed is one of tolerance, respect and constructive criticism. This culture is devoted to allaying fears and countering negative images of Islam. The culmination of this process is the fostering of lively and dynamic online Muslim communities and the democratisation of discourses about Islam. To borrow some lines from Gary Bunt, what these Muslim bloggers have achieved may be 'transformational', qualitatively affecting relationships and personal and communal worldviews and engendering social change'.[58] The Muslim blogosphere in Southeast Asia has without a doubt impacted and affected the Muslim public sphere in real life. Because of the online activism of Muslim bloggers, there now exist in the contemporary virtual world counterchecks against extremist and intolerant individuals and groups that are bent on creating dissension within the Muslim community, and between Muslim and non-Muslim.

Notes

1. Meredith L. Weiss, 'New Media, New Activism: Trends and Trajectories in Malaysia, Singapore and Indonesia', *International Development Planning Review*, 36, 1, (2014), p. 91.
2. Lee Glendinning, 'Malaysian Blogger Raja Petra Kamarudin Goes on Trial for Sedition Charges', *The Guardian*, 6 October 2008.
3. Joe Cochrane, 'Embrace of Atheism Put Indonesian in Prison', *The New York Times*, 3 May 2013.
4. Amir Hussain, 'Sentence Backdated, Amos Yee Released', *The Straits Times*, 7 July 2015.
5. Bruce Lawrence, 'Afterword: Competing Genealogies of Muslim Cosmopolitanism', in Carl W. Ernst and Richard C. Martin (eds), *Rethinking Islamic Studies: From Orientalism to Cosmopolitanism* (Columbia: University of South Carolina Press, 2010), p. 314.
6. See Internet World Stats, 'Asia Marketing Research, Internet Usage, Population Statistics and Facebook Information', <http://www.internetworldstats.com/asia.htm> (last accessed 2 July 2015).

7. Jason Abbott, 'Hype or Hubris? The Political Impact of the Internet and Social Networking in Southeast Asia', in William Case (ed.), *Routledge Handbook of Southeast Asian Democratization* (London: Routledge, 2015), pp. 204–13.

8. Gary Bunt, *iMuslims: Rewiring the House of Islam* (Chapel Hill: University of North Carolina Press, 2009), p. 132.

9. Bunt, *iMuslims*, p. 136.

10. Merlyna Lim, 'Life is Local in the Imagined Global Politics: Islam and Politics in the Indonesian Blogosphere', *Journal of Media and Religion*, 11, 3 (2012), p. 131.

11. Jun-E Tan and Zawawi Ibrahim, *Blogging and Democratization in Malaysia: A New Civil Society in the Making* (Selangor, Malaysia: SIRD, 2008), pp. 33–48.

12. Cherian George, *Contentious Journalism and the Internet: Toward Democratic Discourse in Malaysia and Singapore* (Seattle: University of Washington Press, 2006), p. 3.

13. Jill Walker Rettberg, *Blogging* (Cambridge: Polity Press, 2009), p. 9.

14. Jim Macnamara, *The 21st Century Media (R)evolution: Emergent Communication Practices* (New York: Peter Lang, 2010), p. 39.

15. For a critique of such trends in scholarship, see Natasha Hamilton-Hart, 'Terrorism in Southeast Asia: Expert Analysis, Myopia and Fantasy', *The Pacific Review* 18, 3 (2005), pp. 303–25.

16. Boo Su-Lyn, 'Marina Mahathir: Malaysia Undergoing "Arab Colonialism"', *Malay Mail Online*, 23 May 2015, <http://m.themalaymailonline.com/malaysia/article/marina-mahathir-malaysia-undergoing-arab-colonialism> (last accessed 31 January 2016).

17. Andrew Rippin, *Muslims: Their Religious Beliefs and Practices* (London: Routledge, 2012), p. 329.

18. Mahathir Mohamad, *Blogging to Unblock* (Kuala Lumpur: Berita Publishing, 2013).

19. Andrew J. Shycock, 'Attack of the Islamophobes: Religious War (and Peace) in Arab/Muslim Detroit', in Carl W. Ernst (ed.), *Islamophobia in America: The Anatomy of Intolerance* (Basingstoke: Palgrave Macmillan, 2013), p. 161.

20. Zulkifli Hasan, 'Memahami isu Islamofobia: Antara persepsi dan realiti', Blog of Knowledge, 5 October 2013, <https://zulkiflihasan.wordpress.com/2013/10/05/memahami-isu-islamofobia-antara-persepsi-dan-realiti/> (last accessed 4 July 2015).

21. Mohammad Hashim Kamali, *The Middle Path of Moderation in Islam: The Qur'anic Principle of Wasatiyyah* (New York: Oxford University Press, 2015), pp. 237–8.

22. Hasan, 'Memahami isu Islamofobia'.

23. Hasan, 'Memahami isu Islamofobia'.

24. Edward Said, *Covering Islam: How the Media and the Experts Determine How We See the Rest of the World* (New York: Vintage Books, 1997).

25. Kang Arul, 'Sentimen Media terhadap Islam', kangarul.com [blog], 10 April 2012, <http://kangarul.com/sentimen-media-terhadap-islam> (last accessed 1 February 2016).

26. Arul, 'Sentimen Media'.

27. Clinton Bennett, *Muslims and Modernity: An Introduction to the Issues and Debates* (London: Continuum, 2005), p. 160.

28. Farish A. Noor, 'Reformist Muslim Thinkers in Malaysia: Engaging with Power to uplift the Umma?', in Shireen T. Hunter (ed.), *Reformist Voices in Islam: Mediating Islam and Modernity* (London: M. E. Sharpe, 2009), pp. 222–3.

29. Mohd Asri Zainal Abidin, 'Menangisi Kehilangan Islam di Spain', Minda Tajdid, 10 May 2012, <http://drmaza.com/home/?p=1898> (last accessed 7 July 2015).

30. Zainal Abidin, 'Menangisi Kehilangan Islam di Spain'.

31. Aljunied, 'Writing Reformist Histories', p. 13.

32. Manuel Castells, *The Rise of the Network Society* (Malden, MA: Blackwell, 2000), p. 3.

33. Khairudin Aljunied, 'The "Other" Muhammadiyah Movement: Singapore, 1958–2008', *Journal of Southeast Asian Studies*, 42, 2, (2011), p. 287.

34. Endang Turmudi, *Struggling for the Umma: Changing Leadership Roles of Kiai in Jombang, East Java* (Canberra: ANU E-Press, 2006), p. 177.

35. Zaharuddin Abdul Rahman, 'Tangkapan Mohd Asri: Suatu Pandangan', zaharuddin.net, 3 November 2009, <http://zaharuddin.net/politik-&-dakwah/55/887-tangkapan-dr-mohd-asri--suatu-pandangan.html> (last accessed 9 July 2015).

36. Alexander Knysh, 'A Clear and Present Danger: "Wahabism" as a Rhetorical Foil', *Die Welt des Islams*, 4, 1 (2004), pp. 3–26.

37. Abdul Rahman, 'Tangkapan Mohd Asri'.

38. AngelPakaiGucci [blog], 'Saya Liberal', 25 November 2013, <http://angel-wearsgucci.blogspot.sg/2013/11/saya-liberal.html> (last accessed 9 July 2015).

39. Zulkifli, *The Struggle of the Shi'is in Indonesia* (Canberra: ANU E-Press, 2013), pp. 229–62.

40. See the essays in the following edited volume: Chiara Formichi and Michael Feener (eds), *Shi'ism in Southeast Asia: 'Alid Piety and Sectarian Constructions* (New York: Oxford University Press, 2015).

41. Christoph Marcinkowski, *Facets of Shi'ite Islam in Contemporary Southeast Asia (II): Malaysia and Singapore* (Singapore: Institute of Defence and Strategic Studies, 2006), p. 214.

42. Mohd Faizal Musa, 'The Malaysian Shi'a: A Preliminary Study of Their History, Oppression and Denied Rights', *Journal of Shi'a Islamic Studies*, 4, 4 (2013), pp. 411–63.

43. His blog has been visited by more than 16 million netizens from 2008 to July 2015.

44. Massimo Pendeza, 'Introduction: Is Classical Sociology Still in Vogue? A Controversial Legacy', in Massimo Pendeza (ed.), *Classical Sociology Beyond Methodological Nationalism* (Leiden: Brill, 2014), p. 10.

45. Seyyed Vali Reza Nasr, *The Shia Revival: How Conflicts Within Islam Will Shape the Future* (New York: Norton, 2006).

46. Mahathir Mohamad, 'Sunni dan Syiah', Dr. Mahathir Mohamad: Blogging to Unblock [blog], 30 August 2013, <http://chedet.cc/?p=1052> (last accessed 11 July 2015).

47. Majid Daneshgar, 'The Study of Persian Shi'ism in the Malay-Indonesian World: A Review of Literature from the Nineteenth Century Onwards', *The Journal of Shi'a Studies*, 7, 2 (2014), pp. 191–229.

48. Asef Bayat, *Life as Politics: How Ordinary People Change the Middle East* (Amsterdam: Amsterdam University Press, 2010), p. 187.

49. Satrio Arismunandar, 'Saya bukan Syiah, Tetapi Saya Tidak Merasa Terancam Berhubungan Dengan Muslim Syiah dan Penganut Apa Pun', Satrio Arismunandar: Bangkitlah Indonesia! [blog], 19 March 2015, <http://satrio-arismunandar6.blogspot.sg/2015/04/saya-bukan-penganut-syiah-tetapi-saya.html> (last accessed 11 July 2015).

50. Alia Abdullah, 'The One on Da'wah', Alia Abdullah [blog], 2 April 2015, <http://aliaabdullah.com/2015/04/02/the-one-on-dawah-2/#more-489> (last accessed 11 July 2015).

51. Peter Mandaville, *Transnational Muslim Politics: Reimagining the Umma* (London: Routledge, 2001), pp. 165–70.

52. Religious Rehabilitation Group (RRG), 'About Us', <http://rrg.sg/about-us> (last accessed 11 July 2015).

53. Carrie James, *Disconnected: Youths, New Media, and the Ethics Gap* (Cambridge, MA: MIT Press, 2014), p. 105.

54. Charles Ess, *Digital Media Ethics* (Cambridge: Polity Press, 2009), p. 112.

55. Abah Yasir, 'Etika di Alam Maya', abahyasir.com [blog], 28 March 2015,

<http://abahyasir.com/2015/03/28/etika-alam-maya/> (last accessed 11 July 2015).

56. Nasrudin Hasan Tantawi, 'Etika dan Adab Seorang Blogger', Ustaz Nasrudin Hassan Tantawi [blog], 14 August 2009, <http://www.perjuanganku. com/2009/08/etika-dan-adab-seorang-blogger.html> (last accessed 11 July 2015).

57. Bree McEwan and Miriam Sobre-Denton, 'Virtual Cosmopolitanism: Constructing Third Cultures and Transmitting Social and Cultural Capital Through Social Media', *Journal of International and Intercultural Communication*, 4, 4, (2011), p. 257.

58. Gary R. Bunt, 'Rip. Burn. Pray: Islamic Expression Online', in Lorne R. Dawson and Douglas E. Cowan (eds), *Religion Online: Finding Faith in the Internet* (London: Routledge, 2004), p. 112.

PART II
PERSONAS

4

COSMOPOLITAN MUSLIM PUBLIC INTELLECTUALS

This chapter is concerned with the advent of what I call 'cosmopolitan Muslim public intellectuals'. The term 'public intellectuals' has been used in various ways. The French sociologist Pierre Bourdieu described public intellectuals as those who demonstrate a degree of 'freedom with respect to those in power, the critique of received ideas, the demolition of simplistic either-ors, respect for the complexity of problems'.[1] Edward Said, in turn, argued that public intellectuals are 'the nay-sayers, the individuals at odds with their society and therefore outsiders and exiles so far as privileges, power, and honors are concerned'.[2] Barbara Misztal has listed some of the professional positions occupied by these intellectuals including 'scientists, academics in the humanities and the social and political sciences, writers, artists and journalists who articulate issues of importance in their societies to the general public'.[3] Public intellectuals, according to Misztal, are distinguished by their creativity and civil courage.

Perhaps the most authoritative definition of public intellectuals and their representations is provided by Richard Posner, who sees a public intellectual as a person who

> expresses himself in a way that is accessible to the public, and the focus of his expression is on matters of general public concern of (or inflected by) a political or ideological cast. Public intellectuals may or may not be affiliated

with universities. They may be full-time or part-time academics; they may be journalists or publishers; they may be writers or artists; they may be politicians or officials; they may work for think tanks; they may hold down 'ordinary' jobs. Most often they either comment on current controversies or offer general reflections on the direction or health of society. In their reflective mode they may be utopian in the broad sense of seeking to steer the society in a new direction or denunciatory because their dissatisfaction with the existing state of the society overwhelms any effort to propose reforms. When public intellectuals comment on current affairs, their comments tend to be opinionated, judgmental, sometimes condescending, and often waspish. They are controversialists, with a tendency to take extreme positions. Academic public intellectuals often write in a tone of conscious, sometimes exasperated, intellectual superiority. Public intellectuals are often careless with facts and rash in predictions. [4]

The general impression that emerges from a cursory survey of contemporary studies of public intellectuals in Europe and the United States is that they are in a state of decline and disappearance due to over-specialisation, bureaucratisation, marketisation and marginalisation by states and societies alike.[5] The same inventory of problems faced by public intellectuals in Europe and the United States is found in Muslim Southeast Asia. In Singapore, for example, public intellectuals are a rare breed. The reasons for this have to do with the various constraints that have been laid upon public intellectuals by the authoritarian state since the 1960s.[6] Until the sea change in political climates and the advent of the internet age in the late 1990s, public intellectuals in Malaysia and Indonesia faced similar state impediments and were often subjected to scare tactics and detention.

In light of the above delineations of public intellectuals and the unique context of Muslim Southeast Asia, I define 'cosmopolitan Muslim public intellectuals' in the following manner. They are, first of all, well acquainted with the pertinent local, regional and global issues of their time, just as they are interested in actively engaging ordinary Muslims to discern at first hand the many trials of daily life. They are, therefore, not sitting in an ivory tower bereft of any real contact with the common man. They are not mere armchair theorisers or scholarly priests, whose works no one reads or knows about. Because they see themselves as an integral part of the people that they are writing about, these cosmopolitan Muslim public intellectuals display a strong awareness of (and adherence to) the religious faith. Islam, for them, is not just an inherited identity. It is not something that they are merely born into without any real attachment or meaning. For these intellectuals, Islam is their frame of reference, their basis for thinking and contemplation and their source of inspiration in advocating universal values, inclusivity and social justice in society.

Cosmopolitan Muslim public intellectuals are also activistic in that they campaign for reforms in Muslim societies. This vocation inevitably has implications for non-Muslims, given the multicultural and interconnected social landscapes of contemporary Muslim Southeast Asia. Indeed, the activism of these intellectuals is more often than not amplified and, because of advances in information technology, is felt by those normally beyond their reach. As Dale Eickleman has sharply observed, 'the proliferation and increased accessibility of the means of communication in today's global society, together with the rise of mass education, has increased the power of intellectuals to communicate and of audiences to listen and discuss'.[7] To expand the scope of their activism, these cosmopolitan Muslim public intellectuals affiliate themselves with a plethora of mainstream institutions and independent organisations. However, they also maintain critical stances towards the institutions with which they are associated, especially when the politics, policies and positions of these institutions and organisations run counter to the common good.

More crucially, cosmopolitan Muslim public intellectuals transcend parochial paradigms in their own societies. They censure extreme secularism and oppressive liberalism that gives little space for religious voices in public debates. Yet they are also opposed to the puritanical interpretations of Islam that limit the use of reason and rationality. They are cosmopolitan because they demonstrate a judicious fusion of what is relevant from the intellectual heritage of Islam with what is best from other traditions to devise new solutions to the challenges affecting Muslims.[8]

In what follows, I discuss the ideas of three prominent cosmopolitan Muslim public intellectuals: Chandra Muzaffar, Azyumardi Azra and Hussin Mutalib. I focus on three of the critical concepts that pervade their active writing and advocacy careers: Qur'anic justice, 'Islam Nusantara' (Southeast

Asian Islam) and Islamic assertiveness, concepts which push the boundaries of thinking about Muslim cosmopolitanism in Southeast Asia. There are several reasons selecting these intellectuals, foremost being that all of them correspond to the characteristics outlined above. Moreover, these intellectuals are still vigorous in airing problems and challenges in their respective countries and in Muslim Southeast Asia in general at the present moment. In addition, these figures are linked to a network of intellectuals across the Muslim world and enjoy international reputations. They are members of the sixth generation of Muslim intellectuals in Muslim Southeast Asia, who began their intellectual pursuits in the 1980s and were confronted with 'the deepening penetration of global Islamic fundamentalism as well as global mass-culture and Western liberal values'.[9]

The cosmopolitan Muslim public intellectuals examined here are also selected on the basis that they have lived through different political climates in their home countries and in the Malay world as a whole. They have survived the authoritarian governments of Lee Kuan Yew (Singapore), Mahathir Mohamad (Malaysia) and Suharto (Indonesia). All of these intellectuals showed a remarkable consistency in challenging the authoritarian structures and paradigms they faced throughout those difficult times. In this sense, these intellectuals are 'organic' and they do not succumb to the pressures of being co-opted by states. As explained by Edward Said, who drew upon the writings of the Italian thinker Antonio Gramsci, organic intellectuals 'constantly struggle to change minds and expand markets; unlike teachers and priests, who seem more or less to remain in place, doing the same kind of work year in year out, organic intellectuals are always on the move, on the make'.[10]

Finally, I have chosen the following intellectuals because, although they are academics based in universities, they have resisted the usually inescapable and prevailing tide of 'marketization of the university'[11] by publishing in both scholarly and popular avenues and by writing outside their fields of specialisation. Their ability to straddle the divide between two worlds – the scholarly and popular publics – sometimes at the risk of denial of promotion, constant censure by their own institutions and even imprisonment makes them a fascinating group worthy of critical scrutiny.[12]

Chandra Muzaffar on Qur'anic Justice

Justice is one the pertinent issues to preoccupy cosmopolitan Muslim public intellectuals in Muslim Southeast Asia. This is hardly surprising given that the region has been beleaguered by injustice largely born of authoritarian rule, especially after the rise of nation-states. Media control, the crippling of civil society activism, ethnocracy, crony capitalism and one-party dominance are among the effects of authoritarianism in the region.[13] Several decades of illiberal democracy and harsh rule have given birth to economic disparity, social distancing between groups in society, the widening of underclass populations and the expansion in the proportion of the urban and rural poor. The pro-indigenous Bumiputera and Pribumi policies in Muslim-majority countries such as Malaysia and Indonesia respectively, as well as the continued discriminatory policies against the Muslim minorities in Singapore, have contributed to distinct social inequalities and the migration of discriminated minorities to countries outside Southeast Asia.[14]

A noted cosmopolitan Muslim public intellectual who has spoken truth about such injustices is Dr Chandra Muzaffar. As Hans Köchler puts it in his foreword to Chandra's collection of essays, 'Chandra Muzaffar combines theory with practice in a rather unique fashion: his commitment to global justice and peace is backed by a novel intellectual approach that is deeply-rooted in his essentially cosmopolitan outlook'.[15] Muslim cosmopolitanism, in Chandra's formulation, can be realised when Qur'anic justice is upheld in societies. Before examining Chandra's intellectual elaborations, it is important to note that his personal background shaped his long and firm commitment towards justice and cosmopolitan ideals.

Chandra was born a non-Muslim in 1947. He belongs to Malaysia's minority Indian community and grew up in a relatively privileged household within a multiethnic society. He recounts vividly that his 'family was Indian and Hindu but there was a Chinese amah in our household from the time I was born. A Malay driver was also part of the family. The community I grew up in was also multi-ethnic'.[16] His conversion to Islam preceded his commentaries on religious issues in Malaysia and by his interactions with his doctoral supervisor, Syed Hussein Alatas, a famous Malaysian public intellectual. Upon completing his PhD in Malay Studies in 1977, he established a reputation as a critic of both the state and society by writing many books as well as opinion pieces in local and international newspapers and periodicals. Many of these writings highlight the inequalities caused by the residue of feudalism in Southeast Asia, which had formed the subject of his doctoral thesis.[17]

Because of his unwavering critiques of the existing political and social order, Chandra's appointments as a professor at the Scientific University of Malaysia (Universiti Sains Malaysia) and the University of Malaya were relatively brief. In October 1987, he was arrested under the Internal Security Act (ISA) for his involvement with a Malaysian human rights organisation called Aliran. Released two months later, Chandra left the university and founded the International Movement for a Just World (JUST), a movement that gained him a wide reception among Muslims regionally and internationally. Chandra's ideas on justice reached full maturity thereafter. 'Justice for the weaker segment of society,' Chandra writes, 'has been central to my struggle.'[18] His approach to justice is cosmopolitan, universal, forward-thinking and sophisticated, to an extent that is probably unrivalled by any of his Malaysian peers.

Chandra sees justice as the most important determinant in the making and unmaking of Muslim societies. In addition to drawing upon his life experiences, the importance he places on justice is the upshot of his reading of historical and theological works, more notably, the Qur'an. He describes justice as 'the real goal of religion. It was the mission of every Prophet. It is the message of every Scripture'.[19] The Qur'an is filled with references to the importance of being just. Chandra calls it 'Qur'anic justice', which, if properly conceptualised and implemented, could engender the creation of a cosmopolitan society. By practising Qur'anic justice, Southeast Asian societies can offer a viable alternative to the Western-led global system that 'is so palpably unjust that any human being with an atom of commitment to social justice would want to change it for the good of human beings everywhere'.[20] But what are the characteristics of Qur'anic justice?

A central pillar of Qur'anic justice is fairness to all of mankind. Chandra stressed that the Qur'an lays strong emphasis on the fact that justice should not be confined to Muslims. On the contrary, justice is a right that should be enjoyed by all people. Qur'anic justice therefore transcends religion, class, culture, community, nationality and gender.[21] A universalist conception of justice, according to Chandra, is sorely lacking among Muslims today. Chandra castigates his co-religionists who call out for justice to be served when Muslims are oppressed yet fall silent when it comes to the plights of other communities. Such an exclusivist outlook has worked against the Muslims themselves because it serves to limit the possibilities of forming a united front against oppressive global forces.

By being more inclusive in the approach and implementation of justice, Chandra envisions Muslims and non-Muslims uniting 'to vanquish what is after all a global power structure and create in its stead an egalitarian universal civilisation that is just and compassionate because it respects each and every human person'.[22] Farish Noor has correctly observed that this is one of the underlying themes of Chandra's lifetime pursuit: 'to translate Islam's values and goals into a living reality that is relevant in the here-and-now and to extend its universalism to its utmost inclusive domain, thus bridging the gap between Muslims and non-Muslims'.[23]

Working together in the battle against inequality caused by material-istic systems and ideologies is another important cornerstone of Qur'anic justice. Chandra directs his attention to the hegemony of global capitalism that has corrupted human morality and has given rise to poverty in many parts of the world. Global capitalism has tainted all faiths and, because of this, Chandra calls for interreligious solidarity that involves collaborating with any group, Muslim and/or non-Muslim, in the battle against global capitalism. The coming together of all religious communities to combat capitalism is not an impracticable task. Chandra cites many instances in Southeast Asian and South Asian Islam where Muslims and non-Muslims have worked together to resist colonialism and construct new pathways for their newly founded nations.[24] In Malaysia, for example, non-governmental organizations (NGOs) such as the Inter-faith Spiritual Fellowship and the Malaysian Interfaith Network have brought together many religious groups to address 'societal challenges such as corruption, greed, global hegemony, global justice, the family and the environmental crisis rather than upon theo-logical concerns as such'.[25] Chandra is somewhat silent regarding the reality that these Malaysian NGOs are often regulated by the state. Their impact in society is all too often cut short by the government's policies of discouraging Malays from participating in interreligious activities.

He obliquely addresses the issue of obstacles imposed by states in Southeast Asia by stressing the importance of good governance. Good governance necessitates, first of all, the grooming of enlightened leaders to replace tyrannical ones. Enlightened leaders are men and women who internalise the values found in the Qur'an, who are guided by the idea of unity (*tawhid*) in Islam and who are dedicated towards benefiting all of humanity rather than satisfying their own personal needs. To Chandra, good governance involves paying attention to the demands and concerns of the masses as well as allowing public debate to flourish. In connection to this, he calls upon Islamic civil society activists to struggle against political injustice and to develop leaders who can advise and aid in promoting good governance, especially in Malaysia. He faults these activists for sliding into conservatism and for being averse to opposing authoritarianism, urging them to go beyond their concern with rites and rituals to engage in the larger issues of injustice and inequality caused by despots. Qur'anic justice, from Chandra's vantage point, is closely connected to the flowering of civil society. It is only when the masses, including Muslims and non-Muslims, are involved in the structuring of politics and governing processes of a country that true Qur'anic justice is achieved. This was put into practice, in Chandra's opinion, during the time of the first four caliphs of Islam. [26]

Finally, Chandra argues that Qur'anic justice dictates the upholding of human rights. The notion of human rights has often been defined within the framework of Western ideas of individualism, liberalism and secularism. Chandra contends that such Western conceptions of human rights are partial, selective, sectarian and incongruent with Asian traditions. In this, he is on the same page as Makau Mutua, who rails against the Eurocentric rendering of human rights and encourages the growth of a new human rights movement that is 'multicultural, inclusive and deeply political'. [27] Chandra opines that human rights must be understood within the Qur'anic view that all human beings are responsible towards each other as part of their obligation to Allah. He sees human rights as defined in Islam as sharing a common denominator with other world faiths. In fact, Muslims are encouraged to draw upon other ideas of human rights to illuminate their own conceptions of these rights. The Islamic conception of human rights is, to Chandra, cosmopolitan and open to accepting other traditions to ensure that the rights of the individual and the wider community are protected.

It is because of these and other flaws in the very character of the Western approach to human rights that there is an urgent need to try to evolve a vision of human dignity which is more just, more holistic, and more universal. In Islam, Hinduism, Sikhism, Taoism, Christianity and Buddhism there are elements of such vision of the human being, of human rights and of human dignity. The idea that the human being is vicegerent or trustee of God whose primary role is to fulfill God's trust is lucidly articulated in various religions. As God's trustee, the human being lives life according to clearly established spiritual and moral values and principles. The rights one possesses, like the responsibilities one undertakes, must be guided by these values and principles. What this means is that human rights and human freedoms are part of a larger spiritual and moral worldview. This also means that individual freedom is not the be-all and end-all of human existence. Neither is the individual and community the ultimate arbiter of right and wrong, of good and evil. The individual and community must both submit to spiritual and moral values that transcend both individual and community. It is the supremacy of these values and, in the end, of the Divine which distinguishes our God-guided concept of human dignity from the present individual-centred notion of human rights.[28]

As a public intellectual, Chandra's main contribution to the discourses and dissemination of ideas about Muslim cosmopolitanism lies in his lengthy elaboration of what it means to be just. Muslims, to him, should be the main torchbearers of Qur'anic justice and they must work hand in hand with anyone who does not contradict the message of the Qur'an and of the unity of mankind. Chandra's rendering of Qur'anic justice brings him close to another Muslim thinker, Sayyid Qutb (1906–66). In his book *Social Justice in Islam*, Sayyid Qutb posits that justice is the bedrock of Islamic civilisation and that justice based upon the Qur'an could rid societies of the evils of modern life.[29] But, unlike Sayyid Qutb, Chandra is no radical or revolutionary, nor is he anti-modernity or an Islamic utopian. He is cognizant that, in the realisation of Qur'anic justice, Muslims may fall into developing a 'superficial attachment to identity'.[30] This has come in the form of calls for the 'Islamicisation' of all spheres of society and an obsession with shallow Islamic mottos such as 'Islam is the solution' and ersatz labels such as the

'Islamic car'.[31] Such proclivities will erode the cosmopolitan visions inherent in Islam and result in chaos. However, Chandra is confident that Muslim Southeast Asia will rise against such superficialities towards 'heralding a truly cosmopolitan Islam'.[32]

Azyumardi Azra's 'Islam Nusantara'

While Chandra devotes his attention to the concept of Qur'anic justice, an aspiration that Muslims should work towards in the road to making Muslim Southeast Asia attuned to cosmopolitanism, another prominent Indonesian public intellectual, Azyumardi Azra, focuses on the 'actually existing cosmopolitanism'.[33] He popularised the idea of 'Islam Nusantara' (Southeast Asian Islam) and elaborates how it is closely linked to Muslim cosmopolitanism in Southeast Asia. A brief biography of Azyumardi is in order here. Unlike Chandra, who was educated in secular institutions and became progressively interested in issues concerning Muslim life and faith, Azyumardi was tutored early on in his life in the traditional Islamic sciences. He was born in 1955 into a religious family that adhered to the modernist interpretations of Islam propagated by the Muhammadiyah movement. Educated in Islamic schools and tertiary institutions until the completion of his first degree at the Institut Agama Islam Negeri (IAIN, 'State Institute of Islamic Studies') in Jakarta, he went on to pursue his postgraduate degrees at Columbia University, New York, specialising in history and graduating in 1992.[34]

Azyumardi certainly fits squarely into Richard Posner's definition of public intellectuals being those who obtain 'an audience by engaging with some matter that has the public's attention'.[35] Since his days as a journalist with a local newspaper, *Panji Masyarakat*, Azyumardi has written books and articles seeking to break down the dichotomies between religious and secular sciences as well as between lofty intellectualism and popular activism, by presenting ideas that are accessible to a large segment of the Southeast Asian Muslim community.[36] His intellectual and journalistic output is simply staggering, with more than twenty books and hundreds of articles written in English and the Indonesian languages. Though trained as a *peneliti sejarah* (historical investigator),[37] in his words, Azyumardi has written and commented on topics of contemporary significance surrounding issues such as education, theology, politics, sociology of religions, violence, intellectuals and the intelligentsia, as well as Islamic jurisprudence. One overarching concept that binds all of these writings is the concept of 'Islam Nusantara'. It is a concept that has stirred the imagination of the Southeast Asian public in as much as it has generated polemics among conservatives who felt that Azyumardi was being divisive for having drawn the boundaries between various versions of Islam. Some critics alleged that he was unfair in his judgements of Islam outside Southeast Asia, particularly the ideas and practices of Islam beyond the borders of modern-day Indonesia.[38]

But what is 'Islam Nusantara'? Azyumardi refers to more than just a version of Islam that is unique and distinctive to Southeast Asia. Islam Nusantara points to a variant of Islam that has been 'indigenised' and 'vernacularised' to fit with the *urf* (customs) of the people in Muslim Southeast Asia. The concept of Islam Nusantara shares some affinities with Tariq Ramadan's idea of a 'European Islam', namely, a lived version of Islam that is habituated to the European environment without contravening the core pillars of the Muslim faith.[39] Even though Muslims in Southeast Asia may share the same sacred sources as other Muslims around the world and subscribe to the same basic precepts and beliefs, they interpret and manifest many non-fundamental aspects of Islam in their own cosmopolitan ways.

From dress codes to the interpretation of certain rulings and the treatment of women, Islam Nusantara departs from praxis found in the Arab world. This departure, according to Azyumardi, resulted from the creative exegesis of Muslim scholars that dates back to the thirteenth century. Their close interaction with Southeast Asians informed them that there were aspects of Islam that needed to be reinterpreted to harmonise the faith with local cultures. With the assistance of traders, mystics and wayfarers, these networks of scholars contributed to the rapid spread of Islam in the region by adapting the religion to indigenous traditions.[40]

Azyumardi gives the example of the ritual of fasting in Java and other parts of the Malay world. Some Javanese Muslims stretch the fasting period for three months, beginning with the month of Sya'ban (Sha'ban) and ending it at the end of the month of Syawal (Shawwal). This is radically different from how Ramadan has been understood in other parts of the Muslim world, where it is specific to one month of the Islamic calendar. During Sya'ban, the month preceding Ramadan, Javanese Muslims heighten their devotional activities by organising feasts, conducting religious classes and reaffirming relations with friends and relatives, both Muslim and non-Muslim, in preparation for the fasting month. Following the end of the Ramadan fast, they lengthen the festivity for another month, again differentiating them from Muslims in other parts of the world who normally celebrate the Eidul Fitri holiday on only the first day of Syawal. Javanese Muslims visit their relatives and return to their hometowns during this month as part of their striving to maintain the spirit of Muslim brotherhood.[41] Muslims in Southeast Asia perceive fasting and other religious practices as being more than just devotional acts. These acts are imbricated within the nexus of the kinship relations, community institutions, local traditions and social norms conditioned by Islam Nusantara.

Azyumardi sees Islam Nusantara as being 'easygoing' (*lunak*) and 'gentle' (*jinak*). The reason why Islam Nusantara has such characteristics has to do with the minimal acceptance of Arab cultures by the Malays.[42] On this point, Azyumardi is on the same page as Nurcholish Madjid, who argued that 'Indonesia is the least Arabized of the major Islamic countries, in addition to being geographically farthest from the Holy Lands'.[43] Azyumardi, however, departs from the views of another respected scholar of Southeast Asian Islam, Syed Naquib Al-Attas. The conversion of Southeast Asians to Islam, in Al-Attas's evaluation, brought profound transformations in Malay life, culture and thinking. Among such transformations was the adoption of many aspects of Arab–Persian civilisational elements.[44] Azyumardi does not deny this line of argument and reinforces it by providing evidence of the use of Arabic loanwords in the Malay language.[45] However, the adoption of Arabic words did not change the mild character of Islam Nusantara when compared with the Islam of the Arab world. This mildness has made Islam Nusantara more peaceful, cosmopolitan and inclusive. Azyumardi supported his argument by stating that, excepting isolated internecine conflicts, nominal (*abangan*) and devout (*santri*) Muslims have coexisted well together. The relationship between Muslims and non-Muslims continues to be stable despite the many centuries of Islamisation. The celebration and tolerance of the diverse ways of interpreting Islam is so marked in Southeast Asia that it is unsurpassed by any country in the Arab world.[46]

Azyumardi casts Islam Nusantara as distinctive in yet another aspect: its dialogical character. Indeed, dialogue between fellow Muslims and between

Muslims and non-Muslims has been an inherent feature of Islam in the region. This explains why many aspects of Islam Nusantara are more often than not syncretic and hybrid in nature, fusing past different cultures and beliefs to form a cross-breed Islamic faith. Azyumardi conveys a few forms of dialogue that have defined Islam Nusantara. The first is the dialogue of aesthetics. This is found in the architectural splendours of mosques and other iconic sites, a theme that has been explored in Chapter 2 of this book.[47] The second form of dialogue is an intra-Muslim dialogue that involves groups with competing ideas. Azyumardi divides them into different typologies: modernist Muslims, transformative Muslims, inclusivist Muslims, fundamentalist Muslims and neo-traditionalist Muslims. Each of these groups interprets Islam in its own way. Leaving aside those groups that are extremist and militant, the majority of Muslims in Southeast Asia is often open to discussions pertaining to issues affecting Muslims in general, even if they disagree on the methods of resolving such challenges.[48]

The third form of dialogue is between the different civilisations of Southeast Asia. Azyumardi regards Muslim Southeast Asia as a domain where different religions have coexisted peacefully for many centuries. The change in this harmonious relationship came about with the arrival of colonialism. 'This peaceful relationship often gets tainted by polemics and open protests, particularly after the establishment of Muslim organizations in the beginning of the 20th century.'[49] Although the intercivilisational relations improved greatly, while being kept in check under the iron fist of Suharto's New Order regime, the end of the Suharto's autocratic rule unleashed extremist forces within the religious communities in Indonesia. Azyumardi sees the urgency of reviving dialogue at all levels of society in order to reclaim the friendly relations between Southeast Asians:

> I believe that dialogue that is carried out with much civility, with ethics, will yield many benefits. If nothing else, dialogue can be an ice breaker, breaking the ice between two mutually suspicious parties, or those that have developed prejudices, bias, misperceptions, miunderstanding, and even anxieties and animosity. More than that, dialogue opens up opportunities for a transformation in behaviour and perceptions, aside from imbibing better mutual understanding that transcends the differences that exist between two sides.[50]

Like Chandra, Azyumardi is not a romantic idealist. He does not imagine that Islam Nusantara is a panacea that can free the region of all its problems. Azyumardi acknowledges that there are powerful forces threatening the cosmopolitan nature of Southeast Asian Islam and society. Azyumardi singles out the politicisation of Islam as being the greatest threat to Muslim cosmopolitanism. This conflation of faith and politics is not new to Islam in the region. Muslim sultanates in Southeast Asia during the precolonial period associated politics with Islam in the management of their territories. Azyumardi is concerned, though, with what he calls 'Islam politik' (or political Islam). This is a brand of Islam that is used as 'a framework or basis for political ideology, which would eventually materialize into political parties'.[51] The key setback of political Islam is that it tends to slide into taking a hardline approach in interpreting Islam. The inevitable outcome of this is the rise of communal politics, suspicions between Muslims and non-Muslims, the dismantling of mutual tolerance and, worst of all, the rise in violence. Azyumardi sees the incidents of violence in Aceh, East Timor, Ambon and West Kalimantan as evidence of the politicisation of Islam. These tragic events happened as a result of the influence of radicals and hardliners from militant groups such as Front Pembela Islam (FPI) and Laskar Jihad. These groups may not be popular, but they could grow in number and sow the seeds of hatred between communities.[52]

How, then, can Islam Nusantara be strengthened? Azyumardi agrees with Chandra on the importance of civil society. He draws upon Robert Hefner's concept of 'civil Islam', which is the opposite of the type of Islam imposed by states and regimes. Civil Islam is an Islam that abides by the rule of law but is, at the same time, shaped and conditioned by the work of civil society movements and organisations.[53] Such an Islam, which is at present being steered by the Nahdatul Ulama and the Muhammadiyah, would consolidate and deepen democracy in Indonesia. 'With a strong emphasis on the role of civil society in the democratic process, they are expected not only to consolidate their own organizations in order to be able to function more effectively, but also to disseminate the ideals of democracy; building civic culture and civility among the public in general.'[54]

As a cosmopolitan Muslim public intellectual, Azyumardi places much importance on the intervention of intellectuals. He argues that intellectuals play a crucial role in influencing public perception and understanding about religion in society. Their honesty, humility, public engagement and expertise could help in defining and reconstructing Islam Nusantara to make it relevant to the changing times.[55] They are the vanguard in the march to preserve the inclusive and cosmopolitan legacy of Islam Nusantara. They are also tasked with the responsibility of exposing the root causes of extremism and radicalism. Among the root causes that Azyumardi identifies are 'liberalization of the political system, fragmentation and conflicts among the political elite and parties, failure of law enforcement, economic deprivation, and socio-cultural dislocation and alienation'.[56] Overcoming these causes of radicalism would lead Islam Nusantara towards the middle way (*ummah wasat*), a path that brings Muslim to the ideas and practice of democracy, human rights, justice, gender equality, pluralism and, most crucially, cosmopolitanism.[57]

Hussin Mutalib and Islamic Assertiveness

Until recently, scholars have been confounded by the phenomenon of an Islamic resurgence in Muslim societies. The previously held assumption that religions would inevitably decline with the advent of secularism and high modernity proved to be untenable as successive scholars traced the unexpected return of Islam to the lives of Muslims all over world. Indeed, from the 1970s onwards, 'the old theory of secularization could no longer be maintained'.[58] In place of this discredited theory is the growth of studies about the reassertion of the Islamic way of life in Muslim societies. Chandra Muzaffar wrote a groundbreaking book on the Islamic resurgence in Malaysia.[59] Another cosmopolitan Muslim public intellectual who has delved deeply into the same subject throughout his entire career in academia and public life is Hussin Mutalib.

Hussin shares many defining characteristics with Chandra. Born in 1949, he was a scion of the downtrodden minority Malay community in Singapore. Orphaned at a young age and profoundly affected by the discrimination he suffered in the course of performing his compulsory military service in Singapore, he took on menial jobs and spent a brief period as a radio broadcaster before his eventual entry into the university. Hussin excelled throughout his studies and pursued his doctorate at the University of Sydney in the late 1980s. Through this period, he was strongly involved in Muslim activism. He recalls: 'These activities further helped increase my knowledge about the "real Islam" while also embedding in me the religious calling for qualified Muslims to help others, especially the weak, poor and oppressed the world over'.[60] The subject of his doctoral thesis reflected his own concerns and engagements. Hussin wrote about Islamic resurgence in Malaysia and the interplay between Malay ethnicity, Muslim religiosity and communal politics.[61] He continued to write many opinion pieces to newspapers upon his return to Singapore and was always at the forefront of commenting on critical issues such as Malaysian politics, the marginalisation of the Malays, the future of madrasahs (Islamic schools) in Singapore, the hijab issue, as well as state policies towards minorities. One dominant concept that permeates Hussin's intellectual career is 'Islamic assertiveness'.

Hussin defines 'Islamic assertiveness' through the worldview of its adherents. It is, first of all, a proclamation of Islam as an all-encompassing ideology that addresses all aspects of human life. Islamic assertiveness also involves the promotion of the notion of the global *ummah* (Islamic community) and the will on the part of Muslim activists to establish and forge ties with their brethren in different parts of the world. This 'ummatic paradigm', as Hussin calls it, is based on the Qur'anic injunction that all Muslims belong to a single community and that they should support one another in times of ease and difficulty. The other feature of Islamic assertiveness is the propagation of Islamic values, ideals and solutions to society at large. Such transmission of piety – also termed *dakwah*, or *da'wah* (calling) – entails individuals, groups, organisations and movements uniting to establish of an Islamic political order, Islamic economic system and an Islamically orientated society.[62]

Secular theorists view Islamic assertiveness as being a threat to the modernising world. For them, the return of Islam to the public sphere is antithetical to democracy, human rights and social justice. Islamic assertiveness has been touted as 'the new communism'. It is caricatured as a factor that will lead to a clash between the West and the Islamic civilisations and a chief cause of the rise of militancy throughout the Muslim world. The spectre of the 'Islamic peril' and the 'peril of Islamic resurgence', as Karim H. Karim and John Esposito observe, pervades media coverage of events in the Muslim world and of Muslims in the West, especially after the September 11 attacks on the World Trade Center in New York. At the core of Western bias and fear towards Islam is the belief that an Islamic revival will result in conflict and terrorism on a global scale.[63]

Hussin is critical of such one-sided views of Islamic assertiveness and the spurious link made by some analysts between Islamic assertiveness and 'the hardening of Muslim extremism or radicalism'.[64] He decouples Islamic assertiveness from extremism by documenting its positive effects, for example the flowering of Muslim cultures in Muslim Southeast Asia. This is seen in the realm of devotional popular music such as *nasyid* and a noticeable shift in dress codes as seen in the widespread wearing of *songkok, jilbab*, mini-*telekung* and purdah in many different colours and styles. Another positive effect of Islamic reassertiveness is the strengthening of Muslim institutions. More Muslims are frequenting mosques for prayers, religious classes and community events. After decades of relative neglect, the madrasahs have been given a new lease of life by Muslim activists who are committed to reforming these venerable educational institutions. [65]

Hussin perceives Islamic assertiveness as a constructive enabler in Muslim Southeast Asia because it provides an alternative and a resistance to the incursion of Western and secular values into Muslim societies. Greetings such as the Western 'hello' have been substituted with the Muslim greeting of 'assalaamu'alaikum' (peace be upon you) in forums, talks and the televised news. To curb the hegemony of the West in finance and economics, Islamic banks and shariah-compliant financial institutions have been established. To provide alternatives to Western ideas and ideologies, Muslim activists have established think tanks, universities and research centres that offer new paradigms and theories drawn from Asian and Islamic intellectual traditions.[66]

Another positive consequence of Islamic assertiveness is the growth of civil society in Muslim Southeast Asia. The mushrooming of Islamic organisations and movements has encouraged more Muslims to participate in the shaping of societal affairs and politics. Muslim activists have joined state bodies and achieved positions of authority. They have played crucial roles in upholding justice, social equality, mutual respect and the protection of human rights. Muthiah Alagappa has described this as 'the deep penetration and influence over the state by certain civil society actors'.[67] Civil society actors join various arms of the state and take up strategic positions in state-linked bodies in order to gain access to a range of resources. Islamic assertiveness goes hand in hand with a more vibrant and dynamic Muslim community which was more than ready to engage and work with its co-religionists and also with non-Muslims. Hussin refers to the examples of Anwar Ibrahim from the ABIM, who became part of the ruling government in Malaysia and rose to the rank of deputy prime minister. Anwar set in motion many reforms that addressed educational problems and interracial rifts in Malaysia. While Muslim activists have not penetrated the upper echelons of many state institutions in Singapore, they have developed a strong lobby group that has opposed some of the policies introduced by the state. Hussin cites the case of the madrasah issue in Singapore in 2002 that provoked a strong response by the Muslim community against state attempts to regulate the madrasahs in accordance with the national education policies. Muslim activists involved in the madrasah issue were clearly influenced by the wave of Islamic revivalism sweeping the region. Due to their strong protests against the government's plans regarding the madrasahs, the state relented and changed tack, giving more financial and other forms of support on the road to reforming and bringing the madrasahs up to the standards of mainstream national schools.[68]

In sum, by painting an optimistic picture of Islamic assertiveness in Muslim Southeast Asia, Hussin debunks the adverse assumptions about the effects of the return to Islam in Muslim societies. He offers, therefore, a revisionist conceptualisation of Islamic assertiveness that could further magnify rather than constrict the progress of cosmopolitanism in Southeast Asia. Hussin believes that both Muslims and non-Muslims stand to benefit from the Islamisation of society and from the reinforcement of the Muslim identity. As he puts it: 'The prospect for the Southeast Asian Muslims to become a beacon of hope, if not model, for Muslims elsewhere, is bright provided they have the capacity and ingenuity to manage the process of change in the new century'.[69] And yet, Hussin admits that Islamic assertiveness has had some negative outcomes as well.[70]

Hussin maintains that it would be naive or intellectually dishonest to deny some of the pitfalls of Islamic assertiveness. One of these pitfalls is that it has been hijacked by the state. This was particularly so in Malaysia and Indonesia under Mahathir and Suharto respectively. Both statesmen rode on the wave of Islamic resurgence in an effort to use Islam for their political ends.[71] On the other hand, in Singapore, Islamic assertiveness has been cited as a pretext for clamping down on selected personalities and groups deemed radicals, or who were claimed to have plotted violence and conflict. Hussin stresses that Islamic assertiveness has been a source of justification for states in Southeast Asia to violate the freedom of Muslims, to curtail their privacy, to profile and target them, to label them as fundamentalists and to securitise any problems that are conveniently linked to Islam and Muslims.[72]

Like Chandra, Hussin concedes that Muslim activists can be the nemeses of Muslim cosmopolitanism and that Islamic assertiveness can, at times, lead to communalism and even violence. He is fully aware of the rise of militant groups in Southeast Asia since the advent of the Islamic resurgence in the 1970s. But, Southeast Asian Islam has continued to be, by and large, cosmopolitan and inclusive, so much so that there has been no prospect of establishing any Islamic states in the region. Nor can radical Islam dominate the thinking of the ordinary Muslim because '[i]n fact and in truth, the idea of suicide bombers has never crept into the Islamic literature in the region, simply because Muslims there consider it an act of high sin'.[73] If anything, Islamic assertiveness will lead to a more pluralised society, one that celebrates difference, diversity and distinctiveness. In this sense, Hussin's ideas are in sync with the ideas of the Palestinian Islamic scholar, Ismail al-Faruqi, who posited that Islamic revivalism was not a barrier to the free exchange of ideas between members of different religious and ideological persuasions.[74]

Hussin agrees with Azyumardi on the roles of public intellectuals in shaping Islamic revitalisation towards a more constructive path. They should work together with the traditional *ulama* to relive the legacies of tolerance and openness of past Muslims. They should dispense with the 'emotive slogan-shouting of "Islam is the solution!" in galvanizing the Muslim masses towards some causes. The new age calls for the courage to offer alternative solutions, and the capacity to articulate and rationalize, in clear and pragmatic ways, how such solutions are to be sought and realistically implemented'.[75] For Hussin, Muslim intellectuals, the *ulama* and movement activists should galvanise their resources and expertise to resolve 'manifest tensions in Muslim societies – between traditional–modern ulama, old–new generation, Shia–Sunni, official ulama–autonomous ulama, blind practices, and so on'.[76]

Conclusion

Cosmopolitan Muslim public intellectuals have deeply shaped the texture of Southeast Asian Islam through their writings. They have been able to do so because they write in ways that are accessible and intelligible to the Muslim public, while touching on issues that affect Muslims and non-Muslims alike. The impact of these intellectuals is felt at the grass-roots level owing to the fact that these intellectuals create, as John Esposito and John Voll aptly assert, 'activist programs of reform and social transformation that could be clearly identified as Islamic but, at the same time, went far beyond the traditionalism of the remaining conservative ulama establishment'.[77] By touching on issues such as justice, human rights, equality, politics, marginalisation, religious assertiveness and interreligious tolerance – topics that are seldom broached by the *ulama* class – these intellectuals in Muslim Southeast Asia wield a captive audience of their own. Their reach has expanded further with the advent of digital media.

Another reason why cosmopolitan Muslim public intellectuals command attention from the public is that they hail from humble backgrounds and in much of their writing reveal their personal experiences and struggles. Posner's observations of black intellectuals are instructive here as a basis for comparison.

> Life experiences may be important. One reason so many well-known public intellectuals are black, such as Anthony Appiah, Stephen Carter, Michael Eric Dyson, Henry Louis Gates Jr., Lani Guinier, Thomas Sowell, Shelby Steele, Cornell West, Patricia Williams, and William Julius Wilson, is that blacks are believed to have life experiences that give them insights denied the ordinary white male academic.[78]

Certainly, Chandra, Azyumardi and Hussin have interwoven their personal journeys into their scholarly writings. These three cosmopolitan Muslim public intellectuals are conscious of their minority positions, in terms of ethnicity, paradigms and intellectual posturing. Such a consciousness of marginality adds power and emotion to their works, just as it has committed them to expounding concepts that they hope will bring their societies closer to the ethics of Muslim cosmopolitanism.

Notes

1. Pierre Bourdieu, *Acts of Resistance: Against the New Myths of Our Time*, translated by Richard Nice (Cambridge: Polity Press, 1998), pp. 92.
2. Edward W. Said, *Representations of the Intellectual* (New York: Vintage, 1994), pp. 52–3.
3. Barbara A. Misztal, *Intellectuals and the Public Good: Creativity and Civil Courage* (Cambridge: Cambridge University Press, 2007), p. 1.
4. Richard Posner, *Public Intellectuals: A Study in Decline* (Cambridge, MA: Harvard University Press, 2001), p. 35.
5. Frank Furedi, *Where Have All the Intellectuals Gone?* (London: Continuum, 2004).
6. Koh Tai Ann, 'The Role of Intellectuals in Civil Society: Going against the Grain?', in Gillian Koh and Ooi Giok Ling (eds), *State–Society Relations in Singapore* (Singapore: Oxford University Press, 2000), pp. 156–67.
7. Dale F. Eickelman, 'Clash of Cultures? Intellectuals, their Publics and Islam', in Stéphane A. Dudoigon, Komatsu Hisao, and Kosugi Yasushi (eds), *Intellectuals in the Modern Islamic World: Transmission, Transformation, Communication* (London: Routledge, 2006), p. 291.
8. Some recent studies on Malay Muslim intellectuals and their cosmopolitan tendencies that are worth citing here are: Carool Kersten, 'Islam, Cultural Hybridity and Cosmopolitanism: New Muslim Intellectuals on Globalization', *Journal of International and Global Studies*, 1, 1 (2009), p. 90, and Howard Federspiel, 'Contemporary South-East Asian Muslim Intellectuals: An Examination of the Sources for their Concepts and Intellectual Constructs', in Johan H. Meuleman (ed.), *Islam in the Era of Globalization: Muslim Attitudes Towards Modernity and Identity* (London: RoutledgeCurzon, 2002), pp. 327–50.
9. Yudi Latif, *Indonesian Muslim Intelligentsia and Power* (Singapore: ISEAS, 2008), p. 480.
10. Edward W. Said, *Representations of the Intellectual* (New York: Vintage, 1994), p. 4.
11. Ronald Barnett, 'Academics as Intellectuals', in Dolan Cummings (ed.), *The Changing Role of the Public Intellectual* (London: Routledge, 2005), p. 112.
12. This chapter only deals with male Muslim intellectuals because female Muslim intellectuals are covered in the next chapter.
13. Garry Rodan, *Transparency and Authoritarian Rule in Southeast Asia: Singapore and Malaysia* (London: Routledge, 2004).

14. See, for example, Anis Ananta and Richard Barichello (eds), *Poverty and Global Recession in Southeast Asia* (Singapore: ISEAS Press, 2012).

15. Hans Köchler, 'Foreword', in Chandra Muzaffar, *Hegemony: Justice; Peace* (Selangor, Malaysia: Arah Pendidikan Sdn Bhd, 2008), pp. vi–viii.

16. Chandra Muzaffar, 'The Long Journey to the Just: My Life, My Struggle', *Inter-Asian Cultural Studies*, 12, 1 (2011), p. 110.

17. The thesis was published as Chandra Muzaffar, *Protector? An Analysis of the Concept and Practice of Loyalty in Leader-led Relationships within the Malay Society* (Penang, Malaysia: Aliran, 1979).

18. Muzaffar, 'Long Journey to the Just', p. 111.

19. Chandra Muzaffar, *Muslim Today: Changes Within, Challenges Without* (Islamabad: Emel Publications, 2011), p. 27.

20. Muzaffar, *Muslim Today*, p. 44.

21. Chandra Muzaffar, 'Towards a Universal Spiritual-Moral Vision of Global Justice and Peace', in Chandra Muzaffar (ed.), *Religion Seeking Justice and Peace* (Penang, Malaysia: USM Press, 2010), p. 140.

22. Chandra Muzaffar, *Global Ethic or Global Hegemony? Reflections on Religion Human Dignity and Civilisational Interaction* (London: ASEAN Academic Press, 2005), p. 132.

23. Noor, 'Reformist Muslim Thinkers', p. 218.

24. Chandra Muzaffar, *One God: Many Paths* (Penang, Malaysia: Aliran, 1980).

25. Chandra Muzaffar, *Exploring Religion in Our Time* (Penang, Malaysia: USM Press, 2011), p. 66.

26. Chandra Muzaffar, *Rights, Religion and Reform: Enhancing Human Dignity through Spiritual and Moral Transformation* (London: Routledge, 2002), pp. 173–214.

27. Makau Mutua, *Human Rights: A Political and Cultural Critique* (Philadelphia: University of Pennsylvania Press, 2002), p. 13.

28. Chandra Muzaffar, 'From Human Rights to Human Dignity', in Peter van Ness (ed.), *Debating Human Rights: Critical Essays from United States and Asia* (London: Routledge, 1999), pp. 29–30.

29. See William E. Shepard, *Sayyid Qutb and Islamic Activism: A Translation and Critical Analysis of Social Justice in Islam* (Leiden: Brill, 1996).

30. Muzaffar, *Exploring Religion*, p. 43.

31. Muzaffar, *Exploring Religion*, p. 43.

32. Yoginder Sikand, 'Interview: Chandra Muzaffar on Islamic Inclusivism and Muslim Exclusivism', TwoCircles.net, 19 October 2009, <http://twocircles.

net/2009oct19/interview_chandra_muzaffar_islamic_inclusivism_and_muslim
_exclusivism.html> (last accessed 10 February 2016).

33. Bruce Robbins, 'Actually Existing Cosmopolitanism', in Pheng Cheah and Bruce Robbins (eds), *Cosmopolitics: Thinking and Feeling Beyond the Nation* (Minneapolis, University of Minnesota Press, 1998), pp. 1–19.

34. Azyumardi Azra, *Dari Harvard hingga Makkah* (Jakarta: Penerbit Republika, 2005), pp. 201–4.

35. Posner, *Public Intellectuals*, p. 32.

36. Idris Thaha, 'Memahami Azyumardi Azra', preface to Azyumardi Azra, *Islam Substantif* (Bandung, Indonesia: Penerbit Mizan, 2000), p. 28.

37. Azyumardi Azra, *Historiografi Islam Kontemporer: Wacana, Aktualitas, dan Aktor Sejarah* (Jakarta: Penerbit Gramedia, 2002), p. 84.

38. Heyder Affan, 'Polemik di balik istilah "Nusantara"', Islampos, 28 June 2015, <http://www.islampos.com/mengkritisi-islam-nusantara-versi-azyumardi-azra-192818/> (last accessed 12 February 2016).

39. Tariq Ramadan, *To Be a European Muslim* (Leicester: The Islamic Foundation, 2002), pp. 198 and 250.

40. Azyumardi Azra, *Islam Nusantara: Jaringan Global dan Lokal* (Jakarta: Mizan Press, 2002), p. 61, and *The Origins of Islamic Reformism in Southeast Asia: Networks of Malay-Indonesian and Middle Eastern Ulama in the Seventeenth and Eighteenth Centuries* (Honolulu: University of Hawai'i Press, 2004).

41. Azyumardi Azra, *Jejak-Jejak Jaringan Kaum Muslimin: Dari Australia hingga Timur Tengah* (Jakarta: Penerbit Hikmah, 2007), pp. 51–4.

42. Azyumardi Azra, *Konflik Baru Antar Peradaban: Globalisasi, Radikalisme dan Pluralitas* (Jakarta: PT RajaGrafindo Persada, 2002), pp. 162–3.

43. Nurcholish Madjid, 'Islamic Roots of Modern Pluralism: Indonesian Experiences', *Studia Islamika: Indonesian Journal for Islamic Studies*, 1, 1 (1994), p. 59.

44. Syed Muhammad Naquib Al-Attas, *Preliminary Statement on a General Theory of the Islamization of the Malay-Indonesian Archipelago* (Kuala Lumpur: Dewan Bahasa dan Pustaka, 1969).

45. Azyumardi Azra, *Renaisans Islam Asia Tenggara: Sejarah Wacana dan Kekuasaan* (Bandung, Indonesia: PT Remaja Rosdakarya, 1999), pp. 75–80.

46. Azyumardi Azra, *Konteks Berteologi di Indonesia: Pengalaman Islam* (Jakarta: Penerbit Paramadina, 1999), p. 40; Azra, *Renaisans Islam Asia Tenggara*, p. 24, and Azyumardi Azra, *Reposisi Hubungan Agama dan Negara: Merajut Hubungan Antaraumat* (Jakarta: Penerbit Buku Kompas, 2002), p. 124.

47. Azyumardi Azra, *Paradigma Baru Pendidikan Nasional: Reconstruksi dan Demokratisasi* (Jakarta: Penerbit Buku Kompas, 2002), p. 239.
48. Azra, *Konteks Berteologi di Indonesia*, p. 51.
49. Azra, *Konteks Berteologi di Indonesia*, p. 60.
50. Azra, *Jejak-Jejak Jaringan Kaum Muslimin*, pp. 195–6.
51. Azyumardi Azra, 'Islam di Tengah Arus Transisi Menuju Demokrasi', in Abdul Mun'im D. Z. (ed.), *Islam Di Tengah Arus Transisi* (Jakarta: Kompas, 2000), p. xxiii.
52. Azra, *Konteks Berteologi di Indonesia*, p. 228, and Azyumardi Azra, *Indonesia, Islam, and Democracy: Dynamics in a Global Context* (Jakarta: Solstice Publishing, 2006), pp. 55–88.
53. Hefner, *Civil Islam*, pp. 3–20.
54. Azra, *Konflik Baru Antar Peradaban*, p. 181.
55. Azyumardi Azra, *Esei-esei Intelektual Muslim dan Pendidikan Islam* (Ciputat, Indonesia: PT Logos Wacana Ilmu, 1998), pp. 42–7.
56. Azyumardi Azra, 'Islamic Thought: Theory, Concepts and Doctrine in the Context of Southeast Asian Islam', in K. S. Nathan and Mohammad Hashim Kamali (eds), *Islam in Southeast Asia: Political, Social and Strategic Challenges for the 21st Century* (Singapore: ISEAS Press, 2005), p. 18.
57. Azyumardi Azra, 'Religious Pluralism in Indonesia: The Impact of Democracy on Conflict Resolution', in K. S. Nathan (ed.), *Religious Pluralism in Democratic Societies: Challenges and Prospects for Southeast Asia, Europe, and the United States in the New Millennium* (Singapore: Konrad-Adenauer-Stiftung and Malaysian Association for American Studies [MAAS], 2007), p. 237, and Azra, *Indonesia, Islam, and Democracy*, p. 183.
58. José Casanova, *Public Religions in the Modern World* (Chicago: University of Chicago Press, 1980), p. 19.
59. Chandra Muzaffar, *Islamic Resurgence in Malaysia* (Petaling Jaya, Malaysia: Fajar Bakti, 1987).
60. From an interview conducted with Hussin Mutalib on 30 September 2015.
61. The thesis was eventually published as a monograph. See Hussin Mutalib, *Islam and Ethnicity in Malay Politics* (Kuala Lumpur: Oxford University Press, 1990).
62. Hussin Mutalib, 'Islamic Revivalism in ASEAN States: Political Implications', *Asian Survey*, 30, 9 (1990), p. 878.
63. John L. Esposito, *The Islamic Threat: Myth or Reality?* (New York: Oxford University Press, 1992) and Karim H. Karim, *The Islamic Peril: Media and Global Violence* (New York: Black Rose Books, 2003), p. 175.

64. Hussin Mutalib, *Islam in Southeast Asia* (Singapore: ISEAS Press, 2008), p. 22.

65. Hussin Mutalib, 'Political Islam in Southeast Asia: Shar'iah Pressures, Democratic Measures?', in Hussin Mutalib, *Islam and Democracy: The Southeast Asian Experience* (Singapore: Konrad-Adenauer-Siftung, 2004), p. 13.

66. Mutalib, 'Islamic Revivalism in ASEAN States', p. 880.

67. Muthiah Alagappa, 'Civil Society and Political Change: An Analytical Framework', in Muthiah Alagappa (ed.), *Civil Society and Political Change in Asia: Expanding and Contracting Democratic Space* (Stanford, CA: Stanford University Press, 2004), p. 37.

68. Hussin Mutalib, 'Authoritarian Democracy and the Minority Muslim Polity in Singapore', Johan Saravanamuttu (eds), *Islam and Politics in Southeast Asia* (London: Routledge, 2010), p. 147.

69. Hussin Mutalib, 'Islam in Southeast Asia and the 21st Century: Managing the Inevitable Challenges, Dilemmas and Tensions', *Islamic Studies*, 37, 2 (1998), p. 201.

70. Mutalib, 'Islam in Southeast Asia and the 21st Century', p. 210.

71. Hussin Mutalib, 'Islamisation in Malaysia: Between Ideals and Realities', in Hussin Mutalib and Taj ul-Islam Hashmi (eds), *Islam, Muslims and the Modern State* (New York: St. Martin's Press, 1994), p. 157.

72. Hussin Mutalib, 'The Rise in Islamicity and the Perceived Threat of Political Islam', in K. S. Nathan (ed.), *Perspectives on Doctrinal and Strategic Implications of Global Islam* (Singapore: ISEAS, 2003), p. 19, and Mutalib, 'Political Islam in Southeast Asia', pp. 17–21.

73. Hussin Mutalib, 'Misunderstood: Political Islam in Southeast Asia', *Harvard International Review*, 28, 2 (2006), p. 83.

74. Ismail R. al-Faruqi, *Islam* (Niles, IL: Argus Communications, 1979), p. 65.

75. Mutalib, 'Islam in Southeast Asia and the 21st Century', pp. 210–11.

76. From an interview conducted with Hussin Mutalib on 30 September 2015.

77. John Esposito and John Voll, *Makers of Contemporary Islam* (Oxford: Oxford University Press, 2001), p. 20.

78. Posner, *Public Intellectuals*, p. 56.

5

HIJABIS AS PURVEYORS OF MUSLIM COSMOPOLITANISM

In late 2011, a Malaysian Muslim activist group called the 'Obedient Wives' Club' (OWC) made world headlines when they published a guide on the conduct of married life. Explicitly entitled *Seks Islam: Perangi Yahudi untuk Kembalikan Seks Islam ke Dunia* (Islamic Sex: Fighting Jews to Return Islamic Sex to the World), this provocative book claims that 'Jewish' (read: Zionist) notions of love, sexuality and eroticism have tainted modern-day sexual practices. Women are often approached by their spouses as if they are merely objects or animals, without due consideration of their emotional needs. The book also claims that Jews are responsible for the rampancy of pornography around the world, which has shaped the ways in which men perceive women's bodies. As an alternative, the book provides tips for developing a harmonious married life to keep men away from 'five star hotels that provide "first class service" to their special guests'.[1] This is no place to discuss the controversies surrounding the OWC or the eventual fate of the 'Islamic Sex' book, which was censured by feminist groups and banned by the Malaysian state. My interest is in one factor that undergirds the concerns of the OWC, its detractors as well as its interlocutors: the symbolic importance of Muslim women's bodies in Southeast Asian Islam. To be sure, women's bodies and physical appearances have been, and still are, a highly contested issue in contemporary Islam. Scott Kugle neatly summarises such developments:

Over the past two centuries, Islamic societies have changed dramatically under the impact of European conquest, colonization, and modernity (whether imposed from without or advocated from within). Muslim women's bodies have emerged as the site of contention and the gauge of change, whether as the object of the colonial gaze, the goal of secularist reforms, the concern of the traditionalist reaction, or the target of fundamentalist resurgence.[2]

Kugle's assessment of the growing interest in women's bodies is essentially negative in tone, as if suggesting that the issue has been constructed largely by forces external to the Muslim women themselves. I wish to move in a slightly different direction to develop the argument that women's bodies have also been used productively by female scholars, enthusiasts and activists to air and promote fresh interpretations, inventive practices and innovative programmes to make Southeast Asian Islam more cosmopolitan and inclusive towards its womenfolk in particular and towards Muslims and non-Muslims in general. Nevertheless, the inclusion of Southeast Asian Muslim women in discussions on cosmopolitanism and the ways in which women's discourses and activities have structured the contours of Muslim cosmopolitanism leaves much to be desired.

Despite the call by feminist scholars such as Miriam Cooke for the need to conceptualise 'a new kind of cosmopolitanism marked by religion' through the inclusion of the travails of Muslim women in scholarly writings, very few works on Southeast Asian women have been written in that spirit. [3] The conceptualisation of religious cosmopolitanism through the struggles of Muslim women is all the more urgent, Cooke argues, because these women are increasingly becoming 'outsider/insiders within Muslim communities where, to belong, their identity is increasingly tied to the idea of the veil. As Muslims, they are negotiating cultural outsider/insider roles in societies where Muslims form a minority or they are under threat'.[4]

In this chapter, I focus on a highly debated issue related to women's bodies in Muslim Southeast Asia: the hijab (also referred to as 'tudung', 'jilbab' or, in Javanese, 'kurundung', all of which can be subsumed under the wider category of the 'headscarf').[5] I have left out discussions about the niqab (face veil) because it is not common in Southeast Asian societies. More crucially, in her recent book *What is Veiling?*, Sahar Amer observed that, '[v]eiling is a practice that foments heated debates among ordinary citizens and policy makers in North America and in Europe, as well as in many Muslim-majority societies around the world. It has become a surprisingly powerful symbol'.[6] More than a powerful symbol, delving into the practices, perceptions and politics of the hijab could offer us new pathways in looking at how Muslim women in Southeast Asia have expressed and negotiated their notions of piety while challenging accepted assumptions of what it means to be 'progressive', 'modern' and 'cosmopolitan' Muslim women.

I will first analyse a collective reinterpretation of the meanings, places and functions of the hijab. Such collective reinterpretation comes in the form of life stories that argue for the relevance and necessity of wearing the hijab and that challenge prevailing stereotypes and liberal understandings about wearing the headscarf. The writers also question traditional ideas about why the hijab is obligatory for women. The second part of this chapter turns to how Muslim women keep up with the latest fashion trends. This is evidenced in the wide range of hijab styles that have developed in recent years, adding colour and richness to the meanings of female modesty in Islam. I end with a discussion of online activism and bring into sharp focus the virtual hijab movement in Singapore. Muslim women of different ages and backgrounds have collaborated with men in calling for the acceptance of women wearing the headscarf in many sectors of the country's society and economy to expand the limits of cosmopolitanism in Singapore.

The Hijab Revolution in Muslim Southeast Asia

The donning of the hijab is a relatively new phenomenon in Southeast Asia. The beginnings can be traced back to the end of the 1970s when the headscarf gained prominence during the height of the Iranian Revolution in 1979. Iranian Muslim women wearing their traditional headscarf called the chador (a long black cloak that covers a woman almost completely from head to toe) came out openly to support the revolutionary movement against the ruling shah. These hijab-clad phalanxes were visible in street demonstrations in Iran wielding rifles, guns and clubs in a brazen and belligerent effort to end of many years of state oppression.[7] Iranian women's outward display of defiance through the wearing of the hijab inspired Muslim women the world over. It fuelled and provided much publicity for the proponents of the Islamic resurgence that had already been underway in Southeast Asia since the 1960s. Muslim resurgents urged Muslims to return to the true spirit of Islam that included, among other things, a redefinition of the concept of modesty (*aurah*) among both men and women.

It would not be excessive to posit that one of the ultimate objectives of Islamic resurgence was to regulate Muslim bodies from being influenced by Western consumerism and hedonistic lifestyles. Muslim resurgents maintained that the problems of illicit sex, free interaction between men and women, and the adoption of lewd fashions all had their roots in the exploitation of Muslim women's bodies. The body was thus regarded as an essential marker of the state of societal piety, as the gauge for the progress of Islamisation and as the first line of defence against the incursion of un-Islamic values into Muslim societies. For these reasons, the donning of the hijab became the clarion call of the Muslim resurgents in their 'endeavour to re-establish Islamic values, Islamic practices, Islamic institutions, Islamic laws, indeed Islam in its entirety, in the lives of Muslims everywhere'.[8]

By the 1980s, wearing the headscarf had become increasingly widespread throughout the Muslim world, including in Southeast Asia. In fact, it became an indicator of piety and religious devolution. Katherine Bullock summarises this worldwide trend vividly as follows:

> Women whose mothers did not cover, indeed, whose grandmothers and mothers may have fought to uncover, started wearing the *hijab* and *niqab*. This trend turned into a women's movement that encompasses the entire Muslim world, from Arabia to Asia to Muslims living in the West. It is called the 're-veiling' movement, although it is not really a 're'-veiling movement because the women mostly concerned are covering for the first time, and they are mostly adopting *hijab*, not *niqab*.[9]

More than just a movement, the wearing of the hijab grew to become a revolution regarding what constitutes the *aurah* (the intimate parts of the body). If the *aurah* was limited to covering the body with modest attire without necessarily covering the head, the hijab revolution introduced the idea that only the hands and faces of Muslim women should be left exposed. The idea of *aurah* extended beyond mere dress codes. It encompassed social interactions between men and women. Unmarried persons are enjoined to maintain strict standards of decency when communicating with one another and, except in cases of necessity, men and women should be segregated from one another. They must exhibit the best of manners (*akhlaq*) at all times in line with the essence of the shariah.[10]

The hijab revolution spread like wild fire across Muslim Southeast Asia and gained strength from the growth of *dakwah* movements. Led largely by urban professionals and middle-class youths based in towns and cities in the region, *dakwah* movements were founded in tertiary institutions before beginning to receive support from the wider Muslim population. Young men and women from organisations such as the Himpunan Mahasiswa Islam (HMI, 'Islamic Students' Association') in Indonesia, the Angkatan Belia Islam SeMalaysia (ABIM, 'Muslim Youth Movement of Malaysia') and the Fellowship of Muslim Students Association of Singapore (FMSA) spearheaded and steered the course of the *dakwah* movement right through the 1990s. These young and daring activists faced resistance and criticism from the majority of the Muslim population, particularly those based in suburban and village areas. In Malaysia, many Muslims saw the wearing of the hijab as a regression into fundamentalism and, for some, as a sign of the Arabisation of Malay society.[11] In Indonesia, the headscarf became so prominent within a few years after its emergence in the 1970s that the Suharto state took the drastic measure of banning it in public schools. This was met with strong protest from women activists who saw the wearing of the hijab 'not as a means of protection for women entering public spaces but as a marker of their marginality and the reason for their harassment'.[12] Like their Turkish sisters who wore the headscarf when it was banned in their country, headscarved Indonesian women gained much public attention and support for their acts of courage, influencing many more women to join and support the cause of *jilbalisasi*, or 'veilisation'. So strong was the pressure from Muslims who rallied in support of the headscarf that the regime was forced to formally reverse its policy in 1991.[13]

The end of the twentieth century marked a new phase for the hijab revolution in Southeast Asia. What began as a dress code that was shunned by large segments of the Southeast Asian Muslim communities became accepted as the new normal in the region. With the exception of Singapore, where the hijab is banned in schools, hospitals and the uniformed services, Muslim women in other parts of Muslim Southeast Asia are now allowed to wear headscarves in all sorts of professions and vocations. Female politicians wearing the hijab have become prominent. In Java, Indonesia, as one study suggests, the hijab is, in effect, a powerful symbolic tool used by female politicians to gain support from the Muslim masses.[14] Despite its restrictive policies towards the hijab, the reigning People's Action Party (PAP) fielded three hijab-wearing candidates during the 2015 Singapore general elections. This was part of the ruling party's strategy to court Muslim votes.

The popularity of the hijab expanded rapidly in part due to the changing of fashions. The black and green headscarves that were worn with traditional Malay dress (*baju kurung*) and the mini-*telekung* (triangular headdress) of the 1970s were soon replaced by a hybridised hijab that blends European, Arabian and Southeast Asian motifs.[15] Certainly, the hijab has become normalised to the extent that veiled Muslim women are visible in public places in all parts of Muslim Southeast Asia today. The advent of celebrity 'hijabis' (those who wear the headscarf), such as popular singers like Siti Nurhaliza and Dewi Sandra, supercharged this process of normalisation so much so that now non-veiled women are sometimes regarded by a small and aggressive segment of the community as 'lesser Muslims'.[16]

The omnipresence of the hijab that comes in a variety of styles and colours along with the continued general tolerance and coexistence between those who do and those who do not wear the hijab have made Southeast Asian Islam more pluralised than ever before. While many analysts choose to believe that the post-September 11 world has seen a deepening of divisions within the Muslim community, especially between conservatives and moderates and between so-called 'Islamists' and secularists, in actuality, each of these different persuasions within the Muslim community respects the differing interpretations about the hijab.[17] To wear or not to wear the headscarf is a matter of personal choice for the hijabis. It is to be encouraged, but not enforced; to be culturalised, but not politicised. Undeniably, the headscarf is now part and parcel of the cultural fabric of Southeast Asia. It has morphed beyond being perceived as a foreign importation, as it used to be in the 1970s. Today, it is an indispensable component of Southeast Asian

Islam that is talked and written about. In this sense, the hijab revolution has reached its apogee.

Hijab Confessional Writings and Muslim Cosmopolitanism

Much ink has been spilt on the headscarf since the onset of the hijab revolution in Muslim Southeast Asia. This long list of works can be conveniently categorised as academic, prescriptive and confessional in nature. By 'academic', I mean works that approach the hijab issue from a detached perspective, designed primarily to illuminate rather than to advocate on behalf of the hijabis. These writings draw on sociological, anthropological and political perspectives to explain the hijab revolution. Prescriptive writings on the headscarf, in turn, highlight the plight of hijabis in their societies and advocate for reforms in Muslim thinking about the headscarf. Authors of these works come from a variety of backgrounds, ranging from academics to lay writers to religious activists. Their agenda is to influence public opinion about the hijab. Prescriptive works come in two broad categories. The first of these sees the hijab as a dress code that is compulsory for all Muslim women. For many of these authors, wearing the hijab is a religious ruling to be enforced by Muslims globally in order to ensure the protection of women from harm. Within this body of work, there are writers who manufacture conspiracy theories regarding alleged Western efforts to deculturalise the Muslims through fashion, as seen in the case of the 'Islamic Sex' book which we encountered earlier. The hijab, too, has been turned into mere mass-produced fashion by Western designer firms.[18]

The second category of prescriptive works includes those that advocate the position that scholars are divided (*khilaf*) over the issue of the hijab. Quraish Shihab, for example, deems the headscarf as encouraged by Islam, but not necessarily compulsory.[19] Even though there are personalities and groups advocating the position that hijab is not obligatory and that it is only a part of Arab culture and not Islamic, I have not managed to find any published works explaining such a stance.

In this section, I will focus on the third genre of works on the hijab, or a genre that could be dubbed 'hijab confessional writing'.[20] Despite the wide range of hijab confessional writings in Muslim Southeast Asia, scholars have paid surprisingly little attention to this expansive literature. This neglect may have much to do with the fact that scholars working on the topic of hijab have tended to 'ascribe meaning rather than describe the meaning the veil has for Muslim women'.[21] Hijab confessional writings reveal to us the circumstances that led Muslim women to don headscarves. These works provide inroads into the deeper meanings of the hijab in the everyday lives of Muslim women. Through their confessions, the hijabis also challenge, sometimes obliquely and in many instances blatantly, negative ideas about the hijab. Michel Foucault in his classic *The History of Sexuality* theorises cogently on the function of such confessional writings by stating that

> the confession is a ritual of discourse in which the speaking subject is also the subject of the statement; it is also a ritual that unfolds within a power relationship, for one does not confess without the presence (or virtual presence) of a partner who is not simply the interlocutor but the authority who requires the confession, prescribes and appreciates it, and intervenes in order to judge, punish, forgive, console, and reconcile.[22]

I will show how hijab confessional writings have clarified what the hijab means for Muslim women and the manner in which the hijab does in fact contribute to rather than constrict the growth of Muslim cosmopolitanism in Southeast Asia. The subject of my discussion is a book entitled *Bagaimana Akhirnya Saya Bertudung* (How I Finally Became Headscarved). It is, to my mind, an excellent example of dozens of works of this type.[23] Consisting of twenty-five confessions of why Malay Muslim women took the crucial life-changing step of donning the hijab, the book has been a best-seller since its first publication in 2003. It has been reprinted eight times and has inspired the creation of many blogs covering the confessions of women who have donned the headscarf.[24] With the exception of Katherine Bullock, an Australian academic and a known expert on the subject of veiling, all other contributors are based in Malaysia. These women are cosmopolitan in that they view themselves as belonging to both the Southeast Asian region and the Muslim world as a whole. They have avoided falling into the trap of communal and ethno-nationalist parochialism, couching Islam as not only a Malay or Arab religion but as a universal faith that embraces peoples of all backgrounds. All of these women writers went through the formal secular educational system. A large proportion of them attended tertiary institutions, reaching the level of doctorates and specialised degrees in subjects such as medicine, accountancy, law and engineering. Furthermore, they are well travelled, well connected and well informed about global trends. They have studied and worked for extended periods as professionals in varying occupations and in various countries.

How does this piece of hijab confessional writing contribute to the shaping of Muslim cosmopolitanism? The first answer is found through the writers' deconstruction and demystification of stereotypes about the hijab. In Europe and North America, Katherine Bullock highlights that 'for many in the Western media, *hijab* by and large stands for oppression and as shorthand for all the horrors of Islam (now called Islamic fundamentalism): terrorism, violence, barbarity and backwardness'.[25] Headscarved women are often depicted as the antithesis of the emancipated and liberated Muslim women who have power over their own bodies.[26]

On the contrary, the confessions found in *Bagaimana Akhirnya Saya Bertudung* support the point made by Fadwa El Guindi and Leila Ahmed that headscarved women have had agency and autonomy.[27] The hijab, according to the confessional writers, is a manifestation of the beauty of Islam (*keindahan Islam*). They stress that the hijab serves as a tool of liberation from modern-day ideas of female sexuality. The hijab liberates women from being dehumanised as sexual objects whose bodies are flaunted for men's enjoyment outside the realm of marriage. The hijab liberates women from the predatory capitalism that exploits women's bodies to foster conspicuous spending, which inescapably leads to overspending, arrogance and wastefulness. As the practising lawyer, Zain Azura Abdullah contends that the hijab also ensures the protection of Muslim women from sexual harassment in public places. Wearing the hijab seldom, if ever, excites the passions of men, unlike when women wear revealing clothes.[28] The hijab acts as a reminder and deterrent for Muslim women to not frequent places that would place them in a susceptible situation of being victimised, such as bars, clubs and pubs.[29]

Railing against the stereotype that the hijab hinders Muslim women's freedom of movement and life choices and that the hijab 'perpetuates the culture of gender inequality through symbolic interaction and by the same token instills in a woman an inchoate sense of her insignificance as a social being',[30] the writers explain that headscarves are actually symbols of empowerment and opportunity, and sources of motivation. Associate Professor Dr Harlina Halizah Siraj, in her lengthy confession, contends that the hijab has made her more committed to her religion and to the cause of women. Wearing the hijab has spurred her to excel in her academic pursuits and in her profession as an academic and a specialist doctor. The hijab has made her proactive rather than submissive. She goes on to add:

> No one has or could ever force me to cover my head. My headscarf is not a symbol of marital or parental domination of my personal freedom and rights. My choices are not born of brainwashing throughout my life. On the contrary, many women throughout the world who belong to my faith feel that the wearing of the headscarf enables us to become liberated human beings, free from wild stares and discrimination that puts inordinate emphasis on the external appearance of human beings.[31]

Dr Harlina's disclosures corroborate the study conducted by Sheila Mcdonough on veiling among Muslim women in Canada. She notes that many veiled women were conscious of their decision to veil and that one of her respondents showed that she was 'clearly thinking, and thinking for herself'.[32]

Another stereotype that these women have sought to demolish through their confessional writings is the established supposition that the hijab has its origins in Arab culture, or that they have been forced by men in their society to accept an element of a foreign culture as part of their identity. From this, it follows then that the hijab is not an Islamic requirement but that it was part of the cultural heritage of the Arabs that the Malays have uncritically adopted since the 1970s. Dr Ida Idayu Muhammad, who is currently a professor of chemical engineering at the Technological University of Malaysia, concedes that she once felt that the hijab was but an age-old Arab tradition and that it was relevant only for the Arabs.[33] After reading extensively about the origins and purposes of the hijab, she realised that it is not context-specific as argued by some Muslim feminist groups such as Sisters in Islam (SIS) based in Malaysia and Jaringan Islam Liberal (JIL, 'Liberal Islam Network') in Indonesia.[34] The hijab, as another contributor to the book, Mary C. Ali, explains it, is commandment from God as enshrined in the Qur'an in Chapter 24, verses 30–1, and Chapter 33, verse 59. Mary strengthens her argument by referring to Prophetic traditions (Hadith) that emphasise that women should cover their bodies except for their hands and faces when they are in public.[35] Her interpretation draws upon the medieval understandings of the hijab. This interpretation has found a stronger resonance in the Muslim world since the 1970s, as Muslims painfully cope with the challenges of globalisation.[36] More crucially, the points raised by Mary C. Ali are cemented by research done by an anthropologist, who has observed that headscarved women in Malaysia during the height of the hijab revolution were not passive recipients of male power or foreign culture. Hijabis are 'articulate about their own motives in pursuing a religious world-view and lifestyle'.[37] For these women, wearing the hijab is to be as equally modern as everyone else. The hijab is not a retreat from modernity.

These Muslim confessional writers are aware that deflating stereotypes about the hijab would not be enough in their quest to project a cosmopolitan outlook. Another way to show that hijabis are an embodiment of Muslim cosmopolitanism is to narrate how they have handled continuous bouts of discrimination. For them, to be able to deal with prejudice, stigma, bias and intolerance in a composed and respectable way is to manifest openness and confidence. It is definitely a personification of a long-held ideal of Islam that enjoins every Muslim to repel evil with kindness.[38] The writers in the book achieve this by explaining their responses to bias, insults and prejudice. Some write that they were branded as 'ghosts' (hantu) by their relatives and friends when they made the life-changing decision to wear the headscarf.[39] Others were labeled 'extremists', 'radicals' and 'ascetics' who have abandoned the world. Many of the confessional writers also narrated their experiences of being marginalised, jeered at, insulted and even assaulted for wearing the headscarf. Due to all of these pressures, a number of Muslim women who wore the hijab, according to Endok Sempo, removed their headscarves because they could not bear the stigma they faced from their community.[40] How, then, did these women respond to such challenges in a cosmopolitan way? While some admitted that they remained silent in the face of oppression, most contributors in the book highlight that they were proactive in changing perceptions about the hijab. For them, engagement rather than disengagement was the best course of action to transform societal ideas about the hijab.

These hijabis took a few steps to battle the stigma they faced. The first step consisted of exemplary conduct. They showed their friends and families that their character and behaviour had changed for the better when they started wearing the hijab. Suriza Ahmad Zabidi relates how she became more gentle and well mannered upon donning the hijab, such that her colleagues developed a good impression of headscarved women.[41] In addition, they had light-hearted discussions with anyone curious about the headscarf and those who may have misunderstood its meaning and purpose. Such discussions need not take place in formal settings; they can be spontaneous, often unexpected, and can even be ephemeral yet still leave deep impressions on the matter at hand. Umi Kalthum Ngah tells of her own encounter in the late 1970s with a white British lady, who had asked her while she was busy shopping why she was wearing the 'nice hat'. The lady turned out to be a fashion designer and commented prophetically that hijab could someday be an 'in thing'. Thanking the lady for her query and answering her in a placid way, Umi Kalthum explained that she was not wearing a hat. 'I wear this to cover myself like all Muslim women should do.'[42] Similarly, Dr Hafidzah Mustakim was asked by many of her non-Muslim friends while she was studying in Australia about why she wore her hijab. She explained that the headscarf would ensure the protection of women and that it was not an inhibition to her vocation as a student, an activist or a future medical doctor.[43]

Dr Hafidzah's last point deserves further elaboration here. One persuasive way to argue that the hijab is an asset rather than a liability is to engage in 'enhanced striving'. Gordon Allport defines enhanced striving as an attempt 'to redouble one's effort in a healthy response to an obstacle'.[44] The contributors in the book explained that doing well in their professions and pursuits facilitated the dispelling of negativities towards hijabis. Upon seeing that women who wear the hijab can perform as well as, or even better than, their contemporaries, perceptions of the hijab as a regressive custom began to change. Ummu Hanan, for example, went through such an experience. She recounted her mother's resistance towards her decision to wear the hijab to the point that they would argue about it almost daily. Soon, her mother found that she was excelling in school and subsequently received many job offers in spite of her wearing the hijab. Her mother's opinion of the hijab changed completely.[45]

To close this section, hijab confessional writings provide us with windows into the circumstances that have led Muslim women to don the hijab, their coping strategies when faced with social stigma and the ways in which they seek to position the hijab not as a backward and hampering tool of male hegemony but as an empowering device for them to contribute more to their families and societies. Hijab, in the eyes of these women, is a factor that widens the horizons of Muslim cosmopolitanism to include women who choose to wear a piece of clothing that was previously seen as strange and unacceptable by the mainstream society. Southeast Asian Muslim women have gone further than just talking about the hijab in their endeavour to push the frontiers of Muslim cosmopolitanism. They have embodied it by introducing new hijab fashion styles that appeal to Muslim and non-Muslim publics alike. I now turn to these new hijab trends that have recently gone viral in the virtual and real worlds.

Expressing Piety in Multiple Spaces and Varying Styles

If the wearing of the hijab was stigmatising and daunting many decades ago, by the turn of the twenty-first century, headscarves had grown to become the most noticeable form of Muslim women's clothing throughout Southeast Asia. What used to be plain black and green mini-*telekungs* worn with long dark outfits have now been replaced with colourful hijabs donned with skirts, slacks and jeans. The image of a bland, dull-looking hijabi is a thing of the past. In its place is a highly decorative and multicoloured hijab trend that incorporates a multiplicity of influences and styles. Aihwa Ong describes this new hijab fashion as a form of 'subversive bricolages' that combines 'elements of different traditions to register protest over cultural dislocations linked to colonial and postcolonial domination'.[46] But the notion of 'subversive bricolages' to describe the hijab was perhaps relevant only in the 1970s when headscarves were symbols of protest against existing ideas about women's modesty. From the 1990s onwards, wearing the hijab was no longer regarded as subversive, because what used to be a marginal spectacle had become mainstream. The resistance against colonial domination was eclipsed by a new form of cultural ascendancy in the form of trendy headscarves and Muslimah fashion that piqued the public eye, both Muslim and non-Muslim. In a study of Muslim women and the hijab in the United Kingdom,

Figure 5.1   An office-look hijab tutorial on YouTube.

Emma Tarlo paints a picture of parallel developments in Southeast Asia since the 1990s: 'Worn in a diverse range of colours and textures, built using different techniques of wrapping, twisting and layering and held together with an increasing variety of decorative hijab pins designed for the purpose, the headscarf has in recent years become a new form of Muslim personal art'.[47] Together with this growth of Muslim personal art is the proliferation of hijab tutorials uploaded to many online video and social networking sites such as YouTube, Vimeo and various blogs (see Figure 5.1). To date, Indonesian women have produced the hijab tutorial videos that yield the highest viewership on YouTube.[48]

It is, therefore, more accurate to describe the current hijab fashion as an 'expressive pietism' that draws on all sorts of cultures, influences and styles from the local and the global, Eastern and Western, traditional and modern, to project an image of Muslim women's bodies in ways that are appealing to the cosmopolitan sensibilities of the society at large. The current hijab fashion is expressive not only in terms of its colours and designs, but also in terms of where and how these garments are displayed. Rather than being reserved, passive and introverted, women who subscribe to expressive pietism openly flaunt their headscarves while being open to interactions with any member of society. They parade the hijab in creative ways without necessarily compromising the requirements of the Islamic sense of modesty. Nancy J. Smith-Hefner endorses such expressive pietism in her influential study of Muslim women in Java. She notes that,

> rather than an icon of Islamic traditionalism or antimodernization, for most middle-class Muslims, veiling is a symbol of engagement in a modern, albeit deeply Islamic, world. Although its meanings are varied and contested, for most Muslim women, veiling is an instrument for heightened piety and public participation rather than domestic insulation.[49]

One further point that has to be made in the light of Smith-Hefner's observations is that the hijab is no longer a middle-class phenomenon. Muslim women from all classes have now turned to the hijab as a means to express themselves without compromising piety and moral virtue.

There are specific spaces in which expressive pietism is played out in Muslim Southeast Asia, which I would like to discuss here. Before doing so, it is worth mentioning that studying the hijab spatially is important because it shows how the modest fashions of Muslim women have been transmuted to fit into the demands of selected spaces. I focus on those that are ceremonial, professional and casual. The types of headscarves and Muslim fashions worn in these different spaces may overlap. In fact, they exist within a continuum of preferences and styles. Some aspects of hijab styles worn in ceremonies may be found in professional spaces, some headscarves worn at work may also be worn during casual outings, and so on. Altogether, however, they exhibit a high degree of cosmopolitanism – or hijabi cosmopolitanism – in Muslim Southeast Asia.

The wearing of headscarves during ceremonies has become a fad in Muslim Southeast Asia lately, particularly at weddings. A high-profile figure who donned the headscarf during her wedding in ways that reflect her cosmopolitan penchant is the celebrity singer Siti Nurhaliza. Previously known for being a Muslim lady who did not accept the injunction to wear the hijab, she changed her outlook upon her marriage to Datuk Khalid Mohamed in 2006. From then on, she became a national and international symbol for hijabi women in Singapore, Malaysia and Indonesia. By any standards, her wedding was a lavish affair, costing 500,000 ringgit, and was covered live on Malaysian television channels. Such lavish weddings of prominent Southeast Asian hijabi women are not uncommon. The wedding ceremony of Pengiran Anak Sarah, the wife of the current crown prince of Brunei, cost £1 million.[50] Like Pengiran Anak Sarah, Siti Nurhaliza wore many different dresses on the day, but the most iconic one was worn with the hijab.

Upon closer examination, Siti Nurhaliza's decision to wear a hijab with her wedding dress reflects a blend of many influences while remaining true to the Islamic conception of female modesty. As a news editorial vividly described it,

> Siti, as she is affectionately called, was elegantly dressed in *baju kurung* [Malay traditional dress] of white French lace by Soltiss with blue accents and crystals replete with veil and *selendang* [head cover] for the *akad nikah* [marriage solemnisation], specially created by popular designer Radzuan Razwill.[51]

What was apparent to the public eye was not a quintessentially Malay or Western wedding dress, but an amalgamation of styles that was made even more cosmopolitan with the presence of the hijab. Siti's cosmopolitan ceremonial hijab has inspired many Muslim women in Southeast Asia who are ardent fans and followers. In Riau, the adoption of the hijab or *jilbab* in marriage ceremonies and other formal events in the manner which Siti Nurhaliza and her fans have embodied has been described by a local Indonesian scholar as 'making the Malay dress perfect (perfecting *adat*)'.[52]

Other than the ceremonial hijab, the headscarves worn in professional workplaces are a hallmark of cosmopolitanism among Southeast Asian Muslim women. The 'professional' or 'office look hijab', as it has been called by hijabis, consists mainly of headscarves donned with suits and formal blouses for those working in offices and uniforms for women working in frontline services. Since the mainstreaming of Islamic revivalism in the 1990s, Southeast Asian Muslim women have also been allowed to wear their Malay traditional dresses with the hijab as part of their formal office attired.

Today, Indonesian policewomen are allowed to wear the hijab as part of their uniform. The long-standing ban on policewomen wearing the hijab was lifted due to the increasing numbers of women who were wearing the hijab before and after working hours. Muslim women in uniformed services who choose to wear headscarves have to match the colour of their hijab with their uniforms. When asked why many women now prefer to wear the hijab at work, Dewi Fitria from the Malang Police Force responded that, aside from being a religious requirement, it is 'better to wear a hijab, its more efficient. We don't have to comb our hair but we'd still look tidy. It's also good when we have to work at night'.[53] The hijab, in this regard, professionalises the appearance of these women inasmuch as it serves as a way for them to be exemplars to other officers on duty.

No less significant are the hijabs worn casually. Here, we may witness expressive pietism being put into practice in the most pluralistic of ways. Global capitalism and the rapid growth of Muslim consumerism have accelerated the growth of a multitude of 'Muslimah-friendly' accessories and hijab fashions that in many instances appear to be as appealing as other fashion wear. Recent research shows that global expenditure on hijab fashion wear has amounted to an estimated US$96 billion. Within Southeast Asia, this market is powered by the publication of a plethora of hijab magazines in both English and the vernacular languages.[54]

The development of a variety of casual hijab styles bolster Margaret Maynard's conceptualisation of 'hybrid dressing' in a globalising age. According to Maynard, hybrid dressing 'is complicated and never absolute. Alongside customary dress there may be a qualified mixture of features that can include a substantial dissymmetry between the dominance of dress stemming from the US and Europe and elements derived from other cultures, ethnicities and minority groups. So it is often a question of unbalanced ways in which the universal and the particular function in relation to one another, or indeed as the multiplicity of cosmopolitanisms relate to localisms of all kinds'.[55] Seen in this light, we can divide the casual hijab styles into three types: the conservative, the demure and the flamboyant. All of these types are noticeable throughout Southeast Asia and no particular style can be seen to overshadow another.

The conservative styles are usually more Middle Eastern in appearance, in that women who adopt such styles don large headscarves with loose clothing, usually with a *jubbah* and an *abaya*. The colours chosen are normally dark such as black, dark brown, dark blue and dark green. Owing to the growth of this hijab style in Malaysia, some Muslim public figures have highlighted their concerns about 'Arab colonialism' or the 'Arabisation of Islam in Malaysia', loosely understood as a turn to conservatism on the part of the Malays.[56] But such concerns are rather unfounded because only a segment of Muslim women are wearing such hijab styles and, when they do, these hijabs are embroidered with designs that make them more appealing than being 'conservatively Arab' might suggest.

The other hijab style that is pervasive among Southeast Asian women is the demure form. As the term suggests, this hijab fashion is not as plain as the conservative style, yet it is certainly not ostentatious either. This is the most common type of headscarf worn by Muslim women in Southeast Asia. They come in varying colours though not loud hues and are worn with clothes drawn from all parts of the world. The overall impression that one gets from women who prefer the demure hijab style is that these women have put into practice a 'modest fashion' in which Muslim women's bodies are styled to comply with Islamic laws.[57]

The flamboyant style, which is the third and increasingly popular type of hijab, is worth a detailed excursus here. According to Reina Lewis, the flamboyant hijab originated from Britain and Turkey. The dominance of these countries in hijab fashion has, however, been rivalled by Indonesia, which is, by far, a major producer of flamboyant hijab styles, influencing many parts of the globalised Muslim world.[58] This is of course no place to discuss in the detail the plethora of flamboyant hijab styles on the market and seen on the streets of cities across the Muslim Southeast Asia. Readers are encouraged to consult the wide range of popular hijabi magazines, the most prominent being *Muslimah*, *Hijabista*, *Musmagz* and *Noor*. Suffice it to say here that the flamboyant hijab style is largely a youthful phenomenon. Well travelled, constantly exposed to global fashion, daring and expressive, young Muslim women in Southeast Asia who prefer the flamboyant hijab styles clearly demonstrate that they are not mere recipients of global fashion trends. On the contrary, they are combining what is regarded as Western, fashionable and in vogue with motifs that are clearly Asian in origin and that are Islamically modest.

Some controversies have emerged, without doubt, because of the growing attractiveness of the flamboyant hijab style. Many women activists and
religious scholars in Muslim Southeast Asia have highlighted their concerns
over the problem of the hijab being overly commoditised and commercialised,
to such an extent that modesty has been compomised in the name of fashion.
Some writers, for example, argue that, because of the recent flamboyant wave,
the hijab has been used by some hijabis as a 'mere instrument to look fashionable' (*hanya untuk berfesyen*).[59] Indeed, in Indonesia, a new style of hijab called
the *jilbab gaul* (the 'free-mixing *jilbab*') has appeared. The hijab is worn in a
manner that exposes the neck and sometimes part of the hair. Some of these
women have also been spotted wearing tight jeans and blouses, causing many
Muslim activist groups and religious authorities in the country to respond by
introducing programmes that raise awareness about what the hijab actually
means in Islam.[60] Regardless of all of these debates for or against the flamboyant hijab style, what remains clear is that there is a celebration of all sorts of
expressive pietism among Muslim Southeast Asians in everyday life.

Expanding the Cosmopolitan Space through Online Hijab Activism

In November 2013, a group of hijabis set up a Facebook group page that gained
26,000 'likes' within a few weeks, raising the anxieties of the Singaporean
state that is constantly on the lookout for the 'radicalisation' of Muslims
in the country. Called the 'Singapore Hijab Movement', the group urged
the Singapore government to allow headscarves in public schools and the
uniformed services.[61] The Singapore government, much like its Indonesian
counterpart, has maintained a strict policy against the wearing of the hijab in
selected sectors of the country's economy and society since the 1970s when
headscarves emerged as a new trend. The state's policy is based on its distrust
of non-secular ideologies, including *all* religions and religious groups. Islam
and Muslims are not specifically targeted, but they are a major source for
concern because of the Singapore's location within a Muslim archipelago.
This is so because the ruling regime subscribes to an authoritarian stance
that engenders it to demand compliance from all religious believers. Hence,
the ostensibly one-sided attempts to ban the hijab should be read as nothing more than examples of the Singaporean government's ambivalence and
apprehension towards religions in general.[62]

We dig deeper into the issue of states imposing stumbling blocks for Muslim cosmopolitanism again in the next chapter. For now, the Singapore Hijab Movement Facebook page should be analysed within the context of the persistence of state prejudice towards hijabis. It comes from previous failed appeals to allow the wearing of headscarves in public schools. In early January 2002, a Muslim Singaporean made headlines when he decided to send his seven-year-old hijab-clad daughter to a national school where standard uniforms are required. Contrary to the perceptions of many at the time – that such an act of defiance indicated a person who hailed from a religious, conservative or traditional background – the man was reported to be a modern working professional who embraced the ideals of nationhood and multiculturalism promoted by the long-reigning PAP government. Wearing the hijab at such an early stage in life, according to the man, was a way of eventually making his daughter a good Muslim. But such obligations should not have prevented her from receiving the best form of education available; the girl's father saw secular schools as offering his daughter the best preparation for survival and employment in the modern world.[63]

The Singapore Hijab Movement page disappeared mysteriously after only a few months of activism.[64] Still, its brief existence provided evidence of courage on the part of ordinary citizens in calling for more room to be given to Muslim women to maintain their modesty in a country that purports to be a cosmopolitan city-state. Soon after the disappearance of the Facebook page, similar pages such as I Want Hijab – Singapore, Singapore Hijab Movement X, World Hijab Day Singapore, Embrace Hijab and many influential blogs were created, garnering thousands of 'likes', and many more shared the postings. A large number of the supporters of the hijab movement were non-Muslims who felt that the banning of the hijab contravened the rights of women.[65]

What is most fascinating about this online hijab activism is that it shares some commonalities with Muslim women's activism in other parts the world. One stark commonality is the non-violent means that these activists have used to change the state's stance regarding women's rights. We can thus call these online hijab activists 'velvet jihadists', as described by Faegheh Shirazi in her study of Muslim women's activism in the Middle East.[66] Velvet jihadists hold that agitating for women's rights is a step towards widening the scope of cosmopolitanism in society. When women's rights are respected and their voices are heard and taken seriously, societies move closer to the cosmopolitan ideal of equal consideration for all. Velvet jihadists achieve their ends through reasoned discussions and peaceful engagements. By virtue of the Singaporean state's strict policies towards any public forums and talks about the hijab, hijabis and their supporters – both male and female, Muslim and non-Muslim – turned to the virtual world to make their voices heard. But how exactly did the online hijab activists in Singapore communicate their ideas in ways that could solicit support from the wider society so rapidly?

One intelligent discursive strategy is to compare the predicament of hijabis in Singapore with the experiences of their sisters overseas. Online hijab activists highlight that many developed and even developing countries all over the world have already allowed the wearing of the hijab in schools and the civil service. I Want Hijab – Singapore featured hijabi women working in hospitals as nurses, doctors, firefighters and police officers in Europe, the United States, Australia and, closer to Singapore, in Thailand. Even countries that have previously banned the hijab such as Germany have now overturned such policies. Muslim girls in these countries are also allowed to wear the hijab in public schools. Given all of these examples, why then should the hijab ban be maintained in Singapore? In response to such comparisons, a cabinet minister reasoned in an ironic way: 'Muslim women enjoy many freedoms in Singapore. They don the hijab in many situations, including in Parliament, the highest elected chamber in the land'.[67] Online hijab activists contended against the minister's response by using empirical evidence. They provided cases of clear-cut discrimination in many occupations towards hijabis. One highly publicised incident involved a hijabi sales promoter who worked at ISETAN department store. The sales promoter was told by a manager to leave the store on her first day of work because she was wearing the headscarf. Although ISETAN eventually apologised for what had happened, the episode revealed that bias against hijabis could result in malpractice in employment situations and in the workplace.[68] The second case involved a hijabi, Nury MJ, who worked as an events manager. She was not permitted to enter the premises of an event that she was organising because the security guards objected to her headscarf. Nury MJ's post was shared by close to 2,000

Facebookers, many of whom were appalled by the incessant discrimination against hijabis by many Singaporean employers.[69]

Hijab activists have also culturalised the headscarf in their online postings in order to normalise it among non-Muslims. What I mean by this is that, rather than presenting the hijab as a religious requirement, they maintain that the hijab is part and parcel of the culture of the Malays. Although Malay women may not have worn hijab in the past, their dress codes have evolved over time with a large segment of the Malay women in contemporary Singapore now adopting the hijab. These online hijab activists have impressed upon the Singaporean public that Malay culture and attire is not static. Culture is malleable, changeable and dynamic, and can be reimagined to suit the needs of different times and contexts. Malay culture is formed and reformed through contact with new ideas about what it means to be a Muslim in the modern world. To make it apparent that the hijab is now an indispensable facet of Malay culture, online hijab activists have established the 'Embrace Hijab' Facebook page. This page seeks to promote the idea that 'women with Hijab can contribute better to the development of society and the success of a country'.[70] The page is filled with pictures and stories about many Malay women from all walks of life who regard the hijab as a core element of their identity.

This leads us to another line of discursive strategy used by online activists to further the case for the expansion of the cosmopolitan space for headscarved women: invoking Singapore's constitution. Online hijab activists have invoked Article 152(2) of Singapore's constitution, which states:

> The Government shall exercise its functions in such a manner as to recognize the special position of the Malays, who are the indigenous people of Singapore, and accordingly it shall be the responsibility of the Government to protect, safeguard, support, foster and promote their political, educational, religious, economic, social and culture interest and the Malay language.[71]

The same recognition of the special position of the Malays is found in the Malaysian constitution. However, while the Malaysian state uses it to implement affirmative action policies for the Malays, in Singapore, this constitutional provision has been interpreted as a duty on the part of the government to provide opportunities for Malays to compete with other races on an equal footing. To achieve that end, the government has provided Malays with special assistance in the realm of education.[72] However, online hijab activists interpret Article 152(2) in a different way. For example, active social media activist Walid Jumblatt has opined that, although 'like most laws these articles are ambiguous and often subject to the interpretive discretion of the authorities, one thing is clear: there is a legal basis for the government to allow Muslim females to adorn the tudung [hijab] in public schools or the civil service'.[73] In other words, online hijab activists argue that the state's protection of the Malay Muslims should include not only education but all aspects of Malay Muslim life, including the hijab. Article 152(2) in Singapore's constitution, from the perspective of these activists, is not just symbolic or abstract, included merely as a token acknowledgement that the Malays are the indigenous peoples of Singapore. For the hijab activists, Article 152(2) is a law that could be invoked to broaden the space for hijabis in all sectors of Singaporean society.

How successful have these online hijab activists been? If success is measured in terms of a change in state policy on hijab, then they have failed in their efforts. The hijab ban in schools and the uniformed services is still in full force, with little prospect of the government ever agreeing to acquiesce to the demands of the online hijab activists. However, they have managed to raise public awareness about the importance of hijab among the majority non-Muslim population in Singapore, and they have also made the issue known globally. More local and global non-Muslims are showing their sympathies and support for the hijab cause in Singapore. That non-Muslims are now more open to, or at least have a better understanding of, hijab and why it matters is a battle half won. The online hijab activists' greatest challenge will now be to influence the thinking of policymakers who, although keen on transforming Singapore into a cosmopolis and a cosmopolitan city-state, are still largely trapped within the ideology that 'assumes and requires individuals to have a declared, unambiguous and unchanging ethnic identity'.[74]

Conclusion

More than just a piece of cloth draped over a woman's head, hijab is the litmus test of the future complexion of cosmopolitanism in society. In Muslim

Southeast Asia, the confessional writings and life stories of the hijabis, their creative embodiments of hijab in varying colours and styles, as well as their efforts at online activism have aided in the process of mainstreaming hijab and in making the people around them more conscious that hijab is a significant transformation for the Muslim community, especially for Muslim women. Indeed, the debates, discourses and disputes over hijab fortify the importance of Muslim women in Southeast Asian Islam. Hijabis and non-hijabis alike have played active and proactive roles in shaping their own destinies and ways of life. They have stood hand in hand with their fellow non-Muslim cosmopolitans in defence of the right to be religiously modest. It is, therefore, not unwarranted to posit that no study of Muslim cosmopolitanism in Southeast Asia can ever be adequate without considering the hijabis as its ardent purveyors.

Notes

1. Ummu Hammah, *Seks Islam: Perangi Yahudi Untuk Kembalikan Seks Islam Kepada Dunia* (Selangor, Malaysia: Kelab Taat Suami, 2011), p. xii.
2. Scott Kugle, *Sufis and Saints' Bodies: Mysticism, Corporeality and Sacred Power in Islam* (Chapel Hill: University of North Carolina Press, 2007), p. 9.
3. Miriam Cooke, 'Deploying the Muslimwoman', *Journal of Feminist Studies in Religion*, 24, 1 (2008), pp. 91–9.
4. Miriam Cooke, 'The Muslimwoman', *Contemporary Islam*, 1, 2 (2007), p. 140.
5. In what follows, I use the terms 'hijab' and 'headscarf' interchangeably to refer to the same thing.
6. Sahar Amer, *What is Veiling?* (Chapel Hill: University of North Carolina Press, 2014), p. 2.
7. Haleh Esfandiari, *Reconstructed Lives: Women and Iran's Islamic Revolution* (Baltimore, MD: Johns Hopkins University Press, 1997), p. 133.
8. Muzaffar, *Islamic Resurgence*, p. 2.
9. Katherine Bullock, *Rethinking Muslim Women and the Veil: Challenging Historical and Modern Stereotypes* (London: International Institute of Islamic Thought, 2002), p. 85.
10. Sylvia Frisk, *Submitting to God: Women and Islam in Urban Malaysia* (Copenhagen: NIAS Press, 2009), p. 170.
11. Judith Nagata, 'The Impact of Islamic Revival (Dakwah) on the Religious Culture of Malaysia', in Bruce Matthews and Judith Nagata (eds), *Religion,*

Values and Development in Southeast Asia (Singapore: ISEAS Press, 1986), pp. 37–50.

12. Suzanne Brenner, 'Reconstructing Self and Society: Javanese Muslim Women and "The Veil"', *American Ethnologist*, 23, 4 (1996), pp. 673–97.

13. Sonja van Winchelen, *Religion, Politics and Gender in Indonesia: Disputing the Muslim Body* (London: Routledge, 2010), p. 44.

14. Kurniawati Hastuti Dewi, *Indonesian Women and Local Politics: Islam, Gender and Networks in Post-Suharto Indonesia* (Singapore: NUS Press, 2015), pp. 69–70.

15. Aihwa Ong, 'State Versus Islam: Malay Families, Women's Bodies, and the Body Politic in Malaysia', in Aihwa Ong and Michael G. Peletz (eds), *Bewitching Women, Pious Men: Gender and Body Politics in Southeast Asia* (Berkeley: University of California Press, 1995), p. 160, and Zainah Anwar, *Islamic Revivalism in Malaysia:* Dakwah *Among the Students* (Petaling Jaya, Malaysia: Pelanduk Publications, 1987), p. 31.

16. Elizabeth M. Bucar, *The Islamic Veil: A Beginner's Guide* (Oxford: Oneworld Publications, 2012), p. 169.

17. For a critique of the alarmist tendencies in scholarship about Southeast Asian Islam and Muslims, see John T. Sidel, *The Islamist Threat in Southeast Asia: A Reassessment* (Singapore: ISEAS, 2007).

18. Ulfa Indrawati, *Jilbab itu Indah* (Kuala Lumpur: Synergy Media, 2011), pp. 11–32. See also Shahidah Nafishah Az-Zahra, *Persoalan Wanita: Pemakaian Hijab, Batas-Batas Aurat dan Pergaulan, serta Urusan Dalam Rumahtangga* (Penang, Malaysia: Mulia Terang, 2012).

19. Quraish Shihab, *Jilbab: Pakaian Wanita Muslimah, Pandangan Ulama Masa Lalu dan Cendekiawan Kontemporer* (Ciputat, Indonesia: Penerbit Lentera Hati, 2004).

20. There is now a wide and rapidly growing selection of works in this genre. Some popular examples that have become best-sellers in Southeast Asia include the following: Asma Nadia (ed.), *Jilbab Pertamaku* (Bandung, Indonesia: Lingkar Pena Publishing House, 2005); Siti Muslimah and Laili Nihayati (eds), *Spiritual Journey of a Muslimah* (Bandung, Indonesia: Penerbit Mizania, 2008); Irma Hasmie et al., *Hijabista Hijrahsista: Bagaimana Akhirnya Saya Bertudung* (Kuala Lumpur: PTS Litera Utama, 2015).

21. Rachel Droogsman, 'Redefining Hijab: American Muslim Women's Standpoints on Veiling', *Journal of Applied Communication Research*, 35, 3 (2007), p. 295.

22. Michel Foucault, *The History of Sexuality, Volume One: An Introduction*, translated by R. Hurley (Harmondsworth: Penguin, 1981), pp. 61–2.

23. Ir. Endok Sempo Mohd Tahir (ed.), *Bagaimana Akhirnya Saya Bertudung* (Selangor, Malaysia: PTS Millenia, 2010).

24. See, for example, Nadia Fitri Mohamad Havez, 'Bagaimana saya bertudung', Nadia Fitri Mohamad Hafez [blog], 15 July 2011, <http://nadiafitrihavez.blogspot.sg/2011/07/bagaimana-akhirnya-saya-bertudung-part.html> (last accessed 16 February 2016) and Eiza GreenAppleKu, 'Kenapa aku bertudung', Eiza GreenAppleKu: Story of Our Life [blog], 7 June 2011, <http://www.greenappleku.com/2011/06/kenapa-aku-bertudung.html> (last accessed 16 February 2016).

25. Bullock, *Rethinking Muslim Women and the Veil*, p. 123.

26. Irene Zempi and Neil Chakraborti, *Islamophobia, Victimisation and the Veil* (Basingstoke: Palgrave Macmillan, 2014), p. 10.

27. Fadwa El Guindi, *Veil: Modesty, Privacy and Resistance* (Oxford: Berg, 2009) and Leila Ahmed, *A Quiet Revolution: The Veil's Resurgence, from the Middle East to America* (New Haven, CT: Yale University Press, 2011).

28. Zain Azura Abdullah, 'Saya Dipengaruhi Majalah Nida'ul Islam', in Ir. Endok Sempo Mohd Tahir (ed.), *Bagaimana Akhirnya Saya Bertudung* (Selangor, Malaysia: PTS Millenia, 2010), pp. 84–5.

29. Fizi Has, 'Kawan dari Pakistan Pengaruhi Saya', in Ir. Endok Sempo Mohd Tahir (ed.), *Bagaimana Akhirnya Saya Bertudung* (Selangor, Malaysia: PTS Millenia, 2010), p. 88.

30. Marnia Lazreg, *Questioning the Veil: Open Letters to Muslim Women* (Princeton, NJ: Princeton University Press, 2009), p. 109.

31. Harlina Halizah Siraj, 'Saya Anak Seorang Kadi', in Ir. Endok Sempo Mohd Tahir (ed.), *Bagaimana Akhirnya Saya Bertudung* (Selangor, Malaysia: PTS Millenia, 2010), pp. 84–5.

32. Sheila Mcdonough, 'Voices of Muslim Women', in Sajida Alvi, Homa Hoodfar and Sheila Mcdonough (eds), *The Muslim Veil in North America: Issues and Debates* (Toronto: Women's Press, 2003), p. 106.

33. Ida Idayu, 'Saya Disindir Hantu Kum-kum', in Ir. Endok Sempo Mohd Tahir (ed.), *Bagaimana Akhirnya Saya Bertudung* (Selangor, Malaysia: PTS Millenia, 2010), p. 140.

34. Azza Basarudin, *Humanizing the Sacred: Sisters in Islam and the Struggle for Gender Justice* (Seattle: University of Washington Press, 2016), p. 198, and Ulil Abshar-Abdalla, 'Menyegarkan Kembali Pemahaman Islam', *Kompass*, 18 November, 2002.

35. Mary C. Ali, 'Tudung Menindas Wanita?', in Ir. Endok Sempo Mohd Tahir

(ed.), *Bagaimana Akhirnya Saya Bertudung* (Selangor, Malaysia: PTS Millenia, 2010), pp. 143–5.

36. Anne Sofie Roald, *Women in Islam: The Western Experience* (London: Routledge, 2001), pp. 254–94.

37. Judith Nagata, 'Modern Malay Women and the Message of the "Veil"', in Wazir Jahan Karim (ed.), *'Male' and 'Female' in Developing Southeast Asia* (Oxford: Berg, 1995), p. 104.

38. Mohammed Abu-Nimer, 'Framework for Nonviolence and Peacebuilding in Islam', in Abdul Aziz Said, Mohamed Abu-Nimer and Meena Sharify-Funk (eds), *Contemporary Islam: Dynamic Not Static* (London: Routledge, 2006), p. 150.

39. Puteri Yusman, 'Saya Tidak Tahu Mengapa Saya Bertudung', in Ir. Endok Sempo Mohd Tahir (ed.), *Bagaimana Akhirnya Saya Bertudung* (Selangor, Malaysia: PTS Millenia, 2010), p. 135.

40. Ir. Endok Sempo Mohd Tahir, 'Ayah Saya Pejuang Melawan Belanda', in Ir. Endok Sempo Mohd Tahir (ed.), *Bagaimana Akhirnya Saya Bertudung* (Selangor, Malaysia: PTS Millenia, 2010), p. 105.

41. Suriza Ahmad Zabidi, 'Saya Takut Dirota Ustaz', in Ir. Endok Sempo Mohd Tahir (ed.), *Bagaimana Akhirnya Saya Bertudung* (Selangor, Malaysia: PTS Millenia, 2010), p. 52.

42. Umi Kalthum Ngah, 'Dinasihati Supaya Tidak Mendekati Pelajar Dakwah', in Ir. Endok Sempo Mohd Tahir (ed.), *Bagaimana Akhirnya Saya Bertudung* (Selangor, Malaysia: PTS Millenia, 2010), p. 80.

43. Hafidzah Mustakim, 'Saya Terpengaruh di Semenanjung', in Ir. Endok Sempo Mohd Tahir (ed.), *Bagaimana Akhirnya Saya Bertudung* (Selangor, Malaysia: PTS Millenia, 2010), p. 93.

44. Gordon Allport, *The Nature of Prejudice* (Reading: Addison-Wesley, 1979 [1954]), p. 159.

45. Ummu Hanan, 'Ibu Membenci Saya Bertudung', in Ir. Endok Sempo Mohd Tahir (ed.), *Bagaimana Akhirnya Saya Bertudung* (Selangor, Malaysia: PTS Millenia, 2010), p. 71.

46. Ong, 'State Versus Islam', p. 160. See also Anwar, *Islamic Revivalism*, pp. 178–9.

47. Emma Tarlo, *Visibly Muslim: Fashion, Politics, Faith* (Oxford: Berg, 2010), p. 1.

48. YouTube, search results for 'Hijab tutorials', <https://www.youtube.com/results?sp=CAM%253D&q=hijab+tutorials> (last accessed 17 February 2016). Detailed elaborations on the popularity of these hijab tutorials are found in Annisa R. Beta, 'Hijabers: How Young Muslim Women Redefine Themselves

in Indonesia', *The International Communication Gazette*, 76, 4–5 (2014), pp. 382–3.

49. Nancy J. Smith-Hefner, 'Javanese Women and the Veil in Post-Soeharto Indonesia', *Journal of Asia Studies*, 66, 2 (2007), p. 395.

50. Sebastien Berger, 'Golden Day for Brunei's Bride', *The Telegraph*, 10 September 2014, <http://www.telegraph.co.uk/news/worldnews/middleeast/1471439/Gol den-day-for-Bruneis-bride.html> (last accessed 17 February 2016).

51. Editorial, 'Siti Nurhaliza Weds Datuk K', *Bernama*, 21 August 2006.

52. Lugina Setyawati, '*Adat*, Islam and Womanhood in the Reconstruction of Riau Malay Identity', in Susan Blackburn, Bianca J. Smith and Siti Syamsiyatun (eds), *Indonesian Islam in a New Era: How Women Negotiate their Muslim Identities* (Clayton, VIC: Monash University Press, 2008), p. 92.

53. Dyah Ayu Pitaloka, 'Malang Policewomen Allowed to Wear Hijab on Fridays Despite Nationwide Ban', *Jakarta Globe*, 1 November 2013, <http://jakart aglobe.beritasatu.com/news/malang-policewomen-allowed-to-wear-hijab-on-fridays-despite-nationwide-ban/> (last accessed 17 February 2016). The lifting of the ban took effect on 25 March 2015.

54. Nurzihan Hassim, 'A Comparative Analysis on *Hijab* Wearing in Malaysian *Muslimah* Magazines', *The Journal of the South East Asia Research Center for Communications and Humanities*, 6, 1 (2014) pp. 79–96.

55. Margaret Maynard, *Dress and Globalisation* (Manchester: Manchester University Press, 2004), p. 30.

56. Boo, 'Marina Mahathir'.

57. Reina Lewis (ed.), *Modest Fashion: Styling Bodies, Mediating Faith* (New York: I. B. Tauris, 2013).

58. Reina Lewis, *Muslim Fashion: Contemporary Style Cultures* (Durham, NC: Duke University Press, 2015), pp. 4–5.

59. Azimah Ghazali et al., 'Hijab bukan sekadar fesyen', Sinar Online, 8 December 2013, <http://www.sinarharian.com.my/hijab-bukan-sekadar-fesyen-1.228627> (last accessed 3 March 2016).

60. Deny Hamdani, *Anatomy of Muslim Veils: Practice, Discourse and Changing Appearance of Indonesian Women* (Saarbrücken: Lambert Academic Publishing, 2011), pp. 116–21.

61. BBC Monitoring, 'Singapore: Campaigners Bid to Overturn Hijab Ban', 13 November 2013, <http://www.bbc.com/news/blogs-news-from-elsewhere-24932400> (last accessed 18 February 2016).

62. Khairudin Aljunied, 'Tools of Conflict, Levers of Cohesion: Culture and Religion

in Muslim Southeast Asia', in Joseph Camilleri and Sven Schottmann (eds), *Culture, Religion and Conflict in Muslim Southeast Asia* (London: Routledge, 2012), pp. 185–6.

63. Kamaludeen Mohamed Nasir, Alexius A. Pereira and Bryan S. Turner, *Muslims in Singapore: Piety, Politics and Policies* (London: Routledge, 2010), p. 78.

64. Terence Lee, 'Singapore "Hijab Movement" Facebook Page Mysteriously Disappears', Yahoo! News, 14 November 2013, <https://sg.finance.yahoo.com/news/singapore-hijab-movement-facebook-page-043141957.html> (last accessed 18 February 2016).

65. Sahar Pirzada and Jolie Tan, 'Hijab Issue: Whatever Their Choice, Women Deserve Respect, Inclusion', *Today*, 12 November 2013.

66. Faegheh Shirazi, *Velvet Jihad: Muslim Women's Quiet Revolution to Islamic Fundamentalism* (Gainesville: University Press of Florida, 2009).

67. Editorial, 'Allowing Hijab Problematic for Some Jobs: Yaacob', *Today*, 1 November 2013.

68. Azim Azman, 'Isetan Apologises over the Treatment of Promoter in Tudung', *The New Paper*, 15 July 2014.

69. Nury MJ, Facebook update, 9 September 2015, <https://www.facebook.com/nury.aqilah/posts/10153635009169308> (last accessed 18 February 2016).

70. Embrace Hijab [Facebook page], <https://www.facebook.com/EmbraceHijab/info?tab=page_info> (last accessed 18 February 2016).

71. *The Constitution of Singapore* (Singapore: Government Printing Office, 1980 [reprint]), p. 64.

72. Kevin Y. L. Tan, *The Constitution of Singapore: A Contextual Analysis* (Oxford: Hart Publishing, 2015), pp. 237–8.

73. Walid J. Abdullah, 'Secularism in Singapore: The Tudung Issue in 2013' [Facebook note], 22 October 2013, <https://www.facebook.com/notes/walid-j-abdullah/secularism-in-singapore-the-tudung-issue-in-2013/528681723888998> (last accessed 18 February 2016).

74. Brenda S. A. Yeoh, 'Cosmopolitanism and its Exclusions in Singapore', *Urban Studies*, 41, 12 (2004), p. 2442.

--- PART III ---

POLITICS

6

CONSTRICTING COSMOPOLITANISM: SECULAR STATES IN MUSLIM SOUTHEAST ASIA

From markets to mosques to blogs, via the work of intellectuals and hijab-clad women, it is clear by now that Muslim cosmopolitanism has carved a secure place within the hearts and minds of Muslims in Southeast Asia. This has had implications on non-Muslims in the region as well. Because Southeast Asian Muslims are, by and large, inclusive and cosmopolitan in their outlook, the day-to-day interactions and encounters with non-Muslims have generally been peaceful. Indeed, beyond the isolated episodes of conflict and violence that have so often been sensationalised by the media, the reality of life in Muslim Southeast Asia is such that people of varying backgrounds get along well in everyday life because the majority of the Muslim population understands Islam as a religion that is open towards and tolerant of people of different backgrounds, respectful towards strangers and foreigners, while remaining committed to (and rooted in) their own faith and community.

The state is yet another entity that needs to be scrutinised in the making and unmaking of Muslim cosmopolitanism in Southeast Asia. Most studies of cosmopolitanism have neglected the role of the state. The reasons for overlooking the state are twofold. The foremost reason is the prevailing assumption that globalisation has effectively shifted the agency of states to interest groups, lobby organisations and grass-roots movements. These non-state actors have captured the attention of social theorists who have showed how they have shaped societal receptivity towards cosmopolitan ideals and defined cosmopolitanism from a bottom-up viewpoint, rather than a top-down perspective.[1] A related reason why states have largely been ignored has to do with the supposition that each state is generally concerned with the protection of its own security and citizenry. This has conditioned how states function; that is, they are generally insular regarding cosmopolitan projects because such efforts run contrary to state goals of inculcating national loyalty, commitments to the local culture and the defence of state sovereignty. Noting these trends in scholarship and in state–civil society practices, Garrett Wallace Brown argues that, 'for cosmopolitans, the agenda should be to think more inventively about how to make these everyday state practices increasingly more cosmopolitan'.[2]

This chapter follows Brown's insights by pursuing the following question: Are Southeast Asian states 'responsible cosmopolitan states'?[3] Or, to put it more specifically, do these states support, foster and provide the necessary conditions for Muslim cosmopolitanism to flourish? To address these questions, this chapter looks back at the history of Southeast Asian Muslim states prior to the advent of secular modernity. I propose that the Muslim polities that existed in Southeast Asia before the arrival of European colonialism displayed a high degree of inclusivity and encouraged Muslim cosmopolitanism in the region. The chapter then considers the modern period, which saw the weakening and breaking down of local polities under colonial rule. Even though European powers fostered their own versions of colonial cosmopolitanism and gave Muslim communities the space to develop their own forms of vernacular cosmopolitanisms, the legacies of Western secular colonial statecraft and the racialisation of local communities by the colonial states have lingered. We then move on to the postcolonial period, a time of intense struggles between secular states and Muslim cosmopolitans across Southeast Asia. I contend that the three states that this book considers – Singapore, Malaysia and Indonesia – have displayed differing stances towards Muslim cosmopolitanism. The secular and nationalist outlook of these states and their strategic biases has conditioned these stances. To determine whether these states are indeed responsible cosmopolitan states, I analyse each state's political rhetoric and the laws that are in place that relate to the vitality of Muslim cosmopolitanism, as well as each state's responses to grass-roots efforts to promote cosmopolitan visions and outlook.

Muslim Cosmopolitanism and Early Modern Polities

That Southeast Asian Muslim polities during the precolonial period were cosmopolitan is now an established fact within the expansive historiography on the subject. Since the era of mass conversion to Islam in the eleventh century, kings and other rulers in the region have generally been open to different ideologies and influences. This was clearly manifested in the political organisation of the Malay kingdoms. These polities were based on a mixture of Hindu–Buddhist, Persian and Ottoman Turkish ideas of divine kingship supported by a coterie of priests, merchants and the warrior class.[4] Because the conceptions of territory and political boundaries were porous and permeable, people from all sorts of backgrounds could move between kingdoms and within each kingdom with relative ease. The decentralised nature of governance and the relative absence of any definitive form of citizenship made Southeast Asian states during the precolonial period supportive of, or at least neutral towards, the development of Muslim cosmopolitanism in society. Muslims and non-Muslims, Malays and non-Malays intermarried with one another with few restrictions. Many eventually settled in Southeast Asia to form hybrid or creole communities, with the Jawi Peranakans and Hadhrami Arabs being the most notable ones that exist today.[5]

By the time Muslim rule in the region was fully consolidated in the late fifteenth century, the focus was less on waging war against the remnants of the Hindu–Buddhist kingdoms than on ensuring the strengthening of the Islamic sultanates through peace, diplomacy and trade. '*Kerajaan* economics' dominated the modus operandi of kingdoms where rulers viewed wealth as a means to acquire followers rather than for its own sake. This made possible the establishment of cosmopolitan societies in all major port cities in Southeast Asia.[6] Muslim travellers such as Ibn Battuta witnessed the various trading, religious, familial and political networks that intersected in the region. Southeast Asia became increasingly Islamic with Muslim conquests of Hindu–Buddhist polities. However, the vestiges of the pre-Islamic past endured and coexisted harmoniously within the Islamised societies.[7]

Localised ideas about Islam and what was appropriate for pluralised societies underpinned Muslim states' support for the growth of Muslim cosmopolitanism in Southeast Asia. Granted, there were exceptional episodes of persecution of sects such as the outlawing of the Wujudiyyah movement in Aceh and, granted, some rulers were tyrants who exploited their Muslims subjects; however, the general impression that emerges from the history of Southeast Asian Muslim kingdoms is the development of a statist interpretation of Islam coloured by Sufi notions of tolerance towards all faiths and cultures.[8] Muslim rulers allowed local and vernacular versions of Islam to flourish and left pre-Islamic customs (*adat*) largely undisturbed, as long as those customs did not threaten the state or social harmony and stability. Muslim polities sent missionaries to reach out to non-Muslims, usually by way of peaceful preaching and seldom through the use of force. Even though the *hudud* (punishments for crimes against God) formed part of the state laws, in reality they were rarely put into practice. Because the Islamic states – with exception of Aceh in the seventeenth century – generally followed a mild version of Islam, local Hindus and Buddhists converted in large numbers in the centuries following the establishment of the first Muslim kingdom in Pasai in 1267. By the end of the sixteenth century, almost all parts of island Southeast Asia had either been converted or had at least been made aware of the message of Islam.[9]

The arrival of the Portuguese fleets in 1498 and their subsequent take-over of Malacca in 1511 changed the cosmopolitan landscape of Southeast Asia. Muslim–Christian rivalry, in the realms of both warfare and proselytisation, became more marked than in the years before. The coming of the Dutch in the early seventeenth century further exacerbated the enmity between Muslim and Christian powers in the region. Still, in many parts of what was later known as Indonesia, this conflict did not totally divide the common people into warring religious tribes. In Makassar, for example, communities of varying beliefs existed side by side even after the Dutch colonisation of this Muslim port in 1669. Well aware of the cosmopolitan practices of the Muslim kingdom that preceded it, the Dutch officials based in the port maintained the general order of things to the extent of limiting Christian missionary activities so as to avoid Muslim resentment.[10]

The presence of European powers in Southeast Asia did not weaken Southeast Asian states until the early eighteenth century, when colonialism reached a more aggressive and interventionist stage. The Dutch East India Company (Vereenigde Oostindische Compagnie, or VOC), for example, placed little emphasis on the administration of Muslims; the company was more concerned with maximising profits through trade. Such posturing changed soon after the Napoleonic Wars in Europe and the entry of Britain as an emerging military and trading power in Southeast Asia. By the nineteenth century, what came to be known as Indonesia came largely under Dutch administration while Malaya (known today as Malaysia and Singapore) came under British rule. While the Dutch sought to put in place a bureaucracy that had been established in other colonies, the British developed a highly sophisticated colonial administrative system based on the British experience in India.

Both colonial powers grafted secular technologies of rule onto the existing indigenous governing structures. What developed from this imposition was a three-tier legal-bureaucratic system that acknowledged the continued existence of Islamic laws as well as the customary (*adat*) laws. However, the scope of these religious and customary laws were circumscribed and made subservient to the demands of colonial laws and institutions. For example, shariah laws and courts that had previously regulated all aspects of Muslim life were reduced to covering only Muslim personal laws, including marriage, divorce and the administration of Muslim endowments (*waqf*). The Malaysian historical anthropologist, Shamsul Amri Baharuddin, has succinctly described this three-tier system:

> As a member of the *Adat Perpatih* community, I still remember how this situation was best summarized anecdotally by my elders. They said, 'should you commit a crime you go to the *orang putih*'s (lit. white man's) court, should you want to marry you go to the *Kadi* (local Islamic official), and should you want your mother's *tanah pesaka* (lit. ancestral communal land) after her demise, sorry, you can't, it's your sister's, so says our *adat perpatih*'.[11]

The scope of the shariah, in particular, was further reduced as colonialism reached its height in the aftermath of the First World War and as native rulers became mere symbols of authority. What used to be kingdoms of power and supremacy that aided in the development of Muslim cosmopolitanism became kingdoms of ceremonies with no real control over most matters pertaining to Muslims and non-Muslims in local societies.[12] By the eve of the Second World War, colonial states had effectively eroded much of the political influence of local rulers throughout Southeast Asia. The Japanese occupation did not reverse this state of affairs. The new occupiers maintained the very structures that had been established by the Western colonisers to entrench their imperial ambitions in the region. When European powers regained their Southeast Asian territories following the end of the war, their first priority was to reinstate the bureaucracies that were left in considerable disarray. State secularism and European systems of justice were reinforced.

Even though anti-colonialists and nationalists sought to gain freedom and independence from the Western powers, they did not seek to revive the precolonial forms of statehood. Instead, upon the declarations of Indonesian (1949), Malaysian (1957) and Singaporean (1965) independence, local leaders of these newly independent countries maintained the frameworks and instruments of governance left behind by their colonial predecessors. Postcolonial Southeast Asian states maintained a secular disposition while imposing nationalist politics upon their people. Although religions – particularly Islam – occupied an important place in these states, the tripartite forces of secularism, nationalism and authoritarianism were leviathans that constantly held sway over these faiths.[13]

It follows, then, that each of these three countries developed its own version of state secularism. These different versions of state secularism nonetheless shared an essential feature, namely, the regulation of 'all aspects of individual life – even the most intimate, such as birth and death – no one, whether religious or other can avoid encountering its ambitious powers'.[14] Muslims, whose universalising visions and transnational ambitions were seen as affronts, had to bear the brunt of the punitive and regulative powers of these secular states that embraced nationalism as a vehicle for promoting unity in their countries. The next section explores these versions of state secularism, focusing on their approaches to (and impact on) Muslim cosmopolitanism. It should be mentioned that, when I refer to the 'state', I am referring to the central government or the federal state in these countries. I am aware that policies at the local, provincial or state levels can differ from those at the federal or central level, but that is a topic that requires a lengthy treatment of its own. Moreover, I subscribe to Max Weber's classic portrayal of the state:

The primary formal characteristics of the modern state are as follows: It possesses an administrative and legal order subject to change by legislation, to which the organized activities of the administrative staff, which are also controlled by regulations, are oriented. This system of order claims binding authority, not only over the members of the state, the citizens, most of whom have obtained membership by birth, but also to a very large extent over all action taking place in the area of its jurisdiction. It is thus a compulsory organization with a territorial basis. Furthermore, today, the use of force is regarded as legitimate only so far as it is either permitted by the state or prescribed by it.[15]

Indonesia: Pragmatic Secular State

Since the late 1940s, a few types of state secularism have prevailed in Muslim Southeast Asia. The first is what I call a pragmatic form of state secularism that has taken root in Indonesia. The second is a partisan version enforced by the Malaysian state. The third variant is the provincial type of state secularism that has been applied in Singapore. Before I explain the characteristics of these three types of secularism, it useful to note here that all of these forms of state secularism share a common denominator in that those of Malay-Indonesian stock (who constitute the bulk of the Muslim population in Muslim Southeast Asia) have been and still are regarded by the three states as the indigenous people of these countries. This recognition entails the protection, whether symbolic or through laws and other policies, of the religion, customs and ways of life of the local Muslims. The safeguarding and acknowledgement of their unique position is largely a residue of the colonial past. The British and Dutch colonial rulers devised the categories of 'natives' and 'indigenous' people of Muslim Southeast Asia, and these categories became an integral feature of postcolonial statecraft and constitutions.[16]

The Indonesian state, which is the biggest state in Muslim Southeast Asia, is a quintessentially pragmatic secular state. In contrast with the Malaysian and Singaporean states that have each been defined by one dominant party system – UMNO and PAP respectively – from their independence to the present day, the Indonesian state has gone through a number of regime changes. Because of the volatile political climate, the Indonesian state has maintained a functional secular approach to all matters pertaining to public order and morality, in order to balance the demands of its diverse population. Pragmatism in the management of state secularism has been necessary because of the sheer size of the country, which has presented challenges to the authority and reach of the central government. Dependent on loyal local elites who were devoted to pursuing their own political and economic interests, the Indonesian state was thus 'fragmented, overwhelmed, and ineffective – characteristics it shares with states in most developing countries. Intense political forces traverse its various parts'.[17] One can add that the state's pragmatic secular visions traversed uneasily across the country, varying from province to province in accordance with the relative strength of secular as opposed to religious groups in government and society.

Indonesian politicians were sensitive to the danger of casting religion aside, thus acknowledging its place in the constitution without letting any single religion structure the overall governance of the country. Such a pragmatic secular stance was based on the state's ideology of Pancasila (Five Principles) that was crafted by the founding fathers of the nation, Sukarno, Hatta, Muhammad Yamin and other members of the revolutionary generation of the 1940s. Pancasila was to serve as a common ideological framework for all communities in Indonesia to identify themselves as part of the nation. Pancasila is based on five basic principles: *Ketuhanan Yang Maha Esa* (Belief in the Almighty God), *Kemanusiaan Yang Adil dan Beradab* (Just and Civilised Humanity), *Persatuan Indonesia* (the Unity of Indonesia), *Demokrasi* (Guided Deliberations among Representatives) and *Keadilan Sosial* (Social Justice). Even after a series of changes in government from the time of Sukarno (1945–67) to the New Order period led by Suharto (1967–98) and then the post-Suharto period (1998 to the present), Pancasila is still ensconced as the state's ideology, although it has been subjected to varying interpretations according to the ideological temperaments and political persuasions of different heads of state.

It would not be wrong to characterise Pancasila as a form of 'civil religion' that integrates the essential elements of the major religions in the country.[18] The fact that the words 'Almighty God' are still part of Pancasila to this day implies that the state must play a direct role in matters pertaining to religion and that religious groups can influence matters pertaining to statecraft. Be that as it may, prominent Indonesian statesmen have stressed that the country must remain neither a theocratic Islamic state nor an unabashedly secular state. Or, as Muhammad Hatta put it so coherently:

> We will not establish a state with a separation of religion and state, but a separation of religious affairs and state affairs. If religious affairs are also handled by the state, then the religion will become state equipment and . . . its eternal character will disappear. State affairs belong to all of us. The affairs of Islam are exclusively the affairs of the Islamic ummah and the Islamic society.[19]

In other words, the importance of Islam in nation-building was well acknowledged but it has seldom played a big role in determining the shape of Indonesian politics as a whole.[20] Since Muslims form the majority of the Indonesian population, and since Islam has been the dominant faith in the country since its declaration of independence, the state has had to project itself as being supportive of Islam as a religion, even if this support is only symbolic. At the same time, as it endeavoured to maintain national unity, the state has had to manage (and often resist) the demands of both ultra-secularists and religious radicals. My concern here is with the shifts in the Indonesian state's pragmatic secular outlook and the impact of these shifts on Muslim cosmopolitanism from the 1970s onwards. Four overlapping periods may be discerned: the restrictive period (1966–89), the limited liberalisation period (1989–98), the capricious period (1998–2004) and the stabilisation period (2004–15).

From 1966 to 1989, the Suharto government interpreted Pancasila in a narrow way to mean that only the statist conception of religiosity was appropriate for society. Although pragmatic in nature, state secularism during this period was intrusive into the lives of Muslims and restricted the growth of Muslim cosmopolitanism throughout Indonesia. Muslim presses and publications were subjected to close monitoring and some of them were banned for publishing anti-government materials. Intellectuals, clerics and influential writers were regularly warned by law-enforcement agencies to steer clear of activities that went against the state's visions. Many intellectuals and activists were subjected to detention and imprisonment. The state was particularly suspicious of Islamic groups and movements with political aspirations, such as those that had launched rebellions in many parts of Indonesia in the name of establishing the *darul Islam* (house of Islam).[21]

Although the military had effectively crushed or at least severely crippled what was known as the 'Darul Islam' movement and its militant splinter groups by the end of the 1970s, the Suharto regime remained wary of prominent Muslim personalities and civil society groups and their drive to Islamise society and the state. The state appointed top officials who were either secularist in orientation or culturalist in their approach to Islam and Muslims. Edward Aspinall explains:

> Much of the bitterest Islamic resentment arose from the cultural gap between the leaders of the *umat* and the new ruling elite and centered on government social policies which those leaders interpreted as attempts to legitimate secular and Javanist norms (such as the proposed introduction of uniform marriage and divorce laws in 1973).[22]

Between 1973 and 1978, a series of mass incidents of unrest involving students and Muslim activists were quashed. The Majelis Ulama Indonesia (MUI, 'Indonesian Ulama Council') that was founded in 1975 primarily to issue *fatwas* (religious edicts) for the benefit of ordinary Muslims in the country also served as a mouthpiece for the state's concept of a non-political and benign Islam. Dissenters of the state's brand of Islam within the MUI itself were not spared from the state's heavy hand, as seen in the case of the famous popular preacher and the first general chairman of MUI, Hamka (Haji Abdul Malik bin Abdul Karim Amrullah). Hamka disagreed with Muslims celebrating Christmas or any other non-Muslim religious events because this would endanger their faith at a time of intensive Christian missionary activity in Indonesia. Hamka, however, promoted good relations and cooperation with Christians in other spheres of life, that is, other than in religious events. A long and controversial debate ensued between him and the Ministry of Religion that culminated in his abrupt resignation in 1981.[23]

Through the combined use of repression and coercion, the Suharto regime managed to emasculate Muslim groups and individuals during this restrictive phase of Muslim cosmopolitanism in Indonesia. The tough measures taken against many Muslim groups and personalities fragmented the Islamic community, driving many underground and forcing those who were left unscathed to engage in activities that did not directly threaten the power of the secular state. Commanding millions of members and sympathisers, influential Islamic movements such as the Muhammadiyah and the Nahdatul Ulama focused on welfare, educational and social programmes and avoided political activities to safeguard themselves from state tyranny. The reach of these two movements actually expanded, albeit at a slower rate than before, because the leaders of these movements were careful to avoid being seen as nemeses of the state. The state, in turn, encouraged the leaders of youth groups such as the Himpunan Mahasiswa Islam (HMI, the 'Islamic Students' Association'), giving them wide press coverage and inducting prominent members into the reigning political party, GOLKAR (Partai Golongan Karya, the 'Functional Group Party').[24]

This policy of co-option was part of the state's programme to depoliticise the Muslim community. The HMI as an organisation, however, split into two in the 1980s after major internal disagreements over accepting Pancasila as an ideological base. The Suharto regime forced all Muslim associations and movements to pledge their loyalty to Pancasila above all other ideologies.[25] Wherever and whenever Muslim cosmopolitanism endured, it could be found in social spaces, such as markets, malls and mosques. The Suharto regime, which was devoted to achieving the unity of the nation during this hampering phase, permitted the construction of mega shopping centres, mammoth markets and grand mosques as a mirage that the state was not as despotic as the alternative media and the foreign media described it. By permitting the construction of grand mosques, the state cultivated the image that Islam was still espoused as an important aspect of Indonesian life.[26]

Suharto, however, changed his dictatorial tack from 1989 onwards in ways that puzzled many analysts at that time. Among the plausible reasons for this shift was the global wave of Islamic revivalism, which, combined with rapid economic growth during this period, gave birth to a crop of middle-class Muslim Indonesians. Suharto was shadowing the policies of Prime Minister Mahathir Mohamad in Malaysia. Instead of resisting the surge of Islamisation, Mahathir held it by its horns, rode upon its back and channelled it to the advantage of the Malaysian secular state.[27] The other reason for this shift in policy was linked to the increasing unhappiness among Suharto's old allies regarding the corruption, nepotism and cronyism that characterised his autocratic regime. They were turning their backs on him and this encouraged Suharto to lean closer towards Islamic organisations, movements and intellectuals that he had once held at bay. Suharto was also conscious of the advent of globalisation, the advances in media technologies and also the increasing ease of travel. A policy of *keterbukaan* (openness) towards Muslim cosmopolitanism and its purveyors was thus adopted to ensure the continuity of his rule.

During this limited liberalisation era, the state expanded the scope of Muslim cosmopolitanism through the formation of the Ikatan Cendekiawan Muslim se-Indonesia (ICMI, the 'Indonesian Muslim Intellectuals' Association'). Established in 1990, the ICMI was intended to be a hub for intellectuals and activists to discuss contemporary issues affecting Muslims. Many Muslim intellectuals who were former critics of the Suharto regime joined the ICMI. They saw the state-founded body as an avenue to Islamise society and, by implication, the state itself. Led by the vice-president, B. J. Habibie, these intellectuals soon took up prominent positions in the military, bureaucracy and political positions across the country. Indeed, through the agency of the ICMI, pluralistic and democratic pulses within Islam blossomed among a broad section of the Indonesian Muslim middle classes. One of the intellectuals who demarcated the ideological course of the ICMI in the 1970s was an intellectual giant named Nurcholish Madjid. Trained in Islamic studies both in Indonesia and the United States and a former national leader of the HMI, Nurcholish promoted the separation of religion from politics. The state, according to him, must remain secular. His secularist stance invited wide criticism from his former mentors and many leading Islamic thinkers in Indonesia at that time.[28]

The Indonesian state also established Islamic economic institutions, founded and supported the creation of Islamic schools and universities, while lifting many restrictions that had been imposed upon Muslim printing presses prior to the limited liberalisation period. Previously suppressed, missionary groups such as the Dewan Dakwah Islamiyah Indonesia (DDII), which had once been branded as radical, could now organise more activities to promote Islam. Such support did not entail state tolerance towards radical Muslims. They were continually watched and suppressed when necessary. But, as Arskal Salim notes, 'the formal depoliticization of Islam by the Soeharto regime was a blessing in disguise, as it encouraged a deepening Islamization of Indonesian society in non-political contexts'.[29] Through its pragmatic secularist predisposition during this period, the Indonesian state received much support from Muslim organisations and intellectuals, leading to the creation of a cosmopolitan and pluralist interpretation of Islam. Nurcholish Madjid confidently declared that Indonesia in the early 1990s could offer itself 'as a laboratory for developing modern tolerance and pluralism. With approximately 90 per cent of a population of about 180 million people being Muslims, Indonesia provides a good opportunity to experiment with the bringing of Islam into a positive and constructive dialogue with the demands of this age'.[30]

The downfall of the New Order regime in 1998 placed the newly elected coalition government in an uneasy position as it strove to balance the demands of powerful forces in the Muslim society that were previously inhibited through the force of law and oppression. Vehement debates regarding the expansion of the shariah within the state constitution arose. Some of the Muslim groups that called for the implementation of shariah in Indonesia without considering the plight of minorities in the country included Komite Indonesia untuk Solidaritas Dunia Islam (KISDI, the 'Committee for the Solidarity of the Muslim World'), Majelis Mujahidin Indonesia (MMI, the 'Indonesian Mujahidin Council'), Dewan Dakwah Islamiyah Indonesia (DDII, the 'Islamic Propagation Council'), Front Pembela Islam (FPI, the 'Muslim Defenders Front'), Hizbut Tahrir Indonesia (HTI, the 'Party of Liberation Indonesia'), Laskar Jihad (Warriors of Jihad), among others. During this capricious, fast-moving six-year period when three presidents – B. J. Habibie (1998–9), Abdul Rahman Wahid (1999–2001) and Megawati Sukarno (2001–4) – struggled to keep the country in order, civil society groups came to the fore to counterbalance the influence of radical groups. Indeed, it was the expansion of Muslim cosmopolitanism during the later years of the Suharto regime that empowered movements such as the Muhammadiyah, Nahdatul Ulama, Paramadina and Jaringan Islam Liberal (JIL) to play more significant roles during these years. These movements argued that the shariah, although relevant and revered as the overarching legal frame of reference for all Indonesian Muslims, ought not to be the *raison d'être* of the state. They publicly castigated the calls by some Islamic groups for the revival and implementation of the Jakarta Charter of June 1945 that called for the construction of an Islamic state in Indonesia.[31] These movements, rather than the state, therefore served as alternatives to the build-up of extremism and radicalism in the country.

However, the frailties of the state permitted the rapid spread of religious and ideological parochialism that gained more media attention than the efforts to bring Muslims back to 'the multiform, cosmopolitan and pluralist character of Indonesian nationalism and nation-building'.[32] Immediately after the demise of Suharto's regime, violence between Muslims and non-Muslims broke out in Jakarta and then spilled over into parts of Surakarta, Aceh, the Moluccas, East Timor, Sulawesi, Kalimantan, West Papua and Aceh. There was also a series of car and suicide bombings, the most infamous of which was the Bali bombing in 2002. One factor that underscores all of these instances of *amuk massa* (crowds running amok) was the growth of intolerance between privileged individuals and communal groups against those who had been marginalised for many decades. Such animosities cascaded into large-scale killings. Another factor that could help explain the descent into chaos was the lack of a strong state that, at the height of its powers, had previously held the frustrations of the common people in check.[33] Many analysts predicted the progressive disintegration of Indonesia and the eclipse of the cosmopolitanism that had once defined the country.[34]

These dire predictions did not come true. Apart from East Timor's declaration of independence from Indonesia in 2002, the country remained intact as the unified entity it has been since 1949. The advent of President Susilo Bambang Yudhoyono as the new Indonesian president in 2004 heralded the beginning of a decade of stability, although stagnation did occur in many aspects of the political, economic and the social lives of Indonesians. Perhaps one of the hallmarks of Yudhoyono's rule was the restoration of order in society. This provided the necessary conditions for the growth of Muslim cosmopolitanism in the Indonesian context. Intellectuals were able to voice their dissenting opinions more openly than ever before and civil society movements became more vivacious after the end of the Suharto regime. Freedom of the press was guaranteed.

The pragmatic secular Indonesian state under Yudhoyono nonetheless failed in its battle against the growing intolerance of radical Muslims towards minorities in particular. The attacks against a heterodox Muslim sect, the Ahmadiyya, have continued unabated. Christian churches were also targeted by intolerant Muslims, and such acts have often escaped the tentacles of the law because the state was anxious to avoid backlashes and reprisals from terrorist groups if they were proscribed.[35] Notwithstanding these various failures, the Indonesian state has succeeded in keeping the ideals of Pancasila alive. The continued support for secular parties among the general public attests to the strength of secular democracy in Indonesia. Islamic parties regained their ground in the 2014 elections, following their relative decline in 2009, but they are still not influential enough to field a viable presidential candidate. That there are a number of Islamic parties (also known as 'PARPOL ISLAM' (Parti Politik Islam, or 'Islamic Political Parties') that are still actively vying for power in Indonesia indicates the general acceptance of a diverse Muslim political landscape in the country.[36]

Viewed from this broad canvas of time, the pragmatic secular state in Indonesia has provided much space and room for Muslim cosmopolitanism to subsist and grow in the country. Undeniably, Muslim political activism was severely restricted in the early Suharto years and this stifled lively conversations about democracy and freedom in many ways. But, because communal and religious-based politics were kept at bay, Muslims and non-Muslims learnt to coexist with one another and avoided large-scale conflicts, in part driven by state phobia though, in most instances, out of a genuine mutual respect for each other. The Indonesian example shows that pragmatic rather than dogmatic secular states can provide some leeway for religious groups to participate vigorously in the structuring of the everyday lives of the common people as well as in politics. It is probably the most viable form of state that would ensure the effervescence of Muslim cosmopolitanism in Southeast Asia. The pragmatic secular state comes close to the cosmopolitan state, as outlined by Garrett Wallace Brown above. Whether such a state acts responsibly or not is contingent upon the character of its leadership and the strength of the state in managing the populace and allowing space for the development of civil society activism.

Malaysia: The Partisan Secular State

The pragmatic secularist stand of the Indonesian state has not been replicated anywhere else in Muslim Southeast Asia. The Malaysian state projects a different outlook, taking on what I call the 'partisan' variant of state secularism, which has prevailed since the declaration of the country's independence in 1957. By a 'partisan secular state', I refer to a state that confers special privileges, benefits and rights upon a particular group of people within a given territory. Along the path of bolstering the significance of one particular group, partisan secular states often act unjustly towards other groups that are deemed to be less favoured citizens. These other or outsider groups are cast as threats to the future and well-being of the preferred group that the state seeks to protect and promote. Furthermore, partisan secular states may or may not be supportive of religions in society. This is contingent on the background of the group that the state backs, whether it is secular in orientation or otherwise. In the case of the Malaysian partisan secular state, it is supportive of and even promotes a particular brand of Islam in preference to other versions and at the expense of other religions in the country. This, as we shall see later, has implications for the advancement of Muslim cosmopolitanism in the country.

Unlike the Indonesian state's changing leadership and impartial pronouncements towards all religions in the country, as reflected in Pancasila, the Malaysian state has always been under the secure rule of the Barisan National (National Front) that is dominated by the ruling Malay nationalist party UMNO. UMNO sees itself as a protector of Islam and this has been enshrined in the constitution since 1957. Article 3 of the Malaysian constitution states that Islam is the official religion of Malaysia, but the constitution also guarantees the freedom to practise other religions. Article 153, in turn, guarantees the special position and privileges enjoyed by the Malays as the indigenous people of the country. Article 160 defines 'a Malay' as one who professes Islam, speaks the Malay language, conforms to Malay customs and resides in Malaysia. A Malaysian Malay who renounces Islam is no longer considered a Malay under these constitutional arrangements. In discussing the position of Islam in the Malaysian constitution, Abdul Aziz Bari posits that '[c]ontrary to public perception, the issue of Islam is obviously quite central to the Constitution. Indeed, it may be said that Islam forms part of the essence and foundation of the constitutional framework'.[37]

Under the constitution, local states within Malaysia are permitted to enforce their own laws to govern Muslims in their own state territories. Such laws usually cover personal and family matters as well as minor criminal offences as stipulated in Islam. Because shariah covers specific segments of the overall legal framework, there have been many contestations over whether secular or Islamic laws are to be given the higher priority. Johan Saravanamuttu has described the Malaysian state as a 'hybridized or hybrid state which functions on the basis of a fundamentally secular constitution which, however, has seen the increasing penetration of Islamic precepts in both the discursive and practical realms of state practices'.[38]

Alternatively, I would argue that the Malaysian state is essentially a partisan secular state because its support for Islam is motivated solely by the state's will to protect and advocate the rule and supremacy of the majority ethnic group (the Malays). This is evidenced in the introduction and enlargement of the New Economic Policy (NEP) in 1971. Under the NEP, Bumiputeras ('sons of the soil', a category which includes Malays and the indigenous peoples) were to be given preferential treatment over other communities in Malaysia in the areas of public administration, education, employment, business, land rights, welfare schemes and various subsidies. This policy emerged after the 1969 race riots, where issues pertaining to Malay poverty and underdevelopment came into sharp relief. The NEP and the Malaysian state's adoption of a partisan secularist stand greatly departed from the founding fathers' vision of a responsible cosmopolitan state. [39]

Tunku Abdul Rahman, the first Malaysian prime minister (1957–70), strongly believed in the construction of a state that treated all citizens equally, even though he did acknowledge differences between Bumiputeras and non-Bumiputeras. His vision of an inclusive state took a different course under the leadership of his successor, Tun Abdul Razak (1970–6), who felt that Malays were underrepresented in many important areas of the economy, politics and society, and that affirmative policies were the most effective tools to reverse this predicament. Aside from creating the conditions for the development of 'money politics' and the 'new rich' among the Malays, the NEP policy from Tun Razak's reign onwards has had the effect of turning the Malaysian state into a racially biased entity rather than an institution than binds the nation as a whole.[40] This partisan secularist policy has prevailed since the 1970s. During the reign of Mahathir Mohamad from 1981 to 2003, the state's partisan secularist stance was given a veneer of Islamicity to obtain the support of the Islamic forces that were gaining influence in society.[41]

The partisan secular state's support for Islamisation in Malaysia has expanded substantially since the 1980s.[42] The pronouncements made by Mahathir Mohamad in 2001 and 2002 and by his successor, Abdullah Badawi, in 2007 that Malaysia was already an 'Islamic state' were interpreted by many as indicative of the reality that the state has been thoroughly Islamicised. Notwithstanding such alarmist analyses, it is worth noting that at no point in the recent history of the country has the Malaysian government depicted itself as a theocratic state – in the manner that the opposition PAS party would – with the shariah as the supreme law of the land. The shariah has remained in a second-tier position in relation to the secular laws and the *hudud* punishments have not gained any real foothold in influencing the overall framework of the constitution, despite pressures from many Islamic factions in the country. Maznah Mohamad confirms this by stating that the 'Malaysian state is not secular in the *laïcité* sense, but the transformation of its religious bureaucracy and institutions is akin to a secularized adaptation of Islam rather than to a process of desecularization'.[43]

However, it cannot be denied that the Malaysian state has been increasingly penetrated and influenced by Muslim activists who were inducted into the state apparatus during Anwar Ibrahim's term as an UMNO politician and a minister in the cabinet from 1982 to 1998.[44] The problem, in my opinion, is not to do with the Islamisation of the state, because Islam prior to the coming of colonialism had defined the functions of the state without jeopardising the development of Muslim cosmopolitanism or the welfare and freedom of the non-Muslims. Rather, the problem is to do with the Malaysian partisan state's exploitation and politicisation of Islam as a legitimating tool for the advancement of the supremacy of Malays over Malaysians of other ethnicities. Such an approach to governance has impacted on Muslim cosmopolitanism, especially from the 1980s onwards.

The first adverse effect of this has been the development of racialised politics in Malaysia. Most Malay Muslim political leaders in Malaysia position themselves as representatives and spokespersons of their own ethnic communities first before factoring in the hopes and aspirations of other communities in the country. The situation is made dire by the reality that political parties within the ruling coalition – the Barisan National – have been organised around communal groups rather than to portray themselves as multiracial fronts. The UMNO considers itself a 'Malay first' party and reiterates its defence of *ketuanan Melayu* (Malay supremacy) during its annual assemblies as a way to remind the other politicians and political parties that the Malays are the rightful rulers of the country. According to *ketuanan Melayu,* the real power in Malaysia lies in the hands of the Malays, while other ethnic groups are second-class citizens who ought to submit to Malay political hegemony. This is in stark contrast to Indonesia's Pancasila, which puts emphasis on the equality of all citizens. *Ketuanan Melayu* has found its way into school textbooks, inviting strong condemnation from civil society activists and opposition politicians.[45]

Pluralist politics is, therefore, left out in the cold in Malaysia. Even opposition parties such as PAS and the Democratic Action Party (DAP) operate within a communal-based political framework, with each party organised or dominated largely by a certain ethnic group, specifically the Malays or the Chinese, with other ethnic groups rarely having any political leverage in these parties. The recent fallout between PAS and the DAP and the breakup of the Pakatan Rakyat (PR, 'People's Alliance') opposition alliance have cemented the reality that ethnic politics will likely persist as a conspicuous feature of the Malaysian political landscape for the foreseeable future. Many voters will likely remain polarised along racial lines as long as politicians and political parties remain racialised.[46] That is to say, political cosmopolitanism in Malaysia lurks far beyond the horizon as a consequence of state policies. It could be said that the partisan state's policy of ruling through racial divisions has been remarkably successful, at least in the sense that even the opposition's alliance has emulated the Barisan National.

In addition to laying the conditions for the development of racial politics, the partisan stance that the state has taken over the years has necessitated the proscription of cosmopolitan intellectuals and activists who criticise the race-based policies and the attendant problems of corruption and cronyism that come with it. The state has also used the strategy of co-optation as a means of incorporating dissidents into the state apparatus to ensure that the 'Malay first' status quo is maintained. Proscription of the government's critics heightened dramatically during the long tenure of Mahathir Mohamad, but has relaxed somewhat since then during the administrations of his two immediate successors, Abdullah Badawi and Najib Tun Razak. Viewed in this light, Mahathir could be likened to Suharto, each of whom took a harsh line towards all forms of dissent and resistance and both of whom were intolerant towards Muslim cosmopolitanism in the early years of their long reigns.

However, resistance by cosmopolitan intellectuals and movements has remained unabated amidst decades of repression and persecution in Malaysia. One notable case concerns the 1,200 university students who were arrested after protesting the demolition of squatters' homes and speaking out for the rights of rural farmers in Baling. Among those who were detained was the internationally renowned Malaysian youth activist, Anwar Ibrahim, who would later become deputy prime minister and, still later, an imprisoned opposition leader.[47] Another iconic use of proscriptive methods to silence dissenters of race-based policies was Operation Lalang, in which 119 politicians, intellectuals, media reporters and social activists (including Dr Chandra Muzaffar) were arrested in 1987 in what has been regarded as the biggest crackdown in Malaysian history. Prime Minister Mahathir Mohamad justified the arrests as necessary to defuse the racial tensions that the detainees were fanning through their writings, speeches and activities. The actual reason for the crackdown was that these detainees were questioning the policies and malpractices of the ruling regime.[48] The use of the laws to mute voices of Muslim cosmopolitanism has endured the passage of time and remained a feature of Malaysian politics to the present day. The partisan state and its avatars are still fiercely guarding the notion of *ketuanan Melayu*, so much so that even former stalwarts of UMNO are questioning the relevance of the idea in a pluralised Malaysian setting. For such defiance, these fallen backers of the state are now on the brink of being charged for sedition.[49]

The state has negatively impacted Muslim cosmopolitanism in Malaysia through its narrow definition, bureaucratisation and enforcement of what is legitimately regarded as a mainstream and progressive form of Islam. Since the 1980s, the version of Islam that the Malaysian state has considered legitimate for Malays is a variant that is modernist in orientation as well as being in keeping with the Sunni Shafi'ite school of jurisprudence and the Ash'arite theology. This version of Islam has been enforced through the National Fatwa Council, the setting up of institutes such as the Jabatan Kemajuan Islam Malaysia (JAKIM, 'Department of Islamic Advancement Malaysia') and the Institut Kefahaman Islam Malaysia (IKIM, 'Institute of Islamic Understanding Malaysia') and the regulation of 'Shari'ah (Islamic) courts and the judicial establishment, mosques, religious schools and zakat (Islamic tithe) collection, as well as religious officialdom in general and ulama (Islamic scholars) in particular'.[50] The ramifications of conferring a preferential status upon only one statist version of Islam are deleterious.

In 1995, members of the Al-Arqam movement were arrested on charges of adhering to 'deviationist' teachings. The movement was categorically banned. The actual reason for the shutdown of the movement was its inter-rogative posture towards state-defined Islam.[51] More recently, state religious officials declared Salafism, also referred to as 'Wahhabism', to be deviant and dangerous. According to the National Fatwa Council chairman, Dr Abdul Shukor Husin, the proponents of Salafism and Wahhabism are 'extremists' and their Arab-centric rendering of Islam is incompatible with the moder-ate majority in Malaysia.[52] Because of this uncompromising stance towards Salafism and Wahhabism and the perceived fear that Malays are susceptible to the influence of such teachings, there developed a sort of 'Wahhabi witch hunt'. Persons suspected of following ideologies that are not in line with the statist version of Islam are either detained or banned from teaching religious classes in private or public domains.

More than that, in sponsoring and imposing a particular version of Islam, the state rules out the possibility of Malays transitioning into and incorporating ideas from other schools of Sunni Islamic thought. This has resulted in the parochialisation of Muslim minds aside from the alienation of large numbers of Malay Muslims who are exposed to other interpreta-tions of Islam via digital media and their travels in the Middle East. Hence, the Malaysian state's insular understanding of Islam is incongruent with the public's increasingly cosmopolitan perception of the faith.

Despite the tough measures that have been taken by the partisan state against promoters of Muslim cosmopolitanism, and in spite of the state's promotion of a limited interpretation of Islam in society, the Malaysian state has not been absolutely opposed to cosmopolitan visions. In other words, it would be unfair to posit that partisan secular states are unconditionally hos-tile towards Muslim cosmopolitanism. If such absolutism were actually put into practice, the state would probably be confronted with mass revolts and civil unrest, as exemplified in the cases of the Iranian Revolution (1979) and the decades of Palestinian resistance against the Israeli state.[53] Hence, at the level of political rhetoric and symbolic displays, the Malaysian state proposed several novel aims and ideas that, if properly implemented and carried out, could have turned Malaysia into a model cosmopolitan Muslim country. Nonetheless, because communal forces and considerations have tended to dominate much of the state's operations, many of the projects are either highly rhetorical or stifled by prejudiced forces within the state itself.[54]

One example of the Malaysian state's efforts to foster cosmopolitanism among Muslims in the country is the *Bangsa Malaysia* (Malaysian Nation) ideal promulgated by Mahathir Mohamad in 1995. This was part of the state's 'Vision 2020', where an inclusive identity would eventually be created such that Malaysians would soon 'identify themselves with the country, speak Bahasa Malaysia and accept the Constitution. To realize the goal of Bangsa Malaysia, the people should start accepting each other as they are, regardless of race and religion'.[55] *Bangsa Malaysia* was soon eclipsed by the ideal of *Islam Hadhari* (Civilisational Islam, 2003–9) promoted by Abdullah Badawi, Mahathir's successor. *Islam Hadhari* was, in turn, overshadowed by the *1Malaysia* policy introduced by Najib Tun Razak in 2012 to promote national unity and tolerance. The state also tried to encourage interreligious dialogue through bodies such as the National Inter-Faith Commission and the Committee for the Promotion of Inter-Religious Understanding and Harmony Among Adherents (CPIRUHAA). But all of these slogans, committees and programmes were short-lived or stillborn. The Malaysian state has yet to lay the groundwork for the creation of a cosmopolitan Malaysia because, time after time, the state has hastily jettisoned its own cosmopolitan plans to appease the conservative and hardcore partisan elements in the country.

Jonathan Fox, in his incisive study of political secularism in 177 countries, situates Malaysia within the category of 'religious states'. According to Fox, a 'religious state' is one that 'strongly supports and enforces the majority religion'.[56] In what follows, I show that the picture is far more complex than this. While the Malaysian state does uphold Islam as the official religion of the state and promotes it to the fullest extent, the overall character of the state is secular. Be that as it may, the main targets of the state's policies linked to religious beliefs have been the Malays more than any other group in the country. The Malaysian state accepts the existence of non-Muslim minorities within the country and acknowledges them as citizens. Even so, the state continually manufactures idioms and ideologies to sustain Bumiputera rule and disciplines the Malays from time to time into accepting the state's brand of Islam. Statist Islam in Malaysia is characterised by ethnic overtones to demarcate differences not only between Muslims and non-Muslims, but also between Malay Muslims and non-Malay Muslims.

It may not be wrong to surmise that, when compared with the pragmatic secular state in Indonesia, the partisan secular state in Malaysia is less friendly towards Muslim cosmopolitanism. This may partly explain why, when faced with the question as to whether Christian Malaysians can use the word 'Allah' to describe 'God' in their Malay-language Bibles, the Malaysian Federal Court ruled that it is illegal to do so because it might mislead Malay Muslims into embracing Christianity.[57] In Indonesia, this is not a matter worthy of public or governmental debate, because God is not Malay nor is He the property of any Muslim. Indonesian Christians are free to use the word 'Allah' for God today, just as they have for many generations.[58]

Singapore: The Provincial Secular State

Scholarship on state secularism in Singapore paints a constructive picture of the Singapore state's approach to managing religions. The prevailing line of argument has it that Singapore is not a 'dogmatic' or 'uncompromising' secular state. Unlike many other states in the region, the Singapore state functions in a strategic and dynamic way to harness 'the powerful potential of religion while ensuring that the secular always takes precedence in political discourse, public policy and governance'.[59] Scholars that subscribe to this 'pragmatic secular state' thesis maintain that the state accommodates religions and adopts a judicious approach to dealing with religious pluralism in Singapore. The implication of such an assertion is that the state does not erect barriers against Muslim cosmopolitanism as long as those who promote it act in accordance with the tactical interests of the state.[60]

However, the state's track record in handling of Islam and Muslims in Singapore undermines the pragmatic secular state thesis. As Kamaludeen, Pereira and Turner have argued in the first full-length study of Muslims in

Singapore, the Singapore state frequently intervenes in the religious life of the Muslim minority community with the 'aim of creating an efficient, trouble-free society'.[61] Indeed, it would be fair to say that Islam and, by implication, the Muslim minority is *the* problem for the postcolonial Singaporean state. Or, to quote the first and longest-serving prime minister of Singapore, Lee Kuan Yew, 'we can integrate all religions and races, except Islam'.[62] The idea that the secular and modernising Singapore state regards Islam and Muslims as potential threats can be traced back to 1950, when riots broke out involving Muslims killing non-Muslims.[63]

Since that fateful incident, what has come to be known as the 'Maria Hertogh controversy' has occupied a vital place within the Singapore government's depiction of the turbulent colonial past, so much so that it has often been singled out and invoked during periods of conflict and social effervescence.[64] Postcolonial statesmen use the riots as a reminder for Singaporeans that religion should never be enmeshed with secular and radical politics. The riots provide a potent historical lesson that excessive ideological fervour, missionary zeal and moral assertiveness are undesirable and have no place within a progressive society. Constant references to the riots have also served as a subtle warning to the press that any attempts to incite racial and religious tensions will result in cessation of publication and criminal prosecution. Presented in the mainstream media and school textbooks in such a way as to validate the postcolonial Singapore state's approach to managing religions, the Maria Hertogh controversy has become something of a 'moral panic' that defines the normative boundaries of the Muslim community in Singapore.

When viewed from the perspective that the special position of the Malay Muslims is enshrined within its constitution, the Singapore state's treatment of the minority group is perplexing. What, then, is the best way to describe the state's brand of secularism in relation to Muslim cosmopolitanism? I propose that the Singapore state is best characterised as a 'provincial secular state', one that is territorial in its pronouncements about how world religions – here referring especially to Islam – should be interpreted and lived. The state discourages and even prohibits religious thinkers, scholars and popular preachers from transmitting ideas that would encourage their adherents to imagine themselves as belonging to translocal solidarities, because such solidarities are regarded as having the potential to threaten the sovereignty of the state. Religions, from the point of view of the provincial secular state, must remain local, provincial and national in their overall outlook. Religions must remain local so as to be 'legible' for easier state management.[65]

The provincial secular state is not only territorial; it is also guarded in its liaisons with religious groups. It absorbs religious elites within state structures so as to emasculate them. The state sponsors and promotes compliant members of the religious communities and publicises them as icons so as to gain the acquiescence of the religious masses. Even though the state empowers these individuals, it constantly anticipates betrayals and disloyalty because the state recognises that faithful devotees of any world religions tend to affiliate themselves with their larger global religious communities in moments of crisis, sometimes at the expense of the strategic interests of the state. Above all, the provincial state is intrusive in its policies towards all matters pertaining to the religious life, thought and practices of the clergy and the laity. Through the use of a whole range of surveillance systems, the provincial state maintains control over the activities of all religious groups. The state interferes with religious groups through the use of proxies from within each religious community and it employs the long arm of the law and the judiciary when religious actors become violent.

The parochialist secular posturing which the Singapore state adopts is most apparent when it comes to dealing with Muslims. There are several reasons why the state takes such an approach to Islam, Muslims and Muslim cosmopolitanism. The most important factors are the geopolitical location and demographic complexion of Singapore, which is the only non-Muslim-dominated country within a sea of Muslims in Southeast Asia. Since the early days of independence in 1965, Singapore's political leaders have been apprehensive about split loyalties among its Malay Muslim citizens, especially in times of crisis between Singapore and its two Muslim-majority next-door neighbours, Malaysia and Indonesia. Fears of defection and feelings of distrust towards the Malay Muslims heightened through the years as a result of Islamic revivalism in the region and the post-September 11 'war on terror' that persists today.[66]

Another reason for parochialist posturing could be explained through the postcolonial leaders' experiences with Muslim elites in the region. Singapore was kicked out of Malaysia in August 1965 after much political wrangling between the island-state's politicians and the ultra-Malays of UMNO that led to racial riots in Singapore in 1964. This coincided with the Indonesian Confrontation that lasted for three years from 1963 to 1966. Singapore was threatened by sabotage and invasion by armed groups sponsored by the Sukarno regime. A number of Singaporeans were eventually arrested for their involvement in militant activities. These incidents, combined with the reality that, until the mid-1970s, most members of the armed and uniformed services were Malays, shaped the postcolonial leaders' policies towards Malays in particular and Muslims in general, whom they viewed and treated with suspicion.[67] Singapore's mostly non-Muslim leaders' encounters with Muslims, both within and outside of Singapore, induced the provincial secular state to structure the scope of Muslim cosmopolitanism in the city-state in its image.

This was achieved in a few ways. The state and its agencies limited the interpretive possibilities of what Islam should be by engaging in ideological work. The Singapore Muslim Identity (SMI) project launched in early 2005 under the auspices of MUIS was one such ideological work. It was aimed at creating a breed of Singaporean Muslims who would manifest desired attributes in line with the state's aim of producing progressive Muslims.[68] On the surface, the SMI project appeared benign, affirming the ideal of what it means to be a cosmopolitan Singaporean Muslim. In reality, the SMI serves as a political tool for the state to classify 'moderates' and 'extremists' within the Muslim community. The seventh desired attribute, for example, states that those truly manifesting the SMI should be 'well-adjusted as contributing members of a multi-religious society and a secular state'. The assumption here is that a Muslim who does not contribute to the secular state is therefore problematic and needs to be reformed. Furthermore, the SMI is not an idea that grew out of the Muslim community's collective vision of the identity they hoped to forge. Instead, it is a top-down initiative, born of the state's anxieties about the involvement of a small number of Singaporean Muslims in terrorist networks.[69]

The Singapore state also utilises legal and systemic restrictions to regulate Muslims and the teaching of Islam. Other than the banning of the hijab, as discussed in Chapter 5, the barring of Islamic scholars and teachers from preaching and teaching classes that challenge the state's brand of Islam is another prime example of the state's use of laws to regulate Islam. All Islamic religious teachers in Singapore are required to register themselves with the Asatizah Recognition Scheme (ARS) as a means to verify their religious orientations and qualifications. Islamic religious teachers who are registered with the ARS are required to attend a prescribed number of hours at workshops, talks and training courses conducted by MUIS and its affiliates such as PERGAS (Persatuan Ulama dan Guru-Guru Agama Islam Singapura, the 'Singapore Islamic Scholars and Religious Teachers Association').

The ARS clearly reflects the state's parochialism because it restricts the avenues of religious instruction to those who are formally registered in the scheme.[70] Religious teachers, for example, may have postgraduate degrees from renowned universities but may choose not to register with the ARS because they may not have time to attend the compulsory courses that enable them to remain on the list, or because they fundamentally disagree with the system. As a result, they will be prohibited from teaching in public even if their qualifications surpass those of their peers, and even if Muslim scholars around the world internationally recognise their expertise. This use of legal and systemic restrictions, as Kersten Steiner has highlighted, is made possible through the state's creation of

> a web of interlocking state institutions with decisive interpretative authority regarding law for Muslims in Singapore and a monopoly on its enforcement. The government thus sought control not only over the direction of the administration of law for Muslims but also over who would have the responsibility for implementing it and interpreting it, that is, MUIS and the Syariah (Islamic law) court system.[71]

Besides requiring that religious teachers comply with state-managed registration systems and prohibiting them from teaching if they refuse to comply, the provincial secular state vigorously screens foreign Muslim preachers and scholars who are invited to Singapore to give public lectures. A permit from the Ministry of Manpower has to be obtained before an invited Muslim speaker can actually deliver lectures on the island. In early 2016, for example, a minister in parliament remarked,

> We will not allow anyone, of any religion, who preaches that people of other faiths should be shunned or that people of other faiths should be

ignored . . . And it is not only what he preaches in Singapore. We will also look at what he preaches outside Singapore, because his teachings would be available online.[72]

Certain Muslim preachers have been disallowed from speaking publicly in Singapore, including Dr Zakir Naik, Dr Abu Ameenah Bilal Philips and Mufti Menk. The banning of Mufti Menk from delivering a planned public lecture on the Qur'an generated much speculation about the state's reservations towards Salafi-orientated scholars.[73]

Last but not least, Singapore's provincial secular state employs a whole range of monitoring tactics and fear techniques to ensure that Islam in Singapore does not develop beyond the grasp and legibility of the government. In this regard, the Singapore state is akin to its Indonesian and Malaysian counterparts, in that they are all reputed to be highly securitised states that keep track of the activities of many local Muslim opinion makers, religious groups and influential clerics.[74] Through the use of the Internal Security Act (ISA), the Singapore state has detained Muslims without trial for threatening national security. 'Threats' are defined as broadly as possible from destabilising social harmony to harming the image of the incumbent regime. Muslim preachers, alleged terrorists and potential radicals have been detained from time to time. The most iconic example was the arrest of a former lawyer in 2007, the twenty-eight-year-old Abdul Basheer Abdul Kader, who was described as the first among a series of 'self-radicalised Singaporeans'.[75]

What is crucial here is not the fact that potential suspects and criminals have been arrested, or that many of them have not been put on trial and 'have had no voice'.[76] Rather, what is crucial is the amplification of the dangers that these individuals posed through the use of the media that had a great impact on the development of Muslim cosmopolitanism in the country. Muslim preachers, scholars and writers in Singapore have increasingly developed an unfounded sense of fear of being placed under arrest for questioning state policies or spreading ideas that might contradict the state's vision of Islam. The state's constant issuing of warnings of the possible spread of radical Islamic ideas from overseas, the constant airing of concerns about home-grown terrorism through Friday sermons issued by MUIS and the dissemination of messages for friends and families to always be on the lookout for the indicative signs of radicalisation have resulted in the restraining of open and frank discussions about taboo topics such as 'Islam and politics', 'Islam and secularism', and the notion of a globalised Islam.

Conclusion

It is obvious from the preceding discussion that the three states within Muslim Southeast Asia have yet to fully realise the ideal of being 'responsible cosmopolitan states'. Their inability to be cosmopolitan and to foster Muslim cosmopolitanism is the upshot of their historical experiences with Muslims locally and regionally, just as it is a consequence of the different secular frames of reference which they have adopted for the management of Muslims. That these states have yet to become responsible cosmopolitan states is unsurprising given that the very notion of cosmopolitanism runs contrary to what most states stand for. States often seek to impose a sense of allegiance and loyalty that would glue society together to achieve the state's ends. Conversely, 'cosmopolitanism stands for openness, non-exclusivity, cultural pluralism and citizenship which is – partly at least – decoupled from culture'.[77] This disjuncture becomes even more paralysing when the states embrace secularist stances that are illiberal, authoritarian and prejudiced, and that privilege one group in society over others. We may safely conclude that the survival of Muslim cosmopolitanism in Southeast Asia since the creation of the nation-states has been the product of the will of ordinary Muslims, along with their non-Muslim compatriots, to rise above state provincialism. We can only hope that states in Muslim Southeast Asia will eventually manifest the legacies and cosmopolitan outlooks of their predecessors.

Notes

1. Angela Taraborrelli, *Contemporary Cosmopolitanism* (London: Bloomsbury Academic, 2011), pp. 57–9.
2. Garrett Wallace Brown, 'Bringing the State Back into Cosmopolitanism: The Idea of Responsible Cosmopolitan States', *Political Studies Review*, 9, 1 (2011), pp. 64–5.
3. Brown, 'Bringing the State Back into Cosmopolitanism', p. 55.
4. For a fine study of such fusion of influences, see Maziar Mozaffari Falarti, *Malay*

Kingship in Kedah: Religion, Trade, and Society (Lanham, MD: Lexington Books, 2013).

5. Lakshmi Subramanian, 'Commerce, Circulation and Consumption: Indian Ocean Communities in Historical Perspective', in Shanti Moorthy and Ashraf Jamal (eds), *Indian Ocean Studies: Cultural, Social and Political Perspectives* (London: Routledge, 2010), pp. 136–57.

6. Anthony C. Milner, *The Malays* (Oxford: Wiley-Blackwell, 2008), p. 71.

7. Colin Jack-Hinton, 'Marco Polo in South-East Asia: A Preliminary Essay in Reconstruction', *Journal of Southeast Asian History*, 5, 2, (1964), pp. 64–7.

8. Anthony H. Johns, 'Islamization in Southeast Asia: Reflections and Reconsiderations with Reference to the Role of Sufism', *Southeast Asian Studies*, 30, 1 (1993), pp. 43–61.

9. Al-Attas, *Preliminary Statement*, pp. 29–30.

10. Anthony Reid, *A History of Southeast Asia: Critical Crossroads* (Oxford: Wiley-Blackwell, 2015), p. 110.

11. Shamsul Amri Baharuddin, 'One State, Three Legal Systems: Social Cohesion in a Multi-ethnic and Multi-religious Malaysia', in Adam Possamai, James T. Richardson and Bryan S. Turner (eds), *The Sociology of Shari'a: Case Studies from Around the World* (London: Springer, 2015), p. 21.

12. John M. Gullick, *Rulers and Residents: Influence and Power in the Malay State, 1870–1920* (Kuala Lumpur: Oxford University Press, 1992).

13. Dan Slater, *Ordering Power: Contentious Politics and Authoritarian Leviathan in Southeast Asia* (New York: Cambridge University Press, 2010), pp. 33–54.

14. Talal Asad, *Formations of the Secular: Christianity, Islam, Modernity* (Stanford, CA: Stanford University Press, 2003), p. 199.

15. Max Weber, *Economy and Society: An Outline of Interpretive Sociology*, edited by Guenther Roth and Calus Wittich (Berkeley: University of California Press, 1978), p. 56.

16. Sharon Siddique and Leo Suryadinata, 'Bumiputra and Pribumi: Economic Nationalism (Indiginism) in Malaysia and Indonesia', *Pacific Affairs*, 54, 4 (1981–2), pp. 663–74.

17. Joshua Barker and Gerry van Klinken, 'Reflections on the State in Indonesia', in Gerry van Klinken and Joshua Barker (eds), *State of Authority: The State in Society in Indonesia* (Ithaca, NY: Cornell Southeast Asia Program Publications, 2009), p. 23.

18. Susan S. Purdy, 'The Civil Religion Thesis as it Applies to a Pluralistic Society:

Pancasila Democracy in Indonesia', *Journal of International Affairs*, 36, 2 (1982), pp. 307–16.

19. Quoted in Daniel S. Lev, *Islamic Courts in Indonesia: A Study of Political Bases of Institutions* (Berkeley: University of California Press, 1972), p. 40. See also Eka Darmaputera, *Pancasila and the Search for Modernity and Identity in Indonesian Society* (Leiden: Brill, 1988), p. 163, for an argument that the Indonesian state is neither theocratic nor totally secular.

20. Judith Nagata, 'Authority and Democracy in Malaysian and Indonesian Movements', in Johan Saravanamuttu (ed.), *Islam and Politics in Southeast Asia* (London: Routledge, 2010), pp. 18–45.

21. Chiara Formichi, *Islam and the Making of the Nation: Kartosuwiryo and Political Islam in Twentieth-Century Indonesia* (Leiden: KITLV Press, 2012).

22. Edward Aspinall, *Opposing Suharto: Compromise, Resistance, and Regime Change in Indonesia* (Stanford, CA: Stanford University Press, 2005), pp. 39–40.

23. Melissa Crouch, *Law and Religion in Indonesia: Conflict and the Courts in West Java* (London: Routledge, 2014), p. 88, and Nadirsyah Hosen, 'Behind the Scenes: Fatwas of Majelis Ulama Indonesia (1975–1998)', *Islamic Studies*, 15, 2 (2004), pp. 147–79.

24. Mohammad Kamal Hassan, *Muslim Intellectual Response to New Order Modernization in Indonesia* (Kuala Lumpur: Dewan Bahasa dan Pustaka, 1980), pp. 94–5.

25. Martin van Bruneissen, 'Genealogies of Islamic Radicalism in Post-Suharto Indonesia', *South East Asia Research*, 10, 2 (2002), p. 132, and Taufik Abdullah, *Indonesia: Towards Democracy* (Singapore: ISEAS Press, 2009), p. 454.

26. Hefner, *Civil Islam*, pp. 79–85 and pp. 120–1.

27. David Camroux, 'State Responses to Islamic Resurgence in Malaysia: Accommodation, Co-option, and Confrontation', *Asian Survey*, 36, 9 (1996), pp. 852–68.

28. Nurcholish Madjid, *Islam, Kemodernan, dan Keindonesiaan* (Bandung, Indonesia: Mizan, 1987), p. 204. See also Robert W. Hefner, 'Islam, State, and Civil Society: ICMI and the Struggle for the Indonesian Middle Class', *Indonesia*, 56 (1993), pp. 1–36.

29. Arskal Salim, *Challenging the Secular State: Islamization of Law in Modern Indonesia* (Honolulu: University of Hawai'i Press, 2008), p. 50.

30. Madjid, 'Islamic Roots of Modern Pluralism', pp. 76–7.

31. Verena Beittinger-Lee, *(Un)Civil Society and Political Change in Indonesia: A Contested Arena* (London: Routledge, 2009), pp. 110–11. For more information

on the Jakarta Charter, see Saifuddin Ansari, *The Jakarta Charter of June 1945* (Kuala Lumpur: Muslim Youth Movement of Malaysia, 1979).

32. Robert E. Elson, 'Nationalism, Islam, "Secularism" and the State in Contemporary Indonesia', *Australian Journal of International Affairs*, 64, 3 (2010), p. 328.

33. Kees van Dijk, 'The Good, the Bad and the Ugly: Explaining the Unexplainable: *Amuk Massa* in Indonesia', in Freek Colombijn and J. Thomas Lindblad (eds), *Roots of Violence in Indonesia: Contemporary Violence in Historical Perspective* (Leiden: KITLV Press, 2002), pp. 277–98.

34. See the following collection of essays: Damien Kingsbury and Harry Aveling (eds), *Autonomy and Disintegration in Indonesia* (London: Routledge, 2003).

35. Marcus Mietzner, 'Indonesia: Yudhoyono's Legacy between Stability and Stagnation', in *Southeast Asian Affairs* (Singapore: ISEAS Press, 2012), p. 123.

36. Ben Otto and Sara Schonhardt, 'Islamic Political Parties Make a Comeback in Indonesian Election', *Wall Street Journal*, 10 April 2014, <http://www.wsj.com/articles/SB10001424052702303873604579493311138076926> (last accessed 22 February 2016).

37. Abdul Aziz Bari, 'Religion, Law and Governance in Malaysia', *Islam and Civilisational Renewal*, 2, 1 (2010), p. 75.

38. Johan Saravanamuttu, 'Malaysia: Multicultural Society, Islamic State, or What?', in Michael Heng Siam-Heng and Ten Chin Liew (eds), *State and Secularism: Perspectives from Asia* (Singapore: World Scientific Publishing, 2010), p. 289.

39. Jomo Kwame Sundaram, *The New Economic Policy and Inter-relations in Malaysia* (New York: United Nations Research Institute for Development, 2004).

40. Ariffin Omar, 'Origins and Development of the Affirmative Policy in Malaya and Malaysia: A Historical Overview', *Kajian Malaysia*, 21, 2–3 (2003), pp. 13–29.

41. Sven Schottmann, 'The Pillars of "Mahathir's Islam": Mahathir Mohamad on Being-Muslim in the Modern World', *Asian Studies Review*, 35, 3 (2011), pp. 355–72.

42. See, for example, Clive Kessler, 'Islam, State and Desecularization in Malaysia: The Islamist Trajectory During the Badawi Years', in Norani Othman, Mavis C. Puthucheary and Clive Kessler (eds), *Sharing the Nation: Faith, Difference, Power and the State 50 Years After Merdeka* (Selangor, Malaysia: SIRD, 2008), p. 61.

43. Maznah Mohamad, 'The Ascendance of Bureaucratic Islam and the Secularization of the Sharia in Malaysia', *Pacific Affairs*, 83, 3 (2010), p. 506.

44. Ahmad Fauzi Abdul Hamid, 'Patterns of State Interaction with Islamic Movements in Malaysia During the Formative Years of Islamic Resurgence', *Southeast Asian Studies*, 44, 4 (2007), p. 456.

45. Helen Ting, 'Malaysian Textbooks and the Discourse of *Ketuanan Melayu*', in Daniel P. S. Goh et al. (eds), *Race and Multiculturalism in Malaysia and Singapore* (London: Routledge, 2009), pp. 36–52.

46. Editorial, 'BN, Pakatan Breakdown May Lead to Racial, Religious Splits, Canadian Journalist Warns', *Malay Mail Online*, 27 June 2015, <http://www. themalaymailonline.com/malaysia/article/bn-pakatan-breakdown-may-lead-to-racial-religious-splits-canadian-journalis> (last accessed 24 February 2016) and Bridget Welsh, 'Elections in Malaysia: Voting Behaviour and Electoral Integrity', in Meredith L. Weiss (ed.), *Routledge Handbook of Contemporary Malaysia* (London: Routledge, 2015), pp. 18–19.

47. Charles Allers, *Anwar Ibrahim: The Evolution of a Muslim Democrat* (Singapore: Monsoon Books, 2013), p. 197.

48. Barry Wain, *The Malaysian Maverick: Mahathir Mohamad in Turbulent Times* (Basingstoke: Palgrave Macmillan, 2012), p. 62.

49. Zaid Ibrahim, 'No More Discrimination Please', *The Zaidgeist* [blog], 13 March 2015, <http://www.zaid.my/current/no-more-discrimination-please/> (last accessed 24 February 2016).

50. Hikue Hamayotsu, 'Islam and Nation-building in Southeast Asia: Malaysia and Indonesia in Comparative Perspective', *Pacific Affairs*, 75, 3 (2002), p. 358.

51. Liow, *Piety and Politics*, pp. 57–8.

52. Editorial, 'No Place for Wahabism in Malaysia, Fatwa Council Says', *Malay Mail Online*, 1 March 2015, <http://www.themalaymailonline.com/malaysia/article/no-place-for-wahhabism-in-malaysia-fatwa-council-says> (last accessed 24 February 2016).

53. See Erica Chenoweth and Maria J. Stephan, *Why Civil Resistance Works: The Strategic Logic of Nonviolent Conflict* (New York: Columbia University Press, 2011), pp. 85–197.

54. Baharuddin, 'One State, Three Legal Systems', p. 28.

55. In-Won Hwang, *Personalized Politics: The Malaysian State Under Mahathir* (Singapore: ISEAS Press, 2003), p. 246.

56. Jonathan Fox, *Political Secularism, Religion, and the State* (Cambridge: Cambridge University Press, 2015), p. 44–7.

57. Sophie Brown, 'Malaysian Court to Christians: You Can't Say "Allah"', CNN,

24 June 2014, <http://edition.cnn.com/2014/06/24/world/asia/malaysia-allah-ban/> (last accessed 26 February 2016).

58. Karel Steenbrink, *Catholics in Indonesia: A Documented History, 1808–1900* (Leiden: KITLV Press, 2003), p. 1.

59. Eugene K. B. Tan, 'Keeping God in Place: The Management of Religion in Singapore', in Lai Ah Eng (ed.), *Religious Diversity in Singapore* (Singapore: ISEAS Press, 2008), pp. 66–7.

60. Kenneth Paul Tan, 'Pragmatic Secularism, Civil Religion, and Political Legitimacy in Singapore', in Michael Heng Siam-Heng and Ten Chin Liew (eds), *State and Secularism: Perspectives from Asia* (Singapore: World Scientific Publishing, 2010), pp. 339–57, and Thio Li-Ann, 'Control, Co-optation and Cooperation: Managing Religious Harmony in Singapore's Multi-ethnic, Quasi-secular State', *Hastings Constitutional Law Quarterly*, 33 (2005), p. 200. Critics of such notions of state secularism in Singapore have yet to devise any radical alternatives to the prevailing conceptions, other than to argue that the state approach to secularism is 'muscular'and 'interventionist' and to say that it seeks to calibrate religion to suit its secular interests. See Walid Jumblatt Abdullah, 'Religious Representation in Secular Singapore: A Case Study of MUIS and PERGAS', *Asian Survey*, 53, 6 (2013), pp. 1182–204.

61. Nasir et al., *Muslims in Singapore*, p. 10.

62. Han Fook Kwang et al., *Lee Kuan Yew: Hard Truths to Keep Singapore Going* (Singapore: Straits Times Press, 2011), p. 228.

63. Khairudin Aljunied, *Colonialism, Violence and Muslims in Southeast Asia: The Maria Hertogh Controversy and Its Aftermath* (London: Routledge, 2009), p. 1.

64. The 'Maria Hertogh controversy' was one of the most deadly ethnic riots in Singapore's history, which broke out outside the Singapore High Court on 11 December 1950. The main driving force behind this explosion of violence was a fourteen-year-old girl, Maria Hertogh, who, after having been separated for more than seven years from her Dutch Catholic parents and raised as a Muslim in a Malay family, was ordered by a British judge to return to the Netherlands. Sensational press coverage about the legal case and the girl's brief stay at a Catholic convent heightened Muslim and non-Muslim sensitivities in Singapore. Exacerbating the already volatile situation were the activities of rabble-rousers and the British court's annulment of the marriage between Maria Hertogh and a Malay teacher, Mansoor Adabi, in the midst of the legal proceedings, which, in effect, provoked Muslims in the colony to resort to violence. Sporadic attacks directed against an ineffective police force quickly escalated into widespread

incidents of murder and other forms of brutality, with Europeans and Eurasians the main targets. Dozens of buildings and scores of vehicles were burned as the riots rapidly spread across the entire island. By the time the bloodshed was brought to an end on 13 December, eighteen people were dead, while over a hundred had suffered injuries and at least a thousand others had been incarcerated.

65. James C. Scott, *Seeing Like a State: How Certain Schemes to Improve the Human Condition Have Failed* (New Haven, CT: Yale University Press, 1998), p. 1.
66. Lily Zubaidah Rahim, *Singapore in the Malay World: Building and Breaching Regional Bridges* (London: Routledge, 2009), p. 57.
67. Alon Peled, *A Question of Loyalty: Military Manpower Policy in Multiethnic States* (Ithaca, NY: Cornell University Press, 1998), pp. 93–125.
68. Majlis Ugama Islam Singapura, 'Serving Our Community, Better', MUIS Annual Report 2013, <http://www.muis.gov.sg/documents/Annual_Reports/muis-html/index.html> (last accessed 6 March 2016).
69. Charlene Tan, '(Re)imagining the Muslim Identity in Singapore', *Studies in Ethnicity and Nationalism*, 8, 1 (2008), pp. 33–6.
70. Mutalib, *Islam in Southeast Asia*, p. 55.
71. Kersten Steiner, 'Governing Islam: The State, the Administration of Muslim Law Act (AMLA) and Islam in Singapore', *Australian Journal of Asian Law*, 16, 1 (2015), p. 6.
72. Editorial, 'Collective Effort Needed to Safeguard Racial, Religious Harmony in Singapore: Shanmugam', *The Straits Times*, 19 January 2016.
73. Nurul Izzah Aripin, 'Banned? Well-known Islamic Cleric's Absence from Singapore Conference Leads to Speculation', Yahoo! News, 4 December 2015, <https://sg.news.yahoo.com/banned--well-known-islamic-cleric-s-absence-from-singapore-conference-leads-to-speculation-101926407.html> (last accessed 24 February 2016).
74. Alan Collins, *Security and Southeast Asia: Domestic, Regional, and Global Issues* (Singapore: ISEAS Press, 2003), pp. 63–92.
75. Editorial, 'Self-radicalised Singaporeans Who Were Previously Detained', *The Straits Times*, 29 May 2015.
76. Jothie Rajah, *Authoritarian Rule of Law: Legislation, Discourse, and Legitimacy in Singapore* (New York: Cambridge University Press, 2012), p. 243.
77. Zlatko Skrbiš and Ian Woodward, *Cosmopolitanism: Uses of the Idea* (London: Sage, 2013), p. 29.

CONCLUSION:
THE VISION OF MUSLIM
COSMOPOLITANISM

Vivid and disturbing images of women and children dying in Syria, Yemen and Palestine were flashing across the digital media as this book was being written. The popular press around the world condemned such atrocities as acts of war against humanity. As all eyes are riveted to the Middle East in the aftermath of the Arab Spring, questions are now being asked about the possibility that other parts of the Muslim World, including Southeast Asia, might soon descend into chaos. Tales of fanatical Muslims inspired by their Arab brethren and bent upon overthrowing secular regimes abound in journals and books. The image of religion trying to tear the region apart seems more real than ever before. Seeming to lend credence, yet again, to Samuel Huntington's thesis on the imminent 'clash of civilizations',[1] such prognoses paint a dark picture of the future of Muslim Southeast Asia. Predictions about religious groups losing control over their own kind are used by states to justify interference in all aspects of the religious and cultural lives of Muslims.

However, the experiences on the ground are different from the imaginations of promoters of the 'terrorism industry'.[2] As I have shown in this book, Muslim cosmopolitanism has provided Southeast Asians with the vision and vocabulary to come together, rather than to become increasingly divided, in the age of the networked society. Muslim cosmopolitanism has thrived in numerous places. In markets across Muslim Southeast Asia, people have traded with one another regardless of their backgrounds. The organisation of these markets, coupled with the presence of multicultural populations that have resulted from a long history of travel and migration, made contact between locals and foreigners, men and women, Muslims and non-Muslims all possible without inhibition.

If markets planted the seeds of Muslim cosmopolitanism, mosques further enlivened it. Incorporating styles and forms drawn from different traditions and influences, mosques in Muslim Southeast Asia mirrored the cosmopolitan outlook and temperaments of society at large. Many of these mosques were built close to temples and churches. Mosques have, therefore, functioned not just as sanctuaries for the devoted, but also as bridges for believers from diverse faiths to share their unique worldviews, and as platforms where women can pursue their religious goals.

In the virtual world, blogs are powerful spaces where ideas about Muslim cosmopolitanism are discussed and conveyed in ways that have piqued the sensibilities of Southeast Asians. Muslim bloggers have battled with negative media images of Islam to reinstate the universality of Islam. They have written about transcending the differences within their own communities and agitate for the forging of close ties with non-Muslims. Much like markets and mosques, blogs have served as influential avenues where Muslims and non-Muslims internalise the ethics of mutual respect and reciprocity.

Blogs reveal the importance of personas in amplifying the ideals of Muslim cosmopolitanism. Among those personas are the public intellectuals who deliberated on concepts that shaped Muslim and non-Muslim ideas about Islam and Muslim societies. Qur'anic justice, Islam Nusantara and Islamic assertiveness are among the many concepts that cosmopolitan Muslim public intellectuals have developed and discoursed upon to argue for the creation of an open and inclusive society. Their life experiences and the challenges that they faced as persons who spoke truth to power lent added weight to their writings. The concepts that these public intellectuals deliberated over have been complemented by the work of grass-roots activists.

Most prominent among those activists are women wearing the hijab. Cast aside and stigmatised by their own families and communities for some decades, headscarved Muslim women have engaged in the narration of their life stories to create more awareness about their struggles to gain respect and equality. Beyond their words and thoughts, they have coloured and expanded the frontiers of Muslim cosmopolitanism by introducing new hijab styles and fashions that draw on global influences as well as local culture. In advocating for their rights to wear hijab in the workplace and by showing that head-scarved women can be as successful as other people in their educational, social and professional pursuits, hijabi activists underscore the fact that no country can be considered cosmopolitan if women with pieces of cloth draped over their heads and across their shoulders remain marginalised.

Even though authoritarian regimes have, time and again, placed barriers around communities in order to make them subservient to secularising and nationalist ends, that local societies are still strongly linked is the most profound indication of the continued vitality of Muslim cosmopolitanism in Southeast Asia. Together, Muslim cosmopolitans have struggled to overcome the schemes of powerful states and their attempts to constrict Muslim cosmopolitanism through pragmatic, partisan and provincial secular policies. Muslim cosmopolitans have contested the secular states' 'sovereign power to reorganize substantive features of religious life, stipulating what religion is or ought to be, assigning its proper content, and disseminating concomitant subjectivities, ethnical frameworks, and quotidian practices'.[3] They have used the many tools at their disposal, including religious sites, social media, treatises and dress codes, to keep cosmopolitan ideals alive. They have benefited much from the agency of the non-Muslims in their midst to withstand the intolerance of radical and extremist groups in Muslim Southeast Asia.

Still, much work needs to be done to expand the scope of studies of Muslim cosmopolitanism. One step to achieve this is to radically adjust our scales of observation as we study Muslim societies in Southeast Asia and the world. There is an overarching need, as Veena Das has reminded us, to move beyond the overriding preoccupation with eventful episodes of violence and conflict, to instead look closely at the ordinary and everyday instances of mutual aid between communities.[4] We need to consciously shift away from (but not totally ignore) drawn-out studies of bloodshed and violent groups, to look instead at how Muslims and non-Muslims have come together and forged a common destiny. However, doing so requires us to reframe questions about interactions between peoples of different faiths as experienced at the everyday level and to highlight moments of collaboration, peace and partnership.

There is little doubt that the prevailing intellectual climate may not be too kind towards research on issues that are perceived as mundane or not sensational, or to studies that do not strike a high chord in the ears of policymakers. It is thus the responsibility of intellectuals to resist the pressures of sensationalism, to deflate the overblown fears and unsettle the commonplace assumptions about Muslims. We must put forward a vision of a society that can bind us closer together as human beings. I call it the 'vision of Muslim cosmopolitanism'.

Notes

1. Samuel Huntington, *The Clash of Civilizations and the Remaking of World Order* (New York: Simon & Schuster, 1996).
2. John Mueller, *Overblown: How Politicians and the Terrorism Industry Inflate National Security Threats, and Why We Believe Them* (New York: The Free Press, 2006).
3. Saba Mahmood, *Religious Difference in a Secular Age: A Minority Report* (Princeton, NJ: Princeton University Press, 2016), p. 3.
4. Veena Das, *Violence and the Descent into the Ordinary* (Berkeley: University of California Press, 2007), pp. 7–8.

BIBLIOGRAPHY

Abaza, Mona, 'A Mosque of Arab Origin in Singapore: History, Functions and Networks', *Archipel*, 57 (1993), pp. 61–83.

——, *Debates on Islam and Knowledge in Islam and Egypt: Shifting Worlds* (London: Routledge, 2002).

Abbott, Jason, 'Hype or Hubris? The Political Impact of the Internet and Social Networking in Southeast Asia', in William Case (ed.), *Routledge Handbook of Southeast Asian Democratization* (London: Routledge, 2015), pp. 201–22.

Abdul Hamid, Ahmad Fauzi, 'Patterns of State Interaction with Islamic Movements in Malaysia During the Formative Years of Islamic Resurgence', *Southeast Asian Studies*, 44, 4 (2007), pp. 444–65.

Abdullah, Taufik, *Indonesia: Towards Democracy* (Singapore: ISEAS Press, 2009).

Abshar-Abdalla, Ulil, 'Menyegarkan Kembali Pemahaman Islam', *Kompass*, 18 November 2002.

Abdullah, Walid Jumblatt, 'Religious Representation in Secular Singapore: A Case Study of MUIS and PERGAS', *Asian Survey*, 53, 6 (2013), pp. 1182–204.

Abdullah, Zain Azura, 'Saya Dipengaruhi Majalah Nida'ul Islam', in Ir. Endok Sempo Mohd Tahir (ed.), *Bagaimana Akhirnya Saya Bertudung* (Selangor, Malaysia: PTS Millenia, 2010), pp. 84–5.

Abu-Nimer, Mohammed, 'Framework for Nonviolence and Peacebuilding in Islam', in Abdul Aziz Said, Mohamed Abu-Nimer and Meena Sharify-Funk (eds), *Contemporary Islam: Dynamic Not Static* (London: Routledge, 2006), pp. 131–72.

Ahmad, A. Ghafar, 'The Architectural Styles of Mosques in Malaysia: From Vernacular to Modern Structures', in Muhammad ibn Abdullah ibn Salih, Abdul Hafiz Fida Muhammad Quqani and Jamiᶜat al-Malik al-Saᶜud (eds), *Proceedings of the Symposium on Mosque Architecture: The Historic and Urban Developments of Mosque Architecture*, vol. 2 (Saudi Arabia: King Saud University, 1999), pp. 147–63.

Ahmad, Muhammad Bin, Muhammad Nasri Bin Md. Hussain, Rizal Palil and Noor Hashimah Binti Dolah, 'The Islamic Image of a Marketplace in Malaysia: A Case Study Presentation', *South East Asia Journal of Contemporary Business, Economics and Law*, 2, 1 (2013), pp. 86–8.

Ahmed, Leila, *A Quiet Revolution: The Veil's Resurgence, from the Middle East to America* (New Haven, CT: Yale University Press, 2011).

Alagappa, Muthiah, 'Civil Society and Political Change: An Analytical Framework', in Muthiah Alagappa (ed.), *Civil Society and Political Change in Asia: Expanding and Contracting Democratic Space* (Stanford, CA: Stanford University Press, 2004), pp. 25–60.

Alatas, Syed Hussein, *Intellectuals in Developing Societies* (London: Frank Cass, 1977).

____, *The Myth of the Lazy Native* (London: Frank Cass, 1977).

Al-Attas, Syed Muhammad Naquib, *Preliminary Statement on a General Theory of the Islamization of the Malay-Indonesian Archipelago* (Kuala Lumpur: Dewan Bahasa dan Pustaka, 1969).

Alavi, Seema, *Muslim Cosmpolitanism in the Age of Empire* (Cambridge, MA: Harvard University Press, 2015).

Ali, Mary C., 'Tudung Menindas Wanita?', in Ir. Endok Sempo Mohd Tahir (ed.), *Bagaimana Akhirnya Saya Bertudung* (Selangor, Malaysia: PTS Millenia, 2010), pp. 143–7.

Aljunied, Khairudin, *Colonialism, Violence and Muslims in Southeast Asia: The Maria Hertogh Controversy and its Aftermath* (London: Routledge, 2009).

——, 'The "Other" Muhammadiyah Movement: Singapore, 1958–2008', *Journal of Southeast Asian Studies*, 42, 2 (2011), pp. 281–302.

——, 'Tools of Conflict, Levers of Cohesion: Culture and Religion in Muslim Southeast Asia', in Joseph Camilleri and Sven Schottmann (eds), *Culture, Religion and Conflict in Muslim Southeast Asia* (London: Routledge, 2012), pp. 179–91.

——, 'Writing Reformist Histories: A Cleric as an Outsider-History Maker', *The Public Historian*, 37, 3 (2015), pp. 10–28.

Aljunied, Khairudin, and Rommel Curaming, 'Mediating and Consuming the

Memories of Violence in the Philippines', *Critical Asian Studies*, 44, 1 (2012), pp. 227–50.

——, 'Social Memory and State–Civil Society Relations in the Philippines: Forgetting and Remembering Jabidah "Massacre"', *Time and Society*, 21, 1 (2012), pp. 89–103.

——, 'The Uneven Topography of Personal Memory', in Kah Seng Loh, Stephen Dobbs and Ernest Koh (eds), *Oral History in Southeast Asia: Memories and Fragments* (New York: Palgrave Macmillan, 2013), pp. 83–100.

Allers, Charles, *Anwar Ibrahim: The Evolution of a Muslim Democrat* (Singapore: Monsoon Books, 2013).

Allport, Gordon, *The Nature of Prejudice* (Reading: Addison-Wesley, 1979 [1954]).

Amer, Sahar, *What is Veiling?* (Chapel Hill: University of North Carolina Press, 2014).

Ananta, Aris, and Richard Barichello (eds), *Poverty and Global Recession in Southeast Asia* (Singapore: ISEAS Press, 2012).

Andaya, Barbara, *The Flaming Womb: Repositioning Women in Early Modern Southeast Asia* (Honolulu: University of Hawai'i Press, 2006).

Andaya, Barbara Watson, and Leonard Y. Andaya, *A History of Early Modern Southeast Asia, 1400–1830* (Cambridge: Cambridge University Press, 2015).

Andaya, Leonard Y., *Leaves of the Same Tree: Trade and Ethnicity in the Straits of Melaka* (Honolulu: University of Hawai'i Press, 2008).

Ansari, Saifuddin, *The Jakarta Charter of June 1945* (Kuala Lumpur: Muslim Youth Movement of Malaysia, 1979).

Anwar, Zainah, *Islamic Revivalism in Malaysia:* Dakwah *Among the Students* (Petaling Jaya, Malaysia: Pelanduk Publications, 1987).

Appiah, Anthony, *Cosmopolitanism: Ethics in a World of Strangers* (New York: Norton, 2006).

Arnold, Thomas W., *The Preaching of Islam* (Lahore: Ashraf, 1961).

Asad, Talal, *Formations of the Secular: Christianity, Islam, Modernity* (Stanford, CA: Stanford University Press, 2003).

Aspinall, Edward, *Opposing Suharto: Compromise, Resistance, and Regime Change in Indonesia* (Stanford, CA: Stanford University Press, 2005).

Auda, Jasser, *Maqasid al-Shari'ah: A Beginner's Guide* (London: International Institute of Islamic Thought, 2008).

Azman, Azim, 'Isetan Apologises Over the Treatment of Promoter in Tudung', *The New Paper*, 15 July 2014.

Azra, Azyumardi, *Esei-esei Intelektual Muslim dan Pendidikan Islam* (Ciputat, Indonesia: PT Logos Wacana Ilmu, 1998).

——, *Konteks Berteologi di Indonesia: Pengalaman Islam* (Jakarta: Penerbit Paramadina, 1999).

——, *Renaisans Islam Asia Tenggara: Sejarah Wacana dan Kekuasaan* (Bandung: PT Remaja Rosdakarya, 1999).

——, 'Islam di Tengah Arus Transisi Menuju Demokrasi', in Abdul Mun'im D. Z. (ed.), *Islam Di Tengah Arus Transisi* (Jakarta: Kompas, 2000), pp. xxiii–xxix.

——, *Historiografi Islam Kontemporer: Wacana, Aktualitas, dan Aktor Sejarah* (Jakarta: Penerbit Gramedia, 2002).

——, *Islam Nusantara: Jaringan Global dan Lokal* (Jakarta: Mizan Press, 2002).

——, *Konflik Baru Antar Peradaban: Globalisasi, Radikalisme dan Pluralitas* (Jakarta: PT RajaGrafindo Persada, 2002).

——, *Paradigma Baru Pendidikan Nasional: Reconstruksi dan Demokratisasi* (Jakarta: Penerbit Buku Kompas, 2002).

——, *Reposisi Hubungan Agama dan Negara: Merajut Hubungan Antaraumat* (Jakarta: Penerbit Buku Kompas, 2002).

——, *The Origins of Islamic Reformism in Southeast Asia: Networks of Malay-Indonesian and Middle Eastern Ulama in the Seventeenth and Eighteenth Centuries* (Honolulu: University of Hawai'i Press, 2004).

——, *Dari Harvard hingga Makkah* (Jakarta: Penerbit Republika, 2005).

——, 'Islamic Thought: Theory, Concepts and Doctrine in the Context of Southeast Asian Islam', in K. S. Nathan and Mohammad Hashim Kamali (eds), *Islam in Southeast Asia: Political, Social and Strategic Challenges for the 21st Century* (Singapore: ISEAS Press, 2005), pp. 3–21.

——, *Indonesia, Islam, and Democracy: Dynamics in a Global Context* (Jakarta: Solstice Publishing, 2006).

——, *Jejak-Jejak Jaringan Kaum Muslimin: Dari Australia hingga Timur Tengah* (Jakarta: Penerbit Hikmah, 2007).

——, 'Religious Pluralism in Indonesia: The Impact of Democracy on Conflict Resolution', in K. S. Nathan (ed.), *Religious Pluralism in Democratic Societies: Challenges and Prospects for Southeast Asia, Europe, and the United States in the New Millennium* (Singapore: Konrad-Adenauer-Stiftung and Malaysian Association for American Studies [MAAS], 2007), pp. 225–36.

Az-Zahra, Shahidah Nafishah, *Persoalan Wanita: Pemakaian Hijab, Batas-Batas Aurat dan Pergaulan, serta Urusan Dalam Rumahtangga* (Penang, Malaysia: Mulia Terang, 2012).

Baharuddin, Shamsul Amri, 'One State, Three Legal Systems: Social Cohesion in a Multi-ethnic and Multi-religious Malaysia', in Adam Possamai, James T. Richardson and Bryan S. Turner (eds), *The Sociology of* Shari'a: *Case Studies from Around the World* (London: Springer, 2015), pp. 17–30.

Bari, Abdul Aziz, 'Religion, Law and Governance in Malaysia', *Islam and Civilisational Renewal*, 2, 1 (2010), pp. 60–77.

Barker, Joshua, and Gerry van Klinken, 'Reflections on the State in Indonesia', in Gerry van Klinken and Joshua Barker (eds), *State of Authority: The State in Society in Indonesia* (Ithaca, NY: Cornell Southeast Asia Program Publications, 2009), pp. 17–46.

Barnett, Ronald, 'Academics as Intellectuals', in Dolan Cummings (ed.), *The Changing Role of the Public Intellectual* (London: Routledge, 2005), pp. 108–22.

Basarudin, Azza, *Humanizing the Sacred: Sisters in Islam and the Struggle for Gender Justice* (Seattle: University of Washington Press, 2016).

Bayat, Asef, *Life as Politics: How Ordinary People Change the Middle East* (Amsterdam: Amsterdam University Press, 2010).

Beck, Ulrich, *Cosmopolitan Vision* (Cambridge: Polity Press, 2006).

——, *A God of One's Own: Religion's Capacity for Peace and Potential for Violence* (Cambridge: Polity Press, 2010).

Beittinger-Lee, Verena, *(Un)Civil Society and Political Change in Indonesia: A Contested Arena* (London: Routledge, 2009).

Benda-Beckmann, Keebet von, 'Joint Brockerage of Spouses in Islamic Ambon', in Sita van Bemelen, Madelon Djajadiningrat-Nieuwenhuis, Elsbeth Locher-Scholten and Elly Touwen-Bouwsma (eds), *Women and Mediation in Indonesia* (Leiden: KITLV Press, 1992), pp. 13–32.

Bennett, Clinton, *Muslims and Modernity: An Introduction to the Issues and Debates* (London: Continuum, 2005).

Berenschot, Ward, *Riot Politics: Hindu–Muslim Violence and the Indian State* (New York: Columbia University Press, 2011).

Beta, Annisa R., 'Hijabers: How Young Muslim Women Redefine Themselves in Indonesia', *The International Communication Gazette*, 76, 4–5 (2014), pp. 377–89.

Black, Rachel E., *Porta Palazzo: The Anthropology of an Italian Market* (Philadelphia: University of Pennsylvania Press, 2002).

Bourdieu, Pierre, *Acts of Resistance: Against the New Myths of Our Time*, translated by Richard Nice (Cambridge: Polity Press, 1998).

Bowen, John R., *Muslims through Discourse: Religion and Ritual in Gayo Society* (Princeton, NJ: Princeton University Press, 1993).

Brenner, Suzanne, 'Reconstructing Self and Society: Javanese Muslim Women and "The Veil"', *American Ethnologist*, 23, 4 (1996), pp. 673–97.

Brown, Garrett Wallace, 'Bringing the State Back into Cosmopolitanism: The Idea of Responsible Cosmopolitan States', *Political Studies Review*, 9, 1 (2011), pp. 53–66.

Bruneissen, Martin van, 'Genealogies of Islamic Radicalism in Post-Suharto Indonesia', *South East Asia Research*, 10, 2 (2002), pp. 117–54.

Bucar, Elizabeth M., *The Islamic Veil: A Beginner's Guide* (Oxford: Oneworld Publications, 2012).

Bukhari, Muhammad bin Ismail al-, *Translation of the Meanings of 'Sahih al-Bukhari'*, translated by Muhammad Muhsin Khan (Chicago: Kazi Publications, 1997).

Bullock, Katherine, *Rethinking Muslim Women and the Veil: Challenging Historical and Modern Stereotypes* (London: International Institute of Islamic Thought, 2002).

Bunt, Gary, 'Rip. Burn. Pray: Islamic Expression Online', in Lorne R. Dawson and Douglas E. Cowan (eds), *Religion Online: Finding Faith in the Internet* (London: Routledge, 2004).

——, *iMuslims: Rewiring the House of Islam* (Chapel Hill: University of North Carolina Press, 2009).

Camilleri, Joseph, and Sven Schottmann (eds) *Culture, Religion and Conflict in Muslim Southeast Asia: Negotiating Tense Pluralisms* (Abingdon: Routledge, 2012).

Camroux, David, 'State Responses to Islamic Resurgence in Malaysia: Accommodation, Co-option, and Confrontation', *Asian Survey*, 36, 9 (1996), pp. 852–68.

Cangi, Ellen C., 'Civilizing the People of Southeast Asia: Sir Thomas Stamford Raffles' Town Plan for Singapore: 1819–1832', *Planning Perspectives*, 8, 2 (1993), pp. 166–87.

Casanova, José, *Public Religions in the Modern World* (Chicago: University of Chicago Press, 1980).

Castells, Manuel, *The Rise of the Network Society* (Malden, MA: Blackwell, 2000).

——, *The Networked Society*, 2nd edition (Cambridge: Blackwell, 2000).

Causey, Andrew, *Hard Bargaining in Sumatra: Western Travellers and Toba Batak in the Marketplace of Souvenirs* (Honolulu: University of Hawai'i Press, 2003).

Cavanaugh, William T., *The Myth of Religious Violence: Secular Ideology and the Roots of Modern Conflict* (New York: Oxford University Press, 2009).

Chenoweth, Erica, and Maria J. Stephan, *Why Civil Resistance Works: The Strategic Logic of Nonviolent Conflict* (New York: Columbia University Press, 2011).

Choirul Mahfud, 'The Role of the Cheng Ho Mosque: The New Silk Road, Indonesia–China Relations in Islamic Cultural Identity', *Journal of Indonesian Islam*, 8, 1 (2014), pp. 23–38.

Cochrane, Joe, 'Embrace of Atheism Put Indonesian in Prison', *The New York Times*, 3 May 2013.

Collins, Alan, *Security and Southeast Asia: Domestic, Regional, and Global Issues* (Singapore: ISEAS Press, 2003).

The Constitution of Singapore (Singapore: Government Printing Office, 1980 [reprint]).

Cooke, Miriam, 'The Muslimwoman', *Contemporary Islam*, 1, 2 (2007), pp. 139–54.

——, 'Deploying the Muslimwoman', *Journal of Feminist Studies in Religion*, 24, 1 (2008), pp. 91–9.

Crouch, Melissa, *Law and Religion in Indonesia: Conflict and the Courts in West Java* (London: Routledge, 2014).

Daneshgar, Majid, 'The Study of Persian Shi'ism in the Malay-Indonesian World: A Review of Literature from the Nineteenth Century Onwards', *The Journal of Shi'a Studies*, 7, 2 (2014), pp. 191–229.

Darmaputera, Eka, *Pancasila and the Search for Modernity and Identity in Indonesian Society* (Leiden: Brill, 1988).

Das, Veena, *Violence and the Descent into the Ordinary* (Berkeley: University of California Press, 2007).

Delanty, Gerard, *The Cosmopolitan Imagination: The Renewal of Critical Social Theory* (Cambridge: Cambridge University Press, 2009).

Dewi, Kurniawati Hastuti, *Indonesian Women and Local Politics: Islam, Gender and Networks in Post-Suharto Indonesia* (Singapore: NUS Press, 2015).

Dick, Howard W., 'Urban Public Transport: Jakarta, Surabaya and Malang', *Bulletin of Indonesian Economic Studies*, 17, 1 (1981), pp. 66–82.

Dijk, Kees van, 'The Good, the Bad and the Ugly: Explaining the Unexplainable: *amuk massa* in Indonesia', in Freek Colombijn and J. Thomas Lindblad (eds), *Roots of Violence in Indonesia: Contemporary Violence in Historical Perspective* (Leiden: KITLV Press, 2002), pp. 277–98.

Doorn-Harder, Pieternella van, *Women Shaping Islam: Indonesian Women Reading the Qur'an* (Urbana: University of Illinois Press, 2006).

Droogsman, Rachel, 'Redefining Hijab: American Muslim Women's Standpoints on Veiling', *Journal of Applied Communication Research*, 35, 3 (2007), pp. 294–319.

Duruz, Jean, Susan Luckman and Peter Bishop, 'Bazaar Encounters: Food, Markets, Belonging and Citizenship in a Cosmopolitan City', *Continuum: Journal of Media and Communication Studies*, 25, 5 (2011), pp. 599–604.

Editorial, 'Allowing Hijab Problematic for Some Jobs: Yaacob', *Today*, 1 November 2013.

Editorial, 'Collective Effort Needed to Safeguard Racial, Religious Harmony in Singapore: Shanmugam', *The Straits Times*, 19 January 2016.

Editorial, 'Geylang Serai to Turn into a Street of Tradition and Religion for Hari Raya Light Up 2014', *The Straits Times,* 20 June 2014.

Editorial, 'Self-radicalised Singaporeans Who Were Previously Detained', *The Straits Times*, 29 May 2015.

Editorial, 'Siti Nurhaliza Weds Datuk K', *Bernama*, 21 August 2006.

Editorial, 'Temple-Next-To-Mosque Issue Settled, Says Anwar', *Utusan Malaysia*, 28 March 1998.

Eickelman, Dale F., 'Clash of Cultures? Intellectuals, their Publics and Islam', in Stéphane A. Dudoigon, Komatsu Hisao, and Kosugi Yasushi (eds), *Intellectuals in the Modern Islamic World: Transmission, Transformation, Communication* (London: Routledge, 2006), pp. 289–304.

El Guindi, Fadwa, *Veil: Modesty, Privacy and Resistance* (Oxford: Berg, 2009).

El Shamsy, Ahmed, *The Canonization of Islamic Law: A Social and Intellectual History* (Cambridge: Cambridge University Press, 2013).

Elson, Robert E., 'Nationalism, Islam, "Secularism" and the State in Contemporary Indonesia', *Australian Journal of International Affairs*, 64, 3 (2010), pp. 328–43.

Esfandiari, Haleh, *Reconstructed Lives: Women and Iran's Islamic Revolution* (Baltimore, MD: Johns Hopkins University Press, 1997).

Esposito, John L., *The Islamic Threat: Myth or Reality?* (New York: Oxford University Press, 1992).

Esposito, John, and John Voll, *Makers of Contemporary Islam* (Oxford: Oxford University Press, 2001).

Ess, Charles, *Digital Media Ethics* (Cambridge: Polity Press, 2009).

Falarti, Maziar Mozaffari, *Malay Kingship in Kedah: Religion, Trade, and Society* (Lanham, MD: Lexington Books, 2013).

Faruqi, Ismail R. al-, *Islam* (Niles, IL: Argus Communications, 1979).

Federspiel, Howard, 'Contemporary South-East Asian Muslim Intellectuals: An Examination of the Sources for their Concepts and Intellectual Constructs', in

Johan H. Meuleman (ed.), *Islam in the Era of Globalization: Muslim Attitudes Towards Modernity and Identity* (London: RoutledgeCurzon, 2002), pp. 327–50.

——, *Sultans, Shamans, and Saints: Islam and Muslims in Southeast Asia* (Honolulu: University of Hawai'i Press, 2007).

Fischer, Johan, *Islam, Standards, and Technoscience: In Global Halal Zones* (London: Routledge, 2016).

Foreign Desk, 'Muslims, Christians Hold Joint Break Fast Event at Adjoining Mosque, Church in Sarawak's Miri', *The Straits Times*, 4 July 2015.

Forman-Barzilai, Fonna, *Adam Smith and the Circle of Sympathy: Cosmopolitanism and Moral Theory* (Cambridge: Cambridge University Press, 2010).

Formichi, Chiara, *Islam and the Making of the Nation: Kartosuwiryo and Political Islam in Twentieth-Century Indonesia* (Leiden: KITLV Press, 2012).

Formichi, Chiara, and Michael Feener (eds), *Shi'ism in Southeast Asia: 'Alid Piety and Sectarian Constructions* (New York: Oxford University Press, 2015).

Foucault, Michel, *The History of Sexuality, Volume One: An Introduction*, translated by R. Hurley (Harmondsworth, UK: Penguin, 1981).

Fox, Jonathan, *Political Secularism, Religion, and the State* (Cambridge: Cambridge University Press, 2015).

Frisk, Sylvia, *Submitting to God: Women and Islam in Urban Malaysia* (Copenhagen: NIAS Press, 2009).

Furedi, Frank, *Where Have All the Intellectuals Gone?* (London: Continuum, 2004).

George, Cherian, *Contentious Journalism and the Internet: Toward Democratic Discourse in Malaysia and Singapore* (Seattle: University of Washington Press, 2006).

Gilroy, Paul, *After Empire: Melancholia or Convivial Culture?* (London: Routledge, 2004).

Glendinning, Lee, 'Malaysian Blogger Raja Petra Kamarudin Goes on Trial for Sedition Charges', *The Guardian*, 6 October 2008.

Graaf, H. J. de, 'The Origins of the Javanese Mosque', *Journal of Southeast Asian History*, 4, 1 (1963), pp. 1–5.

Green, Paul, 'British Later-Life Migrants in Malaysia', in Michael Janoschka and Heiko Haas (eds), *Contested Spatialities, Lifestyle Migration and Residential Tourism* (London: Routledge, 2014), pp. 145–57.

Gross, Max L., *A Muslim Archipelago: Islam and Politics in Southeast Asia* (Washington, DC: Center for Strategic Intelligence Research, 2007).

Guha, Ranajit, 'The Small Voice of History', in Shahid Amin and Dipesh Chakrabarty (eds), *Subaltern Studies: Writings on South Asian History and Society* 9 (Delhi: Oxford University Press, 1996), pp. 1–12.

Gullick, John M., *Rulers and Residents: Influence and Power in the Malay State, 1870–1920* (Kuala Lumpur: Oxford University Press, 1992).

Haji Idris, Nor Aini, and Faridah Shahadan, 'The Role of Muslim Women Traders in Kelantan', in Mohamed Arif (ed.), *The Muslim Private Sector in Southeast Asia* (Singapore: ISEAS, 1991), pp. 122–51.

Hamayotsu, Hikue, 'Islam and Nation-building in Southeast Asia: Malaysia and Indonesia in Comparative Perspective', *Pacific Affairs*, 75, 3 (2002), pp. 353–75.

Hamdani, Deny, *Anatomy of Muslim Veils: Practice, Discourse and Changing Appearance of Indonesian Women* (Saarbrücken: Lambert Academic Publishing, 2011).

Hamilton-Hart, Natasha, 'Terrorism in Southeast Asia: Expert Analysis, Myopia and Fantasy', *The Pacific Review* 18, 3 (2005), pp. 303–25.

Han, Fook Kwang, Zuraidah Ibrahim, Rachel Lin, Robin Chan, Chua Mui Hoong, Lydia Lim and Ignatius Low, *Lee Kuan Yew: Hard Truths to Keep Singapore Going* (Singapore: Straits Times Press, 2011),

Hanafiah, Djohan, *Masjid Agung Palembang: Sejarah dan Masa Depannya* (Jakarta: CV Haji Masagung, 1988).

Hannerz, Ulf, *Transnational Connections: Culture, People, Places* (London: Routledge, 1996).

Harsaputra, Indra, 'Cheng Ho Mosque, A Symbol of Peace', *The Jakarta Post*, 28 July 2013.

Haryono, Tri Joko Sri, 'Integrasi Etnis Arab dengan Jawa dan Madura di Kampung Ampel Surabaya', *Biokultur*, 2, 1 (2013), pp. 13–26.

Has, Fizi, 'Kawan dari Pakistan Pengaruhi Saya', in Ir. Endok Sempo Mohd Tahir (ed.), *Bagaimana Akhirnya Saya Bertudung* (Selangor, Malaysia: PTS Millenia, 2010), pp. 86–9.

Hasmie, Irma, Halim Hafidz, Bahruddin Bekri, Diana Amir, Heliza Helmi and Raisyyah Rania Yeap, *Hijabista Hijrahsista: Bagaimana Akhirnya Saya Bertudung* (Kuala Lumpur: PTS Litera Utama, 2015).

Hassan, Haniff, 'Islam tidak melarang wanita menjadi pengerusi masjid', *Berita Harian*, 8 October 2011.

Hassan, Mohammad Kamal, *Muslim Intellectual Response to New Order Modernization in Indonesia* (Kuala Lumpur: Dewan Bahasa dan Pustaka, 1980).

Hassim, Nurzihan, 'A Comparative Analysis on *Hijab* Wearing in Malaysian

Muslimah Magazines', *The Journal of the South East Asia Research Center for Communications and Humanities*, 6, 1 (2014) pp. 79–96.

Hefner, Robert W., 'Islam, State, and Civil Society: ICMI and the Struggle for the Indonesian Middle Class', *Indonesia*, 56 (1993), pp. 1–36.

——, *Civil Islam: Muslims and Democratization in Indonesia* (Princeton, NJ: Princeton University Press, 2000).

Henderson, Joan C., 'Islam and Tourism: Brunei, Indonesia, Malaysia and Singapore', in Noel Scott and Jafar Jafari (eds), *Tourism in the Muslim World* (Bingley, UK: Emerald, 2010), pp. 75–89.

Hew, Wai Weng, 'Cosmopolitan Islam and Inclusive Chineseness: Chinese-style Mosques in Indonesia', in Chiara Formichi (ed.), *Religious Pluralism, State and Society in Asia* (London: Routledge, 2013), pp. 175–97.

Ho, Engseng, 'Before Parochialization: Diasporic Arabs Cast in Creole Waters', in Huub de Jonge and Nico Kaptein (eds), *Transcending Borders: Arabs, Politics, Trade and Islam in Southeast Asia* (Leiden: KITLV Press, 2002), pp. 11–35.

——, *The Graves of Tarim: Genealogy and Mobility across the Indian Ocean* (Berkeley: University of California Press, 2006).

Ho, Shirley S., Waipeng Lee and Shahiraa Sahul Hameed, 'Muslim Surfers on the Internet: Using the Theory of Planned Behaviour to Examine the Factors Influencing Engagement in Online Religious Activities', *New Media and Society*, 10, 1 (2008), pp. 93–113.

Hodge, Robert, and Wilfred D'Souza, 'Museums as a Communicator: A Semiotic Analysis of the Western Australian Museum Aboriginal Gallery, Perth', in Eilean Hooper-Greenhill (ed.), *The Educational Role of the Museum* (London: Routledge, 1999), pp. 53–66.

Hosen, Nadirsyah, 'Behind the Scenes: Fatwas of Majelis Ulama Indonesia (1975–1998)', *Islamic Studies*, 15, 2 (2004), pp. 147–79.

Howell, Julia Day, and Martin van Bruinessen, 'Sufism and the "Modern" in Islam', in Julia Day Howell and Martin van Bruinessen (eds), *Sufism and the 'Modern' in Islam* (London: I. B. Tauris, 2007), pp. 1–18.

Huntington, Samuel, *The Clash of Civilizations and the Remaking of World Order* (New York: Simon & Schuster, 1996).

Hussain, Amir, 'Sentence Backdated, Amos Yee Released', *The Straits Times*, 7 July 2015.

Hwang, In-Won, *Personalized Politics: The Malaysian State Under Mahathir* (Singapore: ISEAS Press, 2003).

Idayu, Ida, 'Saya Disindir Hantu Kum-kum', in Ir. Endok Sempo Mohd Tahir (ed.),

Bagaimana Akhirnya Saya Bertudung (Selangor, Malaysia: PTS Millenia, 2010), pp. 137–42.

Indrawati, Ulfa, *Jilbab itu Indah* (Kuala Lumpur: Synergy Media, 2011).

Iqtidar, Humeira, 'Muslim Cosmopolitanism: Contemporary Theory and Social Practice', in Bryan S. Turner (ed.), *The Routledge International Handbook of Globalization Studies* (London: Routledge, 2010), pp. 622–35.

Ismail, Rahil, 'Ramadan and Bussorah Street: The Spirit of Place', *GeoJournal*, 66, 3 (2006), pp. 243–56.

——, '"Di waktu petang di Geylang Serai" Geylang Serai: Maintaining Identity in a Globalised World', in Rahil Ismail, Brian J. Shaw and Ooi Giok Ling (eds), *Heritage in a Globalising World: Diverging Identities in a Dynamic Region* (Surrey: Ashgate 2009), pp. 19–42.

Jack-Hinton, Colin, 'Marco Polo in South-East Asia: A Preliminary Essay in Reconstruction', *Journal of Southeast Asian History*, 5, 2 (1964), pp. 43–103.

Jacobsen, Frode F., *Hadhrami Arabs in Present-Day Indonesia* (London: Routledge, 2009).

James, Carrie, *Disconnected: Youths, New Media, and the Ethics Gap* (Cambridge, MA: MIT Press, 2014).

Jaschok, Maria, and Shui Jingjun, *The History of Women's Mosques in Chinese Islam: A Mosque of Their Own* (Richmond: Curzon Press, 2000).

Johns, Anthony H., 'Islamization in Southeast Asia: Reflections and Reconsiderations with Reference to the Role of Sufism', *Southeast Asian Studies*, 30, 1 (1993), pp. 43–61.

——, 'Sufism in Southeast Asia: Reflections and Reconsiderations', *Journal of Southeast Asian Studies*, 26, 1 (1995), p. 169–83.

Joseph, Roger, 'The Semiotics of the Islamic Mosque', *Arab Studies Quarterly*, 3, 3 (1981), pp. 285–95.

Kamali, Mohammad Hashim, *The Middle Path of Moderation in Islam: The Qur'anic Principle of Wasatiyyah* (New York: Oxford University Press, 2015).

Karim, Karim H., *The Islamic Peril: Media and Global Violence* (New York: Black Rose Books, 2003).

——, 'Cosmopolitanism: Ways of Being Muslim', in Amyn B. Sajoo (ed.), *A Companion to Muslim Cultures* (London: I. B. Tauris, 2011), pp. 201–20.

Katz, Marion Holmes, *Women in the Mosque: A History of Legal Thought and Social Practice* (New York: Columbia University Press, 2014).

Kenny, Sue, Matthew Clarke, Ismet Fanany and Damien Kingsbury, 'Deconstructing Aceh's Reconstruction', in Sue Kenny, Matthew Clarke, Ismet Fanany and

Damien Kingsbury (eds), *Post-Disaster Reconstruction: Lessons from Aceh* (London: Earthscan, 2010), pp. 3–27.

Kersten, Carool, 'Islam, Cultural Hybridity and Cosmopolitanism: New Muslim Intellectuals on Globalization', *Journal of International and Global Studies*, 1, 1 (2009), pp. 89–113.

——, *Cosmopolitans and Heretics: New Muslim Intellectuals and the Study of Islam* (New York: Columbia University Press, 2011).

Keshani, Hussein, 'Architecture and Community', in Amyn B. Sajoo (ed.), *A Companion to Muslim Cultures* (London: I. B. Tauris, 2012), pp. 117–36.

Kessler, Clive, 'Islam, State and Desecularization in Malaysia: The Islamist Trajectory During the Badawi Years', in Norani Othman, Mavis C. Puthucheary and Clive Kessler (eds), *Sharing the Nation: Faith, Difference, Power and the State 50 Years After Merdeka* (Selangor, Malaysia: SIRD, 2008), pp. 59–80.

Khan, Hassan-Uddin, 'An Overview of Contemporary Mosques', in Martin Frishman and Hassan-Uddin Khan (eds), *The Mosque* (Cairo: American University in Cairo Press, 1997), pp. 247–67.

King, Ross, *Kuala Lumpur and Putra Jaya: Negotiating Urban Space in Malaysia* (Singapore: NUS Press, 2008).

Kingsbury, Damien, and Harry Aveling (eds), *Autonomy and Disintegration in Indonesia* (London: Routledge, 2003).

Knysh, Alexander, 'A Clear and Present Danger: "Wahabism" as a Rhetorical Foil', *Die Welt des Islams*, 4, 1 (2004), pp. 3–26.

Köchler, Hans, 'Foreword', in Chandra Muzaffar, *Hegemony: Justice; Peace* (Selangor, Malaysia: Arah Pendidikan Sdn Bhd, 2008), pp. vi–viii.

Koh, Tai Ann, 'The Role of Intellectuals in Civil Society: Going against the Grain?', in Gillian Koh and Ooi Giok Ling (eds), *State–Society Relations in Singapore* (Singapore: Oxford University Press, 2000), pp. 156–67.

Kong, Lily, and Brenda S. A. Yeoh, *The Politics of Landscapes in Singapore: Constructions of 'Nation'* (New York: Syracuse University Press, 2003).

Koninck, Rodolphe de, Julie Drolet and Marc Girard, *Singapore: An Atlas of Perpetual Territorial Transformation* (Singapore: NUS Press, 2008).

Kreese, Kai, 'Interrogating "Cosmopolitanism" in an Indian Ocean Setting: Thinking Through Mombasa on the Swahili Coast', in Derryl N. MacLean and Sikeena Karmali Ahmed (eds), *Cosmopolitanisms in Muslim Contexts: Perspectives from the Past* (Edinburgh: Edinburgh University Press, 2012), pp. 31–50.

Kreese, Kai, and Edward Simpson (eds), *Struggling with History: Islam and Cosmopolitanism in the Western Indian Ocean* (London: Hurst, 2008).

Kugle, Scott, *Sufis and Saints' Bodies: Mysticism, Corporeality and Sacred Power in Islam* (Chapel Hill: University of North Carolina Press, 2007).

Kusno, Abidin, *The Appearances of Memory: Mnemonic Practices of Architecture and Urban Form in Indonesia* (Durham, NC: Duke University Press, 2010).

Latif, Yudi, *Indonesian Muslim Intelligentsia and Power* (Singapore: ISEAS, 2008).

Lawrence, Bruce, 'Afterword: Competing Genealogies of Muslim Cosmopolitanism', in Carl W. Ernst and Richard C. Martin (eds), *Rethinking Islamic Studies: From Orientalism to Cosmopolitanism* (Columbia: University of South Carolina Press, 2010), pp. 302–24.

——, 'Muslim Cosmopolitanism', *Critical Muslim*, 2 (2012), pp. 18–38.

Lazreg, Marnia, *Questioning the Veil: Open Letters to Muslim Women* (Princeton, NJ: Princeton University Press, 2009).

Lehmann, Uta Christina, 'Women's Rights to Mosque Space: Access and Participation in Cape Town Mosques', in Masooda Bano (ed.), *Women, Leadership and Mosques: Contemporary Changes in Leadership* (Leiden: Brill, 2012), pp. 481–506.

Leichtman, Mara A., and Dorothea Schulz (eds), 'Special Issue on Muslim Cosmopolitanism: Movement, Identity and Contemporary Reconfiguration', *City & Society*, 24, 1 (2012).

Lev, Daniel S., *Islamic Courts in Indonesia: A Study of Political Bases of Institutions* (Berkeley: University of California Press, 1972).

Lewis, Reina (ed.), *Modest Fashion: Styling Bodies, Mediating Faith* (New York: I. B. Tauris, 2013).

——, *Muslim Fashion: Contemporary Style Cultures* (Durham, NC: Duke University Press, 2015).

Lim, Merlyna, 'Life is Local in the Imagined Global Politics: Islam and Politics in the Indonesian Blogosphere', *Journal of Media and Religion*, 11, 3 (2012), pp. 127–40.

Lim, Yan Liang, 'Ministers Join 800 Breaking Fast at Mosque', *The Straits Times*, 23 June 2015.

Lin, Melissa, 'Singapore Named the Most Muslim-friendly Destination among Non-Muslim Countries', *The Straits Times*, 4 March 2015.

Liow, Joseph C., *Piety and Politics: Islamism in Contemporary Malaysia* (New York: Oxford University Press, 2009).

Lockard, Craig A., *Southeast Asia in World History* (Oxford: Oxford University Press, 2009).

Macdonald, Gerard M., 'Indonesia *Medan Merdeka:* National Identity and the Built Environment', *Antipode*, 27, 3 (1995), pp. 270–93.

Mcdonough, Sheila, 'Voices of Muslim Women', in Sajida Alvi, Homa Hoodfar and Sheila Mcdonough (eds), *The Muslim Veil in North America: Issues and Debates* (Toronto: Women's Press, 2003), pp. 105–20.

McEwan, Bree, and Miriam Sobre-Denton, 'Virtual Cosmopolitanism: Constructing Third Cultures and Transmitting Social and Cultural Capital Through Social Media', *Journal of International and Intercultural Communication*, 4, 4 (2011), pp. 252–8.

Macnamara, Jim, *The 21st Century Media (R)evolution: Emergent Communication Practices* (New York: Peter Lang, 2010).

Madjid, Nurcholish, *Islam, Kemodernan, dan Keindonesiaan* (Bandung, Indonesia: Mizan, 1987).

——, 'Islamic Roots of Modern Pluralism: Indonesian Experiences', *Studia Islamika: Indonesian Journal for Islamic Studies*, 1, 1 (1994), pp. 55–77.

Mahmood, Saba, *Religious Difference in a Secular Age: A Minority Report* (Princeton, NJ: Princeton University Press, 2016).

Mandaville, Peter, *Transnational Muslim Politics: Reimagining the Umma* (London: Routledge, 2001).

Marcinkowski, Christoph, *Facets of Shi'ite Islam in Contemporary Southeast Asia (II): Malaysia and Singapore* (Singapore: Institute of Defence and Strategic Studies, 2006).

Maynard, Margaret, *Dress and Globalisation* (Manchester: Manchester University Press, 2004).

Metcalf, Thomas, *An Imperial Vision: Indian Architecture and Britain's Raj* (Berkeley: University of California Press, 1989).

Mietzner, Marcus, 'Indonesia: Yudhoyono's Legacy between Stability and Stagnation', *Southeast Asian Affairs* (Singapore: ISEAS Press, 2012), pp. 119–34.

Mignolo, Walter, 'Cosmopolitan Localism: A Decolonial Shifting of the Kantian Legacies, *Localities,* 1 (2011), pp. 11–45.

Millie, Julian, 'Islamic Preaching and Women's Spectatorship in West Java', *The Australian Journal of Anthropology*, 22, 2 (2011), pp. 151–69.

Milner, Anthony C., *The Malays* (Oxford: Wiley-Blackwell, 2008).

Misztal, Barbara A., *Intellectuals and the Public Good: Creativity and Civil Courage* (Cambridge: Cambridge University Press, 2007).

Mohamad, Mahathir, *Blogging to Unblock* (Kuala Lumpur: Berita Publishing, 2013).

Mohamad, Maznah, 'The Ascendance of Bureaucratic Islam and the Secularization of the Sharia in Malaysia', *Pacific Affairs*, 83, 3 (2010), pp. 505–24.

Mohamad Rasdi, Mohamad Tajudin, *The Architectural Heritage of the Malay World* (Skudai, Malaysia: Penerbit UTM, 2000).

——, *Malaysian Architecture: Crisis Within* (Kuala Lumpur: Utusan Publications, 2005).

Mohd Tahir, Ir. Endok Sempo, 'Ayah Saya Pejuang Melawan Belanda', in Ir. Endok Sempo Mohd Tahir (ed.), *Bagaimana Akhirnya Saya Bertudung* (Selangor, Malaysia: PTS Millenia, 2010), pp. 96–110.

Mohd Tahir, Ir. Endok Sempo (ed.), *Bagaimana Akhirnya Saya Bertudung* (Selangor, Malaysia: PTS Millenia, 2010).

Mohamed, Noriah, 'Malay Language (Bahasa Melayu): Its Early History and Variation in Penang', in Muhammad Haji Salleh (ed.), *Early History of Penang* (Penang, Malaysia: Penerbit USM, 2012), pp. 50–80.

Mueller, John, *Overblown: How Politicians and the Terrorism Industry Inflate National Security Threats, and Why We Believe Them* (New York: The Free Press, 2006).

Mujani, Saiful, 'Civil Society and Tolerance in Indonesia', in Azra Azyumardi and Wayne Hudson (eds), *Islam Beyond Conflict: Indonesian Islam and Western Political Theory* (Aldershot: Ashgate, 2008), pp. 181–210.

Musa, Mohd Faizal, 'The Malaysian Shi'a: A Preliminary Study of Their History, Oppression and Denied Rights', *Journal of Shi'a Islamic Studies*, 4, 4 (2013), pp. 411–63.

Mustakim, Hafidzah, 'Saya Terpengaruh di Semenanjung', in Ir. Endok Sempo Mohd Tahir (ed.), *Bagaimana Akhirnya Saya Bertudung* (Selangor, Malaysia: PTS Millenia, 2010), pp. 90–5.

Mutalib, Hussin, *Islam and Ethnicity in Malay Politics* (Kuala Lumpur: Oxford University Press, 1990).

——, 'Islamic Revivalism in ASEAN States: Political Implications', *Asian Survey*, 30, 9 (1990), pp. 877–91.

——, 'Islamisation in Malaysia: Between Ideals and Realities', in Hussin Mutalib and Taj ul-Islam Hashmi (eds), *Islam, Muslims and the Modern State* (New York: St. Martin's Press, 1994), pp. 152–73.

——, 'Islam in Southeast Asia and the 21st Century: Managing the Inevitable Challenges, Dilemmas and Tensions', *Islamic Studies*, 37, 2 (1998), pp. 201–27.

——, 'The Rise in Islamicity and the Perceived Threat of Political Islam', in K. S. Nathan (ed.), *Perspectives on Doctrinal and Strategic Implications of Global Islam* (Singapore: ISEAS, 2003), pp. 17–21.

——, 'Political Islam in Southeast Asia: Shar'iah Pressures, Democratic Measures?', in Hussin Mutalib, *Islam and Democracy: The Southeast Asian Experience* (Singapore: Konrad-Adenauer-Siftung, 2004), pp. 11–32.

——, 'Misunderstood: Political Islam in Southeast Asia', *Harvard International Review*, 28, 2 (2006), p. 83.

——, *Islam in Southeast Asia* (Singapore: ISEAS Press, 2008).

——, 'Authoritarian Democracy and the Minority Muslim Polity in Singapore', Johan Saravanamuttu (ed.), *Islam and Politics in Southeast Asia* (London: Routledge, 2010), pp. 144–64.

Mutua, Makau, *Human Rights: A Political and Cultural Critique* (Philadelphia: University of Pennsylvania Press, 2002).

Muzaffar, Chandra, *Protector? An Analysis of the Concept and Practice of Loyalty in Leader-led Relationships within the Malay Society* (Penang, Malaysia: Aliran, 1979).

——, *One God: Many Paths* (Penang, Malaysia: Aliran, 1980).

——, *Islamic Resurgence in Malaysia* (Petaling Jaya, Malaysia: Fajar Bakti, 1987).

——, 'From Human Rights to Human Dignity', in Peter van Ness (ed.), *Debating Human Rights: Critical Essays from United States and Asia* (London: Routledge, 1999), pp. 25–31.

——, *Rights, Religion and Reform: Enhancing Human Dignity through Spiritual and Moral Transformation* (London: Routledge, 2002).

——, *Global Ethic or Global Hegemony? Reflections on Religion Human Dignity and Civilisational Interaction* (London: ASEAN Academic Press, 2005).

——, 'Towards a Universal Spiritual-Moral Vision of Global Justice and Peace', in Chandra Muzaffar (ed.), *Religion Seeking Justice and Peace* (Penang, Malaysia: USM Press, 2010), pp. 140–9.

——, *Exploring Religion in Our Time* (Penang, Malaysia: USM Press, 2011).

——, *Muslim Today: Changes Within, Challenges Without* (Islamabad: Emel Publications, 2011).

——, 'The Long Journey to the Just: My Life, My Struggle', *Inter-Asian Cultural Studies*, 12, 1 (2011), pp. 110–21.

Nadia, Asma (ed.), *Jilbab Pertamaku* (Bandung, Indonesia: Lingkar Pena Publishing House, 2005).

Nagata, Judith, 'What is Malay? Situational Selection of Ethnic Identity in a Plural Society', *American Ethnologist*, 1, 2 (1974), pp. 331–50.

——, 'The Impact of Islamic Revival (Dakwah) on the Religious Culture of Malaysia', in Bruce Matthews and Judith Nagata (eds), *Religion, Values and Development in Southeast Asia* (Singapore: ISEAS Press, 1986), pp. 37–50.

——, 'Modern Malay Women and the Message of the "Veil"', in Wazir Jahan Karim (ed.), *'Male' and 'Female' in Developing Southeast Asia* (Oxford: Berg, 1995), pp. 101–20.

——, 'Authority and Democracy in Malaysian and Indonesian Movements', in Johan Saravanamuttu (ed.), *Islam and Politics in Southeast Asia* (London: Routledge, 2010), pp. 18–45.

Nasir, Abdul Halim, *Mosque Architecture in the Malay World* (Bangi, Malaysia: Penerbit UKM, 2004).

Nasir, Kamaludeen Mohamed, *Globalized Muslim Youth in the Asia Pacific: Popular Culture in Singapore and Sydney* (Basingstoke: Palgrave Macmillan, 2016).

Nasir, Kamaludeen Mohamed, Alexius A. Pereira and Bryan S. Turner, *Muslims in Singapore: Piety, Politics and Policies* (London: Routledge, 2010).

Nasr, Seyyed Hossein, *Islam: Religion, History and Civilization* (San Francisco: Harper, 2003).

Nasr, Seyyed Vali Reza, *The Shia Revival: How Conflicts Within Islam Will Shape the Future* (New York: Norton, 2006).

Nasution, *Ekonomi Surabaya pada masa colonial, 1830–1930* (Surabaya, Indonesia: Pustaka Intelektual, 2006).

Ng, Cecilia, Maznah Mohamad and Tan Beng Hui, *Feminism and the Women's Movement in Malaysia: The Unsung (R)evolution* (London: Routledge, 2006).

Ngah, Umi Kalthum, 'Dinasihati Supaya Tidak Mendekati Pelajar Dakwah', in Ir. Endok Sempo Mohd Tahir (ed.), *Bagaimana Akhirnya Saya Bertudung* (Selangor, Malaysia: PTS Millenia, 2010), pp. 55–61.

Nisa, Eva F., 'Female Voices on Jakarta Da'wa Stage', *Review of Indonesian and Malaysian Affairs (RIMA)*, 46, 1 (2012), pp. 55–81.

Noor, Farish A., 'Reformist Muslim Thinkers in Malaysia: Engaging with Power to Uplift the Umma?', in Shireen T. Hunter (ed.), *Reformist Voices of Islam: Mediating Islam and Modernity* (London: M. E. Sharpe, 2009), pp. 208–26.

Omar, Ariffin, 'Origins and Development of the Affirmative Policy in Malay and Malaysia: A Historical Overview', *Kajian Malaysia*, 21, 2–3 (2003), pp. 13–29.

Ong, Aihwa, 'State Versus Islam: Malay Families, Women's Bodies, and the Body Politic in Malaysia', in Aihwa Ong and Michael G. Peletz (eds), *Bewitching Women, Pious Men: Gender and Body Politics in Southeast Asia* (Berkeley: University of California Press, 1995), pp. 159–94.

Onyx, Jenny, Christine Ho, Melissa Edwards, Nina Burridge and Hilary Yerbury,

'Scaling up Connections: Everyday Cosmopolitanism, Complexity Theory and Social Capital', *Cosmopolitan Civil Societies Journal*, 3, 3 (2011), pp. 37–67.

Othman, Mohammad Redzuan, 'The Origins and Contributions of Early Arabs in Malaya', in Eric Tagliacozzo (ed.), *Southeast Asia and the Middle East: Islam, Movement and the* Longue Durée (Stanford, CA: Stanford University Press, 2009), p. 83–107.

Pang, Ching Lin, Sara Sterling and Denggao Long, 'Cosmopolitanism, Mobility and Transformation: Internal Migrant Women in Beijing's Silk Street Market', *Asian Anthropology*, 13, 2 (2014), pp. 124–38.

Papastergiadis, Nikos, *Cosmopolitanism and Culture* (Cambridge: Polity Press, 2012).

Peled, Alon, *A Question of Loyalty: Military Manpower Policy in Multiethnic States* (Ithaca, NY: Cornell University Press, 1998).

Pendeza, Massimo, 'Introduction: Is Classical Sociology Still in Vogue? A Controversial Legacy', in Massimo Pendeza (ed.), *Classical Sociology Beyond Methodological Nationalism* (Leiden: Brill, 2014), pp. 1–24.

Pennycook, Alastair, and Emi Otsuji, *Metrolingualism: Language in the City* (London: Routledge, 2015).

Pires, Tome, *The Suma Oriental of Tome Pires*, translated by Armando Cortesao (London: Hakluyt Society, 1944).

Pirzada, Sahar, and Jolie Tan, 'Hijab Issue: Whatever Their Choice, Women Deserve Respect, Inclusion', *Today*, 12 November 2013.

Posner, Richard, *Public Intellectuals: A Study in Decline* (Cambridge, MA: Harvard University Press, 2001).

Pratt, Mary Louise, *Imperial Eyes: Travel Writing and Transculturation* (London: Routledge, 1992).

Purdey, Jemma, *Anti-Chinese Violence in Indonesia, 1996–1999* (Honolulu: University of Hawai'i Press, 2006).

Purdy, Susan S., 'The Civil Religion Thesis as it Applies to a Pluralistic Society: Pancasila Democracy in Indonesia', *Journal of International Affairs*, 36, 2 (1982), pp. 307–16.

Raffles, Thomas Stamford, *The History of Java*, vol. 1 (London: John Murray, 1817).

Rahim, Lily Zubaidah, *Singapore in the Malay World: Building and Breaching Regional Bridges* (London: Routledge, 2009).

Rahmat, Hadijah, 'Portraits of a Nation: The British legacy for Malay Settlement in Singapore', *Indonesia and the Malay World*, 36, 106 (2008), pp. 359–74.

Raillon, François, 'The Return of the Pancasila: Secular vs Islamic Norms, Another Look at the Struggle for State Dominance in Indonesia', in Michel Picard and

Rémy Madinier (eds), *The Politics of Religion in Indonesia: Syncretism, Orthodoxy, and Religious Contention in Java and Bali* (London: Routledge, 2011), pp. 92–114.

Rajah, Jothie, *Authoritarian Rule of Law: Legislation, Discourse, and Legitimacy in Singapore* (New York: Cambridge University Press, 2012).

Ramadan, Tariq, *To Be a European Muslim* (Leicester: The Islamic Foundation, 2002).

——, 'Cosmopolitan Theory and the Dual Pluralism of Life', in Nina Glick Schiller and Andrew Irving (eds), *Whose Cosmopolitanism? Critical Perspectives, Relationalities and Discontents* (Oxford: Berg, 2015), pp. 57–64.

Reid, Anthony, *Southeast Asia in the Age of Commerce*, vol. 1 (New Haven, CT: Yale University Press, 1988).

——, *Charting the Shape of Early Modern Southeast Asia* (Chiang Mai, Thailand: Silkworm Books, 1999).

——, *A History of Southeast Asia: Critical Crossroads* (Oxford: Wiley-Blackwell, 2015).

Rettberg, Jill Walker, *Blogging* (Cambridge: Polity Press, 2009).

Rippin, Andrew, *Muslims: Their Religious Beliefs and Practices* (London: Routledge, 2012).

Rizvi, Kishwar, *The Transnational Mosque: Architecture and Historical Memory in the Contemporary Middle East* (Chapel Hill: University of North Carolina Press, 2015).

Roald, Anne Sofie, *Women in Islam: The Western Experience* (London: Routledge, 2001).

Robbins, Bruce, 'Actually Existing Cosmopolitanism', in Pheng Cheah and Bruce Robbins (eds), *Cosmopolitics: Thinking and Feeling Beyond the Nation* (Minneapolis: University of Minnesota Press, 1998), pp. 1–19.

Rodan, Garry, *Transparency and Authoritarian Rule in Southeast Asia: Singapore and Malaysia* (London: Routledge, 2004).

Rumford, Chris, 'Theorizing Borders', *European Journal of Social Theory*, 9, 2 (2006), pp. 155–69.

Said, Edward W., *Representations of the Intellectual* (New York: Vintage, 1994).

——, *Covering Islam: How the Media and the Experts Determine How We See the Rest of the World* (New York: Vintage Books, 1997).

Salim, Arskal, *Challenging the Secular State: Islamization of Law in Modern Indonesia* (Honolulu: University of Hawai'i Press, 2008).

Sandhu, Kernial Singh, 'Chinese Colonization of Malacca, 1500 to 1957 AD', *Journal of Tropical Geography*, 15 (1961), pp. 1–26.

Saravanamuttu, Johan, 'Malaysia: Multicultural Society, Islamic State, or What?' in Michael Heng Siam-Heng and Ten Chin Liew (eds), *State and Secularism: Perspectives from Asia* (Singapore: World Scientific Publishing, 2010), pp. 279–300.

Sardar, Ziauddin, *The Consumption of Kuala Lumpur* (London: Reaktion Books, 2000).

Schottmann, Sven, 'The Pillars of "Mahathir's Islam": Mahathir Mohamad on Being-Muslim in the Modern World', *Asian Studies Review*, 35, 3 (2011), pp. 355–72.

Scott, James C., *Seeing Like a State: How Certain Schemes to Improve the Human Condition Have Failed* (New Haven, CT: Yale University Press, 1998).

Seligmann, Linda J., 'Introduction: Mediating Identities and Marketing Wares', in Linda J. Seligmann (ed.), *Women Traders in Cross-Cultural Perspective: Mediating Identities, Marketing Wares* (Stanford, CA: Stanford University Press, 2002), pp. 1–24.

Seo, Myengkyo, *State Management of Religion in Indonesia* (London: Routledge, 2013).

Setiawan, Kartum, *Masjid-masjid Bersejarah di Jakarta* (Jakarta: Penerbit Erlangga, 2011).

Setyawati, Lugina, '*Adat*, Islam and Womanhood in the Reconstruction of Riau Malay Identity', in Susan Blackburn, Bianca J. Smith and Siti Syamsiyatun (eds), *Indonesian Islam in a New Era: How Women Negotiate their Muslim Identities* (Clayton, VIC: Monash University Press, 2008), pp. 69–96.

Shepard, William E., *Sayyid Qutb and Islamic Activism: A Translation and Critical Analysis of Social Justice in Islam* (Leiden: Brill, 1996).

Sheridan, Greg, *Cities of the Hot Zone: A Southeast Asian Adventure* (Sydney: Allen and Unwin, 2003).

Shihab, Quraish, *Jilbab: Pakaian Wanita Muslimah, Pandangan Ulama Masa Lalu dan Cendekiawan Kontemporer* (Ciputat, Indonesia: Penerbit Lentera Hati, 2004).

Shirazi, Faegheh, *Velvet Jihad: Muslim Women's Quiet Revolution to Islamic Fundamentalism* (Gainesville: University Press of Florida, 2009).

Shycock, Andrew J., 'Attack of the Islamophobes: Religious War (and Peace) in Arab/Muslim Detroit', in Carl W. Ernst (ed.), *Islamophobia in America: The Anatomy of Intolerance* (Basingstoke: Palgrave Macmillan, 2013), pp. 145–74.

Siddique, Sharon, and Leo Suryadinata, 'Bumiputra and Pribumi: Economic Nationalism (Indiginism) in Malaysia and Indonesia', *Pacific Affairs*, 54, 4 (1981–2), pp. 662–87.

Sidel, John T., *The Islamist Threat in Southeast Asia: A Reassessment* (Singapore: ISEAS, 2007).

Simone, Abdulmaliq, *Jakarta: Drawing the City Near* (Minneapolis: University of Minnesota Press, 2014).

Siraj, Harlina Halizah, 'Saya Anak Seorang Kadi', in Ir. Endok Sempo Mohd Tahir (ed.), *Bagaimana Akhirnya Saya Bertudung* (Selangor, Malaysia: PTS Millenia, 2010), pp. 78–85.

Siti Muslimah and Laili Nihayati (eds), *Spiritual Journey of a Muslimah* (Bandung, Indonesia: Penerbit Mizania, 2008).

Skrbiš, Zlatko, and Ian Woodward, *Cosmopolitanism: Uses of the Idea* (London: Sage, 2013).

Slater, Dan, *Ordering Power: Contentious Politics and Authoritarian Leviathan in Southeast Asia* (New York: Cambridge University Press, 2010).

Smith-Hefner, Nancy J., 'Javanese Women and the Veil in Post-Soeharto Indonesia', *Journal of Asia Studies*, 66, 2 (2007), pp. 389–420.

Smyth, Ines, 'Indonesian Women as (Economic) Mediators: Some Comments on Concepts', in Sita van Bemelen, Madelon Djajadiningrat-Nieuwenhuis, Elsbeth Locher-Scholten and Elly Touwen-Bouwsma (eds), *Women and Mediation in Indonesia* (Leiden: KITLV Press, 1992), pp. 33–46.

Snellgrove, David, 'Syncretism as a Main Feature of Indonesian Culture, As Seen by One More Used to Another Kind of Civilization', *Indonesian Circle*, 20, 56 (1991), pp. 24–48.

Steenbrink, Karel, *Catholics in Indonesia: A Documented History, 1808–1900* (Leiden: KITLV Press, 2003).

Steiner, Kersten, 'Governing Islam: The State, the Administration of Muslim Law Act (AMLA) and Islam in Singapore', *Australian Journal of Asian Law*, 16, 1 (2015), pp. 1–16.

Subramanian, Lakshmi, 'Commerce, Circulation and Consumption: Indian Ocean Communities in Historical Perspective', in Shanti Moorthy and Ashraf Jamal (eds), *Indian Ocean Studies: Cultural, Social and Political Perspectives* (London: Routledge, 2010), pp. 136–57.

Sundaram, Jomo Kwame, *The New Economic Policy and Inter-relations in Malaysia* (New York: United Nations Research Institute for Development, 2004).

Syuan-yuan, Chiou, 'Building Traditions for Bridging Differences: Islamic Imaginary Homelands of Chinese-Indonesian Muslims in East Java', in Chan Kwok Bun, Jan W. Walls and David Hayward (eds), *East-West Identities: Globalization, Localization, and Hybridization* (Leiden: Brill, 2007), pp. 265–78.

Tan, Charlene, '(Re)imagining the Muslim Identity in Singapore', *Studies in Ethnicity and Nationalism*, 8, 1 (2008), pp. 31–49.

Tan, Eugene K. B., 'Norming "Moderation" in an "Iconic Target": Public Policy and the Regulation of Anxieties in Singapore', *Terrorism and Political Violence*, 19, 4 (2007), pp. 443–62.

——, 'Keeping God in Place: The Management of Religion in Singapore', in Lai Ah Eng (ed.), *Religious Diversity in Singapore* (Singapore: ISEAS Press, 2008), pp. 55–82.

Tan, Jun-E, and Zawawi Ibrahim, *Blogging and Democratization in Malaysia: A New Civil Society in the Making* (Selangor, Malaysia: SIRD, 2008).

Tan, Kenneth Paul, 'Pragmatic Secularism, Civil Religion, and Political Legitimacy in Singapore', in Michael Heng Siam-Heng and Ten Chin Liew (eds), *State and Secularism: Perspectives from Asia* (Singapore: World Scientific Publishing, 2010), pp. 339–57.

Tan, Kevin Y. L., *The Constitution of Singapore: A Contextual Analysis* (Oxford: Hart Publishing, 2015).

Taraborrelli, Angela, *Contemporary Cosmopolitanism* (London: Bloomsbury Academic, 2011).

Tarlo, Emma, *Visibly Muslim: Fashion, Politics, Faith* (Oxford: Berg, 2010).

Tay, Kheng Soon, 'Architecture of Rapid Transformation', in Kernial Singh Sandhu and Paul Wheatley (eds), *Management of Success: The Moulding of Modern Singapore* (Singapore: ISEAS, 1989), pp. 860–78.

Ten, Leu-Jiun, 'The Invention of a Tradition: Indo-Saracenic Domes on Mosques in Singapore', *Biblioasia*, 9, 1 (2013), pp. 17–19.

Thaha, Idris, 'Memahami Azyumardi Azra', preface to Azyumardi Azra, *Islam Substantif* (Bandung, Indonesia: Penerbit Mizan, 2000), pp. 19–30.

Thio, Li-Ann, 'Control, Co-optation and Cooperation: Managing Religious Harmony in Singapore's Multi-ethnic, Quasi-secular State', *Hastings Constitutional Law Quarterly*, 33 (2005), pp. 197–253.

Ting, Helen, 'Malaysian Textbooks and the Discourse of *Ketuanan Melayu*', in Daniel P. S. Goh, Matilda Gabrielpillai, Philip Holden and Gaik Cheng Khoo (eds), *Race and Multiculturalism in Malaysia and Singapore* (London: Routledge, 2009), pp. 36–52.

Toorn, Roemer van, 'Counteracting the Clash of Cultures: Mosque Architecture as an Emancipating Factory', in Ergün Erkoçu and Cihan Buğdacı (eds), *The Mosque: Political, Architectural and Social Transformations* (Rotterdam: Nai Publishers, 2009), pp. 107–13.

Turmudi, Endang, *Struggling for the Umma: Changing Leadership Roles of Kiai in Jombang, East Java* (Canberra: ANU E-Press, 2006).

Ummu Hammah, *Seks Islam: Perangi Yahudi Untuk Kembalikan Seks Islam Kepada Dunia* (Selangor, Malaysia: Kelab Taat Suami, 2011).

Ummu Hanan, 'Ibu Membenci Saya Bertudung', in Ir. Endok Sempo Mohd Tahir (ed.), *Bagaimana Akhirnya Saya Bertudung* (Selangor, Malaysia: PTS Millenia, 2010), pp. 65–71.

Veer, Peter van der, 'Colonial Cosmopolitanism', in Robin Cohen and Steve Vertovec (eds), *Conceiving Cosmopolitanism* (Oxford: Oxford University Press, 2002), pp. 165–80.

Wain, Barry, *The Malaysian Maverick: Mahathir Mohamad in Turbulent Times* (Basingstoke: Palgrave Macmillan, 2012).

Weber, Max, *Economy and Society: An Outline of Interpretive Sociology*, edited by Guenther Roth and Calus Wittich (Berkeley: University of California Press, 1978).

Weiss, Meredith L., 'New Media, New Activism: Trends and Trajectories in Malaysia, Singapore and Indonesia', *International Development Planning Review*, 36, 1 (2014), pp. 91–109.

Welsh, Bridget, 'Elections in Malaysia: Voting Behaviour and Electoral Integrity', in Meredith L. Weiss (ed.), *Routledge Handbook of Contemporary Malaysia* (London: Routledge, 2015), pp. 11–21.

Wilson, Ian Douglas, *The Politics of Protection Rackets in Post-New Order Indonesia* (London: Routledge, 2012).

Winchelen, Sonja van, *Religion, Politics and Gender in Indonesia: Disputing the Muslim Body* (London: Routledge, 2010).

Wiryomartono, Bagoes, 'A Historical View of Mosque Architecture in Indonesia', *The Asia-Pacific Journal of Anthropology*, 10, 1 (2009), pp. 33–45.

Wismantara, Pudji Pratitis, 'The Dynamics of the Form of Nusantara Mosque: Architectural Homogeneity vis a vis Architectural Hybridity', *Journal of Islamic Architecture*, 2, 1 (2012), pp. 21–7.

Yeoh, Brenda S. A., 'Cosmopolitanism and its Exclusions in Singapore', *Urban Studies*, 41, 12 (2004), pp. 2431–45.

Yousef Mousa, Wael A., *Modern Mosques in Malaysia: Between Regionalism and Eclecticism* (Penang, Malaysia: Universiti Sains Malaysia Press, 2014).

Yusman, Puteri, 'Saya Tidak Tahu Mengapa Saya Bertudung', in Ir. Endok Sempo Mohd Tahir (ed.), *Bagaimana Akhirnya Saya Bertudung* (Selangor, Malaysia: PTS Millenia, 2010), pp. 129–36.

Zabidi, Suriza Ahmad, 'Saya Takut Dirota Ustaz', in Ir. Endok Sempo Mohd Tahir (ed.), *Bagaimana Akhirnya Saya Bertudung* (Selangor, Malaysia: PTS Millenia, 2010), pp. 50–4.

Zainal Abidin, Mohd Asri, *Mengemudi Bahtera Perubahan Minda* (Kuala Lumpur: Utusan Publications, 2008).

Zaman, Muhammad Qasim, 'The Scope and Limits of Islamic Cosmopolitanism and the Discursive Language of the Ulama', in Miriam Cooke and Bruce Lawrence (eds), *Muslim Networks from Hajj to Hip Hop* (Chapel Hill: University of North Carolina Press, 2005), pp. 84–104.

Zempi, Irene, and Neil Chakraborti, *Islamophobia, Victimisation and the Veil* (Basingstoke: Palgrave Macmillan, 2014).

Zubaida, Sami, 'Cosmopolitanism and the Middle East', in Roel Meijer (ed.) *Cosmopolitanism, Identity, and Authenticity in the Middle East* (Richmond: Curzon Press, 1999), pp. 15–34.

Zulkifli, *The Struggle of the Shi'is in Indonesia* (Canberra: ANU E-Press, 2013).

Internet Sources

Abah Yasir, 'Etika di Alam Maya', abahyasir.com [blog], 28 March 2015, <http://abahyasir.com/2015/03/28/etika-alam-maya/> (last accessed 11 July 2015).

Abdul Rahman, Zaharuddin, 'Tangkapan Mohd Asri: Suatu Pandangan', zaharud din.net, 3 November 2009, <http://zaharuddin.net/politik-&-dakwah/55/887-tangkapan-dr-mohd-asri--suatu-pandangan.html> (last accessed 9 July 2015).

Abdullah, Alia, 'The One on Da'wah', Alia Abdullah [blog], 2 April 2015, <http://aliaabdullah.com/2015/04/02/the-one-on-dawah-2/#more-489> (last accessed 11 July 2015).

Abdullah, Walid J., 'Secularism in Singapore: The Tudung Issue in 2013' [Facebook note], 22 October 2013, <https://www.facebook.com/notes/walid-j-abdullah/secularism-in-singapore-the-tudung-issue-in-2013/528681723888998> (last accessed 18 February 2016).

Affan, Heyder, 'Polemik di balik istilah "Nusantara"', Islampos, 28 June 2015, <http://www.islampos.com/mengkritisi-islam-nusantara-versi-azyumardi-azra-192818/> (last accessed 12 February 2016).

AngelPakaiGucci [blog], 'Saya Liberal', 25 November 2013, <http://angelwearsgu cci.blogspot.sg/2013/11/saya-liberal.html> (last accessed 9 July 2015).

Aripin, Nurul Izzah, 'Banned? Well-known Islamic Cleric's Absence from Singapore Conference Leads to Speculation', Yahoo! News, 4 December 2015, <https://

sg.news.yahoo.com/banned--well-known-islamic-cleric-s-absence-from-sin-gapore-conference-leads-to-speculation-101926407.html> (last accessed 24 February 2016).

Arismunandar, Satrio, 'Saya bukan Syiah, Tetapi Saya Tidak Merasa Terancam Berhubungan Dengan Muslim Syiah dan Penganut Apa Pun', Satrio Arismunandar: Bangkitlah Indonesia! [blog], 19 March 2015, <http://satrio arismunandar6.blogspot.sg/2015/04/saya-bukan-penganut-syiah-tetapi-saya. html> (last accessed 11 July 2015).

Arul, Kang, 'Sentimen Media terhadap Islam', kangarul.com [blog], 10 April 2012, <http://kangarul.com/sentimen-media-terhadap-islam> (last accessed 1 February 2016).

Awang, Siti Fatihah, 'Pasar Siti Khadijah berwajah baru', Sinar Online, 22 February 2014, <http://www.sinarharian.com.my/edisi/kelantan/pasar-siti-khadijah-ber wajah-baru-1.253370> (last accessed 22 January 2016).

BBC Monitoring, 'Singapore: Campaigners Bid to Overturn Hijab Ban', 13 November 2013, <http://www.bbc.com/news/blogs-news-from-elsewhere-24932400> (last accessed 18 February 2016).

Berger, Sebastien, 'Golden Day for Brunei's Bride', *The Telegraph*, 10 September 2014, <http://www.telegraph.co.uk/news/worldnews/middleeast/1471439/Gol den-day-for-Bruneis-bride.html> (last accessed 17 February 2016).

Boo, Su-Lyn, 'Marina Mahathir: Malaysia Undergoing "Arab Colonialism"', *Malay Mail Online*, 23 May 2015, <http://m.themalaymailonline.com/malaysia/arti cle/marina-mahathir-malaysia-undergoing-arab-colonialism> (last accessed 31 January 2016).

Brown, Sophie, 'Malaysian Court to Christians: You Can't Say "Allah"', CNN, 24 June 2014, <http://edition.cnn.com/2014/06/24/world/asia/malaysia-allah-ban/> (last accessed 26 February 2016).

Chooi, Clara, 'Keep Husbands Sexually Satisfied to Curb Infidelity, Says Wives Club', The Malaysian Insider, 4 June 2011, <http://www.themalaysianinsider. com/malaysia/article/keep-husbands-sexually-satisfied-to-cu#sthash.8jrG8ho9. dpuf> (last accessed 15 February 2016).

Editorial, 'Bersebelahan dengan Masjid, Ini Cara Gereja Mahanaim Atur Kebaktian Natal', *Tribun Pekanbaru*, 25 December 2015, <http://pekanbaru.tribunnews. com/2015/12/25/sebelahan-dengan-masjid-ini-cara-gereja-mahanaim-atur-kebaktian-natal> (last accessed 7 February 2015).

Editorial, 'BN, Pakatan Breakdown May Lead to Racial, Religious Splits, Canadian Journalist Warns', *Malay Mail Online*, 27 June 2015, <http://www.themalay

mailonline.com/malaysia/article/bn-pakatan-breakdown-may-lead-to-racial-religious-splits-canadian-journalis> (last accessed 24 February 2016).

Editorial, 'No Place for Wahabism in Malaysia, Fatwa Council Says', *Malay Mail Online*, 1 March 2015, <http://www.themalaymailonline.com/malaysia/article/no-place-for-wahhabism-in-malaysia-fatwa-council-says> (last accessed 24 February 2016).

Eiza GreenAppleKu, 'Kenapa aku bertudung', Eiza GreenAppleKu: Story of Our Life [blog], 7 June 2011, <http://www.greenappleku.com/2011/06/kenapa-aku-bertudung.html> (last accessed 16 February 2016).

Embrace Hijab [Facebook page], <https://www.facebook.com/EmbraceHijab/info?tab=page_info> (last accessed 18 February 2016).

Ghazali, Azimah, Syahidatul Akmal Dunya and Wan Amalia Wan Mhd Daud, 'Hijab bukan sekadar fesyen', Sinar Online, 8 December 2013, <http://www.sinarharian.com.my/hijab-bukan-sekadar-fesyen-1.228627> (last accessed 3 March 2016).

Hasan, Zulkifli, 'Memahami isu Islamofobia: Antara persepsi dan realiti', Blog of Knowledge, 5 October 2013, <https://zulkiflihasan.wordpress.com/2013/10/05/memahami-isu-islamofobia-antara-persepsi-dan-realiti/> (last accessed 4 July 2015).

Ibrahim, Zaid, 'No More Discrimination Please', *The Zaidgeist* [blog], 13 March 2015, <http://www.zaid.my/current/no-more-discrimination-please/> (last accessed 24 February 2016).

Ignatius, Dennis, 'Wahhabism in Southeast Asia', Asia Sentinel, 27 March 2015, <http://www.asiasentinel.com/society/wahhabism-in-southeast-asia/> (last accessed 1 March 2016).

Internet World Stats, 'Asia Marketing Research, Internet Usage, Population Statistics and Facebook Information', <http://www.internetworldstats.com/asia.htm> (last accessed 2 July 2015).

Izwan, Md, 'In "Touch a Dog" Issue, Scholars See Modernisation of Muslim Youth', The Malaysian Insider, 23 October 2014, <http://www.themalaysianinsider.com/malaysia/article/in-touch-a-dog-issue-scholars-see-modernisation-of-muslim-youth> (last accessed 10 February 2016).

Koh, Jun Lin, 'Daily Death Threat Avalanche Hits Syed Azmi', Malaysiakini, 25 October 2014, <http://www.malaysiakini.com/news/278581> (last accessed 10 February 2016).

Lee, Terence, 'Singapore "Hijab Movement" Facebook Page Mysteriously Disappears', Yahoo! News, 14 November 2013, <https://sg.finance.yahoo.

com/news/singapore-hijab-movement-facebook-page-043141957.html> (last accessed 18 February 2016).

Leo, P. J., 'Bargains Galore at Tanah Abang', *The Jakarta Post*, 1 June 2011, <http://www.thejakartapost.com/news/2011/06/01/bargains-galore-tanah-abang.html> (last accessed 22 January 2016).

Libo-on, Lily B., 'Indonesia Targets UAE, Middle East as Potential Tourism Markets', *Khaleej Times*, 29 May 2009, <http://www.khaleejtimes.com/article/20090528/ARTICLE/305289919/1002> (last accessed 27 January 2016).

Lim, Ida, 'Syed Azmi, the "Touch-A-Dog" Organiser Who Turned Hero and Villain in a Week', *Malay Mail Online*, 26 October 2014, <http://www.themalaymailonline.com/malaysia/article/syed-azmi-the-touch-a-dog-organiser-who-turned-hero-and-villain-in-a-week> (last accessed 10 February 2016).

Lim, Kit Siang, 'Media Statement', Indian-Malaysian Online, 31 March 1998, <http://www.indianmalaysian.com/demolition.htm> (last accessed 6 February 2016).

Majlis Ugama Islam Singapura, 'Mosque Directory', <http://www.mosque.sg/mosque-directory.html> (last accessed 3 March 2016).

——, 'Serving Our Community, Better', MUIS Annual Report 2013, <http://www.muis.gov.sg/documents/Annual_Reports/muis-html/index.html> (last accessed on 6 March 2016).

Mohamad, Mahathir, 'Sunni dan Syiah', Dr. Mahathir Mohamad: Blogging to Unblock [blog], 30 August 2013, <http://chedet.cc/?p=1052> (last accessed 11 July 2015).

Mohamad Havez, Nadia Fitri, 'Bagaimana saya bertudung', Nadia Fitri Mohamad Hafez [blog], 15 July 2011, <http://nadiafitrihavez.blogspot.sg/2011/07/bagaimana-akhirnya-saya-bertudung-part.html> (last accessed 16 February 2016).

Nafee, Ibrahim, 'Malaysia's Halal Tourism Attracts Muslims from All Over the World', *Arab News*, 28 May 2014, <http://www.arabnews.com/news/577851> (last accessed 27 January 2016).

Noor, Farish A., 'Kelantan's Multicultural Mosque Laudable', Malaysiakini, 8 November 2000, <http://www.malaysiakini.com/news/66> (last accessed 5 February 2016).

Nugrahani, Novani, 'Walking a Harmonious Life on Harmony Street', Psycho Paradiso [blog], 10 September 2013, <http://psychoparadiso.com/2013/09/10/walking-a-harmonious-life-on-harmony-street/> (last accessed 7 February 2016).

Nury MJ, Facebook update, 9 September 2015, <https://www.facebook.com/nury.
aqilah/posts/10153635009169308> (last accessed 18 February 2016).

Otto, Ben, and Sara Schonhardt, 'Islamic Political Parties Make a Comeback in
Indonesian Election', *Wall Street Journal*, 10 April 2014, <http://www.wsj.com/
articles/SB10001424052702303873604579493311138076926> (last accessed
22 February 2016).

Pitaloka, Dyah Ayu, 'Malang Policewomen Allowed to Wear Hijab on Fridays
Despite Nationwide Ban', *Jakarta Globe*, 1 November 2013, <http://jakart
aglobe.beritasatu.com/news/malang-policewomen-allowed-to-wear-hijab-on-
fridays-despite-nationwide-ban/> (last accessed 17 February 2016).

Religious Rehabilitation Group (RRG), 'About Us', <http://rrg.sg/about-us> (last
accessed 11 July 2015).

Sikand, Yoginder, 'Interview: Chandra Muzaffar on Islamic Inclusivism and
Muslim Exclusivism', TwoCircles.net, 19 October 2009, <http://twocircles.
net/2009oct19/interview_chandra_muzaffar_islamic_inclusivism_and_
muslim_exclusivism.html> (last accessed 10 February 2016).

Soledad and the Sisters Co (SATSCO), 'Pasar Kampung Ampel (2014)'
[YouTube video], posted on 20 March 2015, <https://www.youtube.com/
watch?v=I9ViAfA-WLw> (last accessed 26 January 2016).

Tantawi, Nasrudin Hassan, 'Etika dan Adab Seorang Blogger', Ustaz Nasrudin Hassan
Tantawi [blog], 14 August 2009, <http://www.perjuanganku.com/2009/08/
etika-dan-adab-seorang-blogger.html> (last accessed 11 July 2015).

UCAN Indonesia, 'Gereja dan masjid sebagai symbol toleransi', 22 July 2013,
<http://indonesia.ucanews.com/2013/07/22/gereja-dan-masjid-sebagai-simbol-
toleransi/> (last accessed 7 February 2016).

Winn, Philip, 'Majelis Taklim and Gendered Religious Practice in Northern Ambon',
Intersections: Gender and Sexuality in Asia and the Pacific, 30 (2012), <http://
intersections.anu.edu.au/issue30/winn.htm> (last accessed 9 February 2016).

YouTube, search results for 'Hijab tutorials', <http://www.youtube.com/results?sp=
CAM%253D&q=hijab+tutorials> (last accessed 17 February 2016).

Zaidi, Zainarida Emilia, '70 pelancong bukan Islam sertai majlis berbuka puasa', My
Putrajaya News, 17 July 2014, <http://myputrajayanews.com/v2/70-pelancong-
bukan-islam-sertai-majlis-berbuka-puasa/> (last accessed 8 February 2016).

Zainal Abidin, Mohd Asri, 'Menangisi Kehilangan Islam di Spain', Minda Tajdid,
10 May 2012, <http://drmaza.com/home/?p=1898> (last accessed 7 July 2015).

INDEX

Page numbers in *italics* indicate illustrations; f indicates a figure, n indicates endnote.

The interrelation of Islam, local culture and global forces has created a unique hybrid in Southeast Asia. This new book brings this complicated and compelling question into the present day, revealing a new Islamic cosmopolitanism in the twenty-first century.

Jonathan A. C. Brown, author of *Misquoting Muhammad*

This book offers new insights into the study of the historical fusion of religion and ethnicity in the evolution of Muslim cosmopolitanism in Southeast Asia. Through this critical study its author, who views his own personal life and experiences in the region as a fairly good reflection of the state of this particular cosmopolitanism since the 1970s, has succeeded in portraying it as at once unique and similar to cultural expressions of cosmopolitanism in other parts of the Muslim world. Khairudin Aljunied's current work is a welcome contribution to the study of Muslim cosmopolitanism in Southeast Asia.

Osman Bakar, author of *Classification of Knowledge in Islam*

Muslim Cosmopolitanism looks at Islam's existence in a new and unique manner. Rather than an ethnographic, historical or political study, as studies of the region tend to be, Khairudin Aljunied examines the states of Indonesia, Malaysia and Singapore from the perspective of a theoretical construct generally known as 'Muslim Cosmopolitanism'. In this construct, 'cosmopolitan' Muslims seek to open themselves to the entire world, eschew narrow interpretations of race, religion and culture, and seek new knowledge and insights. The aim is to find peace and harmony within the Muslim community and avenues of understanding with non-Muslims.

Howard M. Federspiel, author of *Sultans, Shamans and Saints*

Muslim Cosmopolitanism is as timely as it is a pleasure to read. Timely because of widely held but mistaken perceptions in much of the non-Muslim world which associate Islam with violence and intolerance. Timely too, because of the current fixation in much academic and public discourse with the trials and tribulations that have beset Islam in the Middle East and West Asia. By refocusing our attention on Southeast Asia the book sheds useful light not just on this region but on the very core of Islamic belief, ethos and culture.

Muslim Cosmopolitanism will delight any reader with an interest in religion, politics and culture and their fascinating interaction in the local sites where people live, pray, converse, trade and reflect. The book does not ignore the less-than-helpful, at times noxious role of the contemporary state in Indonesia, Malaysia and Singapore. But, while conscious of the stunting effects of authoritarianism and the politics of fear and polarisation, Dr Aljunied offers us an inspiring vision of what Islam can contribute to a cosmopolitan future in the making.

Joseph A. Camilleri, author of *Worlds in Transition*